ONE GIRL
ONE DREAM

ONE GIRL
ONE DREAM

LAURA DEKKER

HarperCollins*Publishers*

HarperCollins*Publishers*

First published in Dutch in 2013
by Alk & Heijnen
First published in English in 2014
This edition published in 2016
by HarperCollins*Publishers* (New Zealand) Limited
Unit D1, 63 Apollo Drive, Rosedale, Auckland 0632, New Zealand
harpercollins.co.nz

HarperCollins*Publishers*
Unit D1, 63 Apollo Drive, Rosedale, Auckland 0632, New Zealand
Level 13, 201 Elizabeth Street, Sydney NSW 2000, Australia
A 53, Sector 57, Noida, UP, India
77–85 Fulham Palace Road, London W6 8JB, United Kingdom
2 Bloor Street East, 20th floor, Toronto, Ontario M4W 1A8, Canada
195 Broadway, New York, NY 10007, USA

National Library of New Zealand cataloguing-in-publication data:

Dekker, Laura, 1995–
  Ein Mädchen, ein Traum. English
  One girl, one dream / Laura Dekker.
  ISBN 978 1 77554 099 1 (paperback)
  ISBN 978 1 77549 082 1 (ebook)
  1. Dekker, Laura, 1995– — Travel.
  2. Voyages around the world.
  3. Single-handed sailing.
  I. Title.
910.41—dc 23

Translated from the original Dutch by Lily-Anne Stroobach
Maps and boat diagrams by Michiel van der Eijk
All cover and internal images courtesy of Laura Dekker with the exception of the
following: page 2 top right courtesy of Mike Ruel; page 4 middle and page 7 bottom
left courtesy of Jillian Schlesinger; page 7 middle courtesy of Uwe Moser; and page 8
top courtesy of Karel Heijnen.
Cover design by Christa Moffitt, Christabella Designs
Typeset in Bembo Std by Kirby Jones
Printed and bound in Australia by McPhersons Printing Group
The papers used by HarperCollins in the manufacture of this book
are a natural, recyclable product made from wood grown in sustainable
plantation forests. The fibre source and manufacturing processes meet
recognised international environmental standards, and carry certification.

If you want to see the other side of the world,
you can do two things: turn the world upside down
or travel there yourself.

Acknowledgements

Thank you to everyone who supported me — my sponsors, family, and especially Dad. I couldn't have accomplished the things I did without them. I got to know myself, learnt about the world and fulfilled the dream of my life.

Contents

Foreword

One of my favorite quotes ever comes from one of Laura's sailing heroes, Bernard Moitessier, the legendary Frenchman who participated in the first singlehanded race around the world in the late sixties. Non-stop. Back then, ship to shore communications were primitive, and when he passed Cape Horn and was about to head back north to the finish line, he had no idea he was in first place. What he did know was that he wasn't ready to face life ashore in northern Europe, and so he made the famous decision to continue sailing west back to Polynesia. Off the Cape of Good Hope, he used a slingshot to fire a message home onto the deck of a tanker: *'I am continuing non-stop towards the Pacific Islands because I am happy at sea, and perhaps also, to save my soul.'*

Laura and I are not his only fans. This quote resonated with decades of sailors who wanted to escape the industrial machine and surged south to tropical climates on boats, to catch rainwater, eat fish, rice and bananas, navigate by sun and stars. It was a simple, healthy life that beckoned to many a kindred spirit troubled by the demands of civilisation, and more than 40 years later, one young lady had to fight long and hard for her right to join these ranks and happily sail around the world. And, when Laura Dekker finally broke free to busily prove all the naysayers wrong, I cheered her on.

She was 14 years old when she started, 16 at the end of her solo circumnavigation. If she'd had it her way, she would have left Holland at 13, right after sailing a 22-footer across the English Channel alone, before announcing her dream and intention landed her in the custody of child services. Three other young solo sailors — two 16-year-old boys, and one girl — were successfully completing their own circumnavigations at the time, with corporate sponsorships and hero's welcomes in the US, UK, and Australia — but Laura's story sparked an international debate about irresponsible parents, foolish daughters, and how young is too young. A 13-, 14-, then 15-year-old girl who wanted to be alone at sea needed medication, headlines cried, not indulgence.

Opinions were broadcast around the world. But, instead of crumbling under the weight of so much doubt about her motivation, maturity, or readiness, Laura decided to keep going, even after the boat she originally wanted to go with was confiscated. In between fighting the courts and getting a little older, she purchased and refurbished a super-sweet 38-foot boat for the voyage.

For over a year, at a time during which most 14-year-olds worry way too much about what other people think and what to wear, this amazing girl kept doggedly pursuing a dream, where the greatest challenge was turning out to be not singlehanded sailing but the strong opposition standing between her and the ocean.

Everyone was doing their jobs — the older and wiser people who profess to know what's best for a young girl, and the teenager, professing to know what was best for herself. She held fast, and when the blockade finally dissolved, without the flash of major sponsors and support, she took off. Only 14, the battling had taken longer than her entire subsequent sail around the world.

I followed this little pilgrim's progress, and because I'd circumnavigated alone as a young girl and was now a mother, media types kept calling to ask for my thoughts. At the time, my two teenaged boys were being inspired by the pleasure principle more than any kind of passion that wasn't mainstream, and I thought this lack of imagination was worrisome. So, while allowing for normal parental fears and concerns, because that's what we do, I also couldn't help admiring Laura's spunk, how she was setting a new standard of courage and determination.

If we all feared the same things, and if nobody was willing to take a risk for what they believed in, the world would be a very boring place indeed. In fact, we'd still all be in caves cringing from scary flames. So many conventional young people make decisions that lead to tragic endings (usually after too much of the pleasure principle) that hardly make it out of local newspapers. I couldn't understand the fuss over this girl's dream to sail around the world — a decision that is never made and carried out impulsively, without a lot of serious thought, focused planning and preparation — and why it was meeting with such vocal resistance. I could only imagine the relief Laura must have felt on the day she finally sailed out of that Dutch port and pointed the bow south. Moitessier would have understood. *'You do not ask a tame seagull why it needs to disappear from time to time toward the open sea. It goes, that's all.'*

But, we live in different times, and only seagulls have the luxury of disappearing at sea. Modern sailors are not Bernard Moitessier, sending messages to loved ones with slingshots aimed at passing tankers. They keep daily blogs and use satellite phones to call home. GPS and chart plotters provide up-to-the-minute positions and EPIRBs pinpoint them immediately in the event of a disaster. All this can be a double-edged sword. At the same time that technology has made the high seas feel safer and more accessible to everyone, it also keeps the sailor tethered to land. In the middle of the ocean, Laura was still on stage, and I got the impression she saw this as a necessary evil, the price she had to pay to fulfill her quest.

Periodically, I'd check in on her blog, see how far along she'd got. As the dots steadily tracked across one ocean after another, I visualised her flat calms becoming boring, broken equipment annoying, strong winds exciting, all part of the overall package that had once been mine. The descriptions of her adventure were also full of wonder and gratitude for having been given this opportunity. At sea, this girl was in her element, and most of the time her blog reflected utter contentment, words that strongly echoed more of Moitessier's: *'I am a citizen of the most beautiful nation on earth. A nation whose laws are harsh yet simple, a nation that never cheats, which is immense and without borders, where life is lived in the present. In this limitless nation, this nation of wind, light, and peace, there is no other ruler besides the sea.'*

The real fly in her ointment came from land. At one point, I read, because she admitted the distractions out there were keeping her from applying herself regularly to schoolwork, she received a scolding from the rulers. Imagine that. Imagine swishing westward, hundreds of miles away from terra firma. You've just swatted the last mosquito that hitched a ride aboard in the last port, tweaked the sails, enjoyed a few hours of cockpit time, and are maybe thinking about dinner, when you go below to make another blog posting about how lucky you feel to be out there — the modern equivalent of a log entry — and a message comes in. You are being chastised, and not by your parents. Some governmental authority is commanding you to return to your schoolwork, or face consequences upon your return *from a singlehanded circumnavigation*, for crying out loud. Total killjoy. It made me feel embarrassed to be an adult.

Her story defines valour, and comes to us at yet another time in history when words about right and wrong talk way louder than actions all around the planet. Laura is definitely not too young to teach her elders a thing or two about optimism, perseverance and true individuality, even as over-analysed public opinion tried to stuff her back in a box. She escaped and got out there, very happily, freely, and impressively living her dream.

People worried about her being at sea; she worried about her homecoming. What next? What happens after you've spent a significant percentage of a short life single-mindedly pursuing one goal, and it's over?

When I finished my solo circumnavigation in the late eighties, at the age of 21 — an old maid compared with Laura — my fantasy was to have a house in the country, gardens and children. After sailing to all those islands and countries, meeting the people who belonged to worlds I was just passing through, I wanted a place where I belonged, a community of my own.

Time passes and is measured by what we do with it. In October 2012, nine months after Laura successfully and proudly sailed into Saint Martin, she came to visit me, my house, gardens, and average young-adult boys — who were a little older than her and home from college for a visit. We went for a walk around the hilltop, across fields and into woods crisp with the colours of autumn and foliage littering the paths connecting the part of the world I call home, and shared stories. I felt a certain closeness with her that transcended the difference in our ages, the generational gap with this feisty girl I would be proud to call a daughter inhabited by a timeless watery place somewhere beyond the wooded horizon and words, to a place known by seagulls, Bernard Moitessier, and those who come from all walks of life who want to live fully in the present with wind, light and peace.

As she had written in her blog, she had been back to Holland for some talks, appearances, and time with family, before continuing on to sail back to New Zealand where she had citizenship, planning to build a life there. Now, she was performing the expected duties — compiling a book, figuring out a way to finish up schooling — but was unsure about what to do next. What does one do after becoming a 16-year-old solo circumnavigator?

I could remember how the elation of my own last days at sea before making landfall in New York had been dampened by the very same concern, the pure joy of accomplishing such a huge challenge mitigated by the melancholy of knowing I had just lived my greatest adventure with the most beautiful nation on earth. For two and a half years, the sea had given me the gift of clarity, of knowing exactly what needed to be done every day — whatever it took, in a seamanlike way, to head west and get back home. As I was about to be swept up in life ashore, a young adult faced with many paths into the future, leading in all possible directions, I could see that things would never again be so simple.

The beauty of a journey is how it really has a beginning, a middle and an end. Once I returned to New York, it was important to sit down, write the book, and process the whole experience into the black and white of words; a complete story told for once and for all, that could be put aside before moving on. Meeting and talking with Laura, I saw a very practical and down-to-earth young lady who would do the same for herself, then capably figure out what came next.

A much older Moitessier was never able to reconcile himself with Europe, the politics of Western civilisation. He made several attempts, but it was always a painful struggle, with him torn between responsibility to relationships and a lifelong yearning to be out at sea again, unencumbered by societal expectations, the only place where he ever felt true happiness. '*A sailor's joys are as simple as a child's,*' he said.

When you're a child sailor, you can know the best of both worlds, but no matter who we are and what we've done, we all face the pitfalls of growing up someday. Laura gets to do this with the companionship of a really nice boat, and on the strength of a major success that smashed conventional wisdom about the limitations of youth, proving what focus, guts and determination can accomplish. Once again, I wish her all the best and success, wherever the voyage leads as she resets her focus on new goals, and plots and sails a course from this remarkable adolescence into adulthood.

Tania Aebi
Vermont, April 2013

How it all began

I am Laura and I was born in Whangarei, New Zealand. My parents were sailing around the world at the time and had been in New Zealand for two years. I became the youngest member of the crew when we made our way to Australia. They wanted to take their time to see as much of the world as possible. My sister Kim was born three years after me, and our 12-metre yacht eventually became too cramped for a family with two little girls. So we sailed back to the Netherlands where we moved into a real house for the first time. My parents' journey had taken them seven years, and it was hard for Dad to live on firm land. He immediately started on the construction of an even bigger boat: a 20-metre, seaworthy Norwegian fishing cutter with enough room for everyone. Unfortunately, my parents' marriage broke up and, at the age of six, I chose to stay with my father. We lived in a caravan for some time while he worked on the new boat.

As you can see, my life started very differently to that of my schoolmates. This was evident in the drawings I did as a child. While they drew little houses with trees, I drew boats on the water; while they played in the playground, I played on the water with homemade boats and anything that would float. Living in a caravan with Dad working on a new boat was normal life for me. Within a year of moving onto land, I was back in a boat on the water and it would stay that way. Recognising my interest in sailing, my father bought me an Optimist for my sixth birthday. This is the classic sailing craft for children, and I spent almost every day on it, both in summer and in winter. Later, when I was eight, an acquaintance gave me a Mirror; a great little boat. By now I was crazy about sailing and took part in youth sailing competitions. After a while, I wasn't allowed to compete anymore because I won too often, so I started taking part in the adult sailing class events. I sometimes even sailed against my dad, who was a fanatical sailor himself. I didn't win as often, but I continued to take great pleasure in sailing.

By now I wanted my own cabin yacht. There was a Hurley 700 in our marina that was hardly ever used. One day I approached the owner and asked him if I could try it out. He agreed and, as a 10-year-old, I made my first long-distance solo trip. I sailed his boat across the inland waters in the north of the Netherlands, from the Ijsselmeer — the largest inland lake in the country — to Friesland and the Wadden Islands in the North Sea.

I soon realised that I wanted to sail around the world, just like my parents had. I also knew that I wanted to leave as soon as possible, and this meant that I needed a seaworthy boat of my own. When I was 11, I bought my own boat, a seaworthy Hurley 700. Dad paid for it on condition that I paid back half. I took on all sorts of jobs in order to pay off the boat: two newspaper rounds, cleaning jobs in the afternoons and, at the weekends, work in a chandlery. Anything at all so long as it paid. I even earned money performing tricks on a unicycle!

When I was 13 I sailed my seaworthy Hurley 700 single-handedly to England. Customs clearance was no problem, but after a couple of days in England I suddenly received a visit from the police. Afterwards, I learnt that one of my girlfriends' parents had gone to the Dutch police because they felt I shouldn't have been allowed to sail on my own to England. The Dutch authorities then contacted the British police, who in turn asked my dad to come to England to sail back with me. Once he arrived, the authorities handed the responsibility for my welfare back to my dad and he allowed me to sail solo back to the Netherlands.

In the meantime, I had started making preparations for my round-the-world voyage. My 7-metre yacht was a little small for the trip, and I needed to get hold of a bigger boat. My faithful Hurley 700 was soon sold after a sponsor offered me a Hurley 800. My father and I got cracking to ready the new boat for my long journey. Through the *Wereldschool*, an educational programme for Dutch children living abroad, we also arranged everything that was necessary for me to continue my schooling during my voyage. In the Netherlands it is compulsory for children to attend a real school until they are 16. If kids want to take a day off, they have to ask permission weeks in advance and then it is usually turned down. If they take the day off anyway, their parents get a heavy fine and, if they refuse to pay, then one of them may face prosecution. As I was planning to stop going to school, we had to see an official from the Department of Education. She didn't understand what we were talking about and had never heard of the *Wereldschool*. She stated bluntly that it was compulsory for me to attend school and that Dad would be breaking the law if he allowed me to stop. In short, there was no escaping the education system in the Netherlands.

A few days later, a journalist from a national newspaper contacted us. How on earth had she heard about our appointment with the education official? Surely our meeting should have been confidential? Without any intention on our part, I became front-page news. It was very unpleasant to be telephoned by journalists every day, and there were complete television crews on the jetty asking questions that I didn't feel like answering. I wasn't looking for fame; I just wanted to sail and be left alone.

When Dutch Prime Minister Jan Peter Balkenende announced publicly on TV that I couldn't skip school to sail because it was compulsory for everyone in the Netherlands to attend school, Child Protection also began to meddle in our affairs. Dad and I were called to appear in court, and we needed to engage a lawyer. I'd never been inside a court building before and almost laughed when three (!) judges appeared in their black robes and what looked like white bibs. The Child Protection official asked the judges to have me put into a closed institution immediately and to terminate my dad's parental rights. Fortunately, the court had no good grounds to do so.

In the end, the judges said I was allowed to stay with Dad, but ordered me to remain under the supervision of the authorities. They appointed a guardian to keep an eye on me. This guardian knew nothing about boats or sailing, and he certainly didn't have sea legs! When he came by, we would laugh at how he clambered on board; he was so clumsy, we almost hoped that he would fall overboard. Once on board, I had to keep watch over Spot, my dog, who took an instant dislike to the man. Spot could sense that we didn't want this man on the boat. With the truth twisted in all sorts of official reports, and through all the resulting commotion, negative media reports and court cases, many of the sponsors that I had taken so much trouble to find over the past year pulled out. When we were dealing with a second court case a month later, the judge ordered that I was not allowed to leave on my voyage before being tested to see if I could cope psychologically with the voyage. The judge's decision meant that I stood to lose a whole year, as I'd be unable to leave the Netherlands in the winter. Two months later, a sponsor offered to get my Hurley in top condition for my world voyage, and so I needed to get my boat to a bigger boatyard. This turned out to be too good to be true. It was the last time I would see my Hurley 800: the authorities had taken the boat.

My boat was gone, but the dream lived on. It was so unfair to be fighting against authorities who would go to such lengths. I decided on another plan. I knew that my phone and PC were being monitored by the *Algemene Inlichtingen en Veiligheids Dienst* (the Dutch state intelligence and security service), so I used another PC and a different email address to find information. Using the internet, I found a broker on the island of Saint Martin in the Caribbean who had a Dufour Arpège 9-metre polyester yacht. It had been left behind on the island because the owner didn't ever want to sail again. Within a few days I had all the information I needed about the boat. The price was very low and the specifications were right. I calculated that the money from my Hurley 700, together with my savings, would be enough to buy it; and there would be sufficient money left for me to start sailing from Saint Martin. I figured that once I had a boat again and was sailing, the rest would follow.

On 17 December, I collected my savings and wrote a farewell note to my dad. I was afraid to tell him about my plans in case he stopped me. We were in the middle of court cases and I was under state supervision. I took the train to Paris because I was worried that the Dutch passport control officials would recognise me at the airport and would hold me back. I had said goodbye to no one, except my faithful dog, Spot. He wasn't likely to tell anyone.

Once in France, nobody recognised me, and there were daily flights from Paris to Saint Martin. It all went a lot more smoothly than I had expected. When I arrived at Gare du Nord, I took the shuttle train to Charles de Gaulle airport. It was really easy to buy a last-minute ticket at the airport to Saint Martin with the cash I had and with my new New Zealand passport. Before I knew it, I was on an Air France flight on my way to realise my dream …

At the airport on Saint Martin, I walked straight through Customs, and there I was, 14 years old with the tropical sun beaming down on me. Presenting myself as 17-year-old Jessie Muller, I called the broker, who fetched me from the airport, and the next morning I was on board to inspect the boat. The inside was a huge mess, but I had learnt from Dad to ignore this. It's the structure of the boat that's important, and technically the boat seemed OK. I was sitting in the broker's office ready to sign the sales agreement when the phone rang. During a short conversation, the broker looked at me several times and typed something on his computer. He then turned the screen towards me to show me a life-size picture of myself ... The Dutch authorities had sent out a worldwide search warrant for me — as if I were a serious criminal.

I felt my world crumble. No, I wasn't Jessie Muller and wasn't 17 either. The broker was very nice to me. He said he had to inform the police that I was there, but that it could wait a while. He suggested we go to the beach with his wife and child and have some lunch before doing this. When I told them everything that had occurred over the past six months, I felt that I was finally with people who understood and sympathised with me. They were genuinely sorry for me.

The broker felt bad about having to inform the police, but he was worried about his reputation on the island. Late that afternoon, he took me to the Saint Martin Yacht Club where the police were waiting for me.

The next day I was put onto a flight to the Netherlands under police escort. On the plane, two members of the Military Police took over the guard duties, and at Schiphol, the international airport outside Amsterdam, I was again treated like a criminal and was ushered in through a side entrance. I was interrogated for three hours by police and lawyers working for Child Protection, and wasn't even allowed access to my own lawyer or my parents. I was then taken straight to a court in Utrecht for an emergency hearing, where I was allowed five minutes with Dad and Peter de Lange, my lawyer. I sat in court totally exhausted from my long journey. Child Protection once again demanded that I be placed in protective custody. After a whole day of deliberations, the three judges couldn't reach a consensus and decided to sleep on it before continuing the next day. I wasn't allowed to go home with Dad but was put into the care of a stranger. Why him and not Dad or Mum? I soon found out. The man had contacts with the Child Protection and Child Welfare lawyers. I knew what they were trying to do — they were trying to break my will so that I'd give up. The more they tried, the more I was determined to leave this country, so I put on a brave face and continued to fight for my dream. ·

Then I read in the newspaper that the Child Protection and Child Welfare lawyers had told journalists that my guardian was a family friend. Utter lies! The court session, which took the whole day, was chaotic. Tempers were so high that my mother left the court furious about the proceedings and my lawyer rebuked the judges. When no one could figure out how to continue, I was eventually allowed to go home with Dad. The Child Protection lawyers were seething that they hadn't had their way. They'd thought up a number of ways to outmanoeuvre us, but hadn't succeeded. They had used the media to put me in a bad light but still hadn't managed to put me into protective custody. Unfortunately, the judge did manage to keep me under state supervision. Spot was over the moon when we got home after the two-day court session. It was back to school and back to the weekly visits by the guardian, who, much to our disappointment, still hadn't managed to fall into the water.

They hadn't locked me up, so I managed to continue with my plans. I didn't let the officials, Child Protection, the Child Welfare authorities and lawyers stop me. My biggest problem was that I no longer had a boat and, because of all the negative media reports, there was no new sponsor in sight. My family felt really sorry for me and dug deep into their savings. Within a few weeks, they found a cheap, 33-year-old Jeanneau Gin Fizz, badly neglected but basically sound. I fell in love with her at first sight. She had a beautiful design; a two-master which would make it easier to handle as a solo sailor, because, while there were more sails, they were smaller and easier to handle.

By now it was spring and we lived very far away from my new boat, which needed a lot of work. We sailed Dad's boat, on which we were living, to our new mooring in Den Osse, in the south of the Netherlands, so that we could start work on my new boat. There was a huge amount of work to be done and, if I was to leave by summer, we had only four months left to complete it. Together we worked day and night to get the Jeanneau ready and seaworthy. I didn't mind cycling 13 kilometres to school every day, so long as I could work on my dream. Hans van Dijke, the owner of the water sports business of the same name, helped us when he could. Hans also became my new sponsor.

'*Guppy*, you beauty!' I called when we launched her a few months later on a rainy day in May.

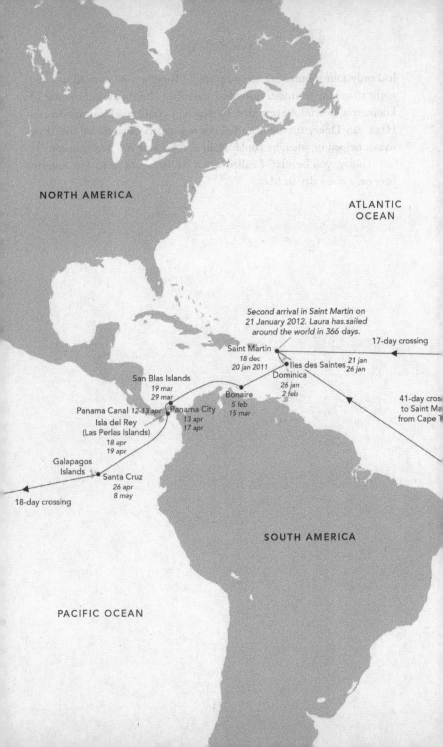

NORTH AMERICA

ATLANTIC
OCEAN

Second arrival in Saint Martin on
21 January 2012. Laura has sailed
around the world in 366 days.

17-day crossing

Saint Martin
18 dec
20 jan 2011

Iles des Saintes   21 jan
                    26 jan

Dominica
26 jan
2 feb

San Blas Islands
19 mar
29 mar

Bonaire
5 feb
15 mar

Panama Canal 12-13 apr
Panama City
13 apr
17 apr

41-day cros
to Saint Ma
from Cape T

Isla del Rey
(Las Perlas Islands)
18 apr
19 apr

Galapagos
Islands

Santa Cruz
26 apr
8 may

18-day crossing

SOUTH AMERICA

PACIFIC OCEAN

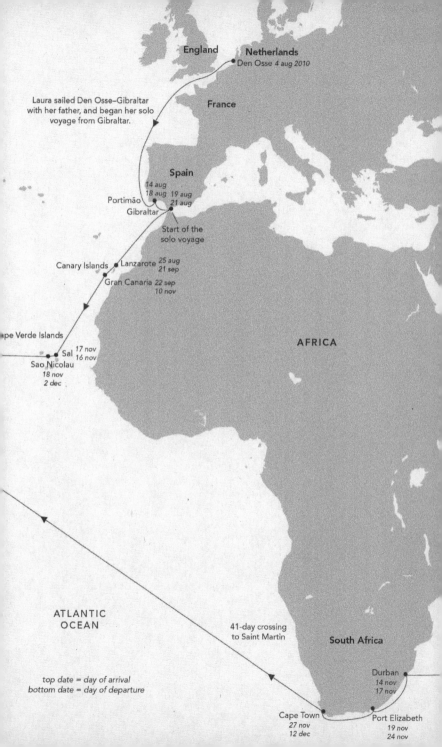

England

Netherlands
Den Osse *4 aug 2010*

France

Laura sailed Den Osse–Gibraltar
with her father, and began her solo
voyage from Gibraltar.

Spain

14 aug
18 aug   *19 aug*
Portimão   *21 aug*
Gibraltar

Start of the
solo voyage

Canary Islands   • Lanzarote   *25 aug*
21 sep

Gran Canaria *22 sep*
10 nov

AFRICA

pe Verde Islands

Sal *17 nov*
16 nov
Sao Nicolau
18 nov
2 dec

ATLANTIC
OCEAN

41-day crossing
to Saint Martin

South Africa

Durban
14 nov
17 nov

Port Elizabeth
19 nov
24 nov

Cape Town
27 nov
12 dec

top date = day of arrival
bottom date = day of departure

At last!

I stick my fork into a slice of cake that my gran has brought while she stitches *Guppy*'s canopy. Granddad and Dad have gone outside. I drop my fork and anxiously pace up and down the boat. Right now, the court in Middelburg is swarming with journalists who are waiting to hear the verdict in the sixth court case in the past 11 months. Yes, that's how often the authorities have dragged me before the judges! In a couple of hours one of the judges will probably be telling them, for the umpteenth time, that I'm to remain under the supervision of the authorities until kingdom come, and this will mean that I won't be able to start my voyage.

I'm messing about on the boat when I see Dad approaching. He looks a bit dazed.

'Laura, you're free to go,' he says, as if talking about the weather.

He's just been phoned by our lawyer and still can't believe it himself. It takes a while before his words begin to sink in, but when they do I burst into tears and fly into his arms, hug Spot and fling myself around *Guppy*'s mast. My lawyer, Peter de Lange, is on the phone again with Dad to tell him that it will make sense to have all the journalists present at the court come to us in Den Osse, as there will be no way of avoiding them now. In this way, I can give a brief press conference on the terrace of the harbour office and be rid of them all in one go.

I'm told to make myself presentable, and I dive into my cupboard to find a suitable outfit. It appears that I'm making world history and the footage that will be recorded will soon be flashing across the globe. While I'm changing, my mobile phone starts to ring and doesn't stop ringing for the rest of the day. Friends and acquaintances are all phoning to congratulate me. Shit, with all the excitement, I've forgotten to let my mum know! I quickly give her a call. She's happy for me and swears under her breath. Her eldest daughter, who's a mere 14 years old, will soon be going on a two-year voyage all on her own. A little later,

25

dozens of cars arrive with journalists wielding cameras and satellite dishes. They want me to sail *Guppy* around the harbour and I have to smile and pose for the cameras. I have just enough time to gobble down some food before a taxi arrives to take me to the television studio. I once again have to repeat how I feel about the events of this day.

I get to bed very late that night, and that's when I finally have time to absorb the news. One thought is uppermost in my mind: now that I have been acquitted, I need to de-register myself as a Dutch resident immediately so that Child Protection and other authorities are unable to lodge an appeal. They'll have to de-register me, whether they like it or not. I don't want to wait longer than a week before setting off, and don't want to take any more chances with these scheming authorities. There is still so much to do! Getting food supplies, filling up with diesel and stocking up with all the parts and equipment that we haven't got around to installing yet. *Guppy* is not nearly ready, but I want to leave this country NOW. Thoroughly exhausted, I fall into a deep sleep and dream of blue waters and far-off countries.

The journey begins

4 August

The day has finally dawned! I'm actually leaving today and *Guppy* will be my home for the next two years. When I wake up at six in the morning and look outside, I notice that there are a couple of camera crews in motion again. Sigh. There are just a few to start with, but soon there are dozens. Even the Russian state television is present. There is also a growing crowd in the harbour of Den Osse. Everyone wants a glimpse of *Guppy* and me. Hmm. I say farewell to my family for the umpteenth time, and then walk onto the quayside just after nine. Surrounded by dozens of journalists, photographers and television crews who are pushing me closer to the water's edge, I give a short interview. I answer the same questions over and over again in both Dutch and English. They ask me if I'm scared of pirates (no), how long I'll be away (two years), and if I think I'll succeed in being the youngest sailor ever to sail single-handedly around the world (well, I'm about to find out!).

It's been a week since the amazing news that I was acquitted by the court in Middelburg. How lucky I was to have found a judge, at last, who saw through the games the authorities were playing with me. The judge declared that they were wrong and I was free. I'm de-registered as a Dutch resident in the Netherlands and there is nothing more they can do — or so I thought.

On the day of my departure, my mother and sister are on holiday abroad and it pours with rain. Dad is sailing with me as far as Portugal, because *Guppy* is not quite ready and still needs some trial runs. *Guppy* needs to be checked and tested thoroughly before Dad will allow me to continue on my own. Fortunately, Nature's mood changes and the rain actually stops when we finally set off. I'm followed by dozens of hooting boats up to the first lock. My gran, granddad, aunt, uncle and niece also accompany me in their boats. Not that long ago, I couldn't have dreamt of this. Past the lock the water gets rougher; it begins to rain again, and the boats drop away. Yet another yacht approaches and fires a flare in salute while the crew shout their good wishes above the sound of the wind.

The Coast Guard launch follows me closely all the way; probably to check that I'm not sailing on my own. As a 14-year-old, I'm not allowed to sail the inland waters of the Netherlands without adult supervision on this size boat. After having been doused with plenty of water along the way, we finally reach the sea lock. A new crowd has gathered here, and they are also shouting their wishes for a safe journey.

We are beyond the locks and into the North Sea before we know it. I stand at the helm with my wet-weather gear buttoned up to the top. I simply can't sail *Guppy* out on autopilot on a day like today. The weather is awful; it's cold with buckets of rain and a 25-knot wind that we're heading straight into. But this doesn't put *Guppy* off; she's in her element and plunges through the waves. I'm soaked to my underwear within two minutes as the waves wash over the deck. My spirits, too, are a little dampened as I leave this cold and bleak country. This little nation, which has caused me so much misery and hardship over the past year, disappears out of sight and I don't look back.

On our way, I test *Guppy* and push her to her limits. This is real sailing at last! Dad is happy with me and lets me do all the work while he watches, because that's the way it's going to be when he leaves. After a week of sailing, the wind picks up near Portugal and *Guppy* sets record speeds for herself. The log shows a regular 9 to 10 knots. I'm enjoying *Guppy* and the rush of water. Dad says nothing, but frowns.

'It's OK,' I say, 'I know, but this is so cool!'

At one stage the wind, from the starboard quarter, accelerates to 40 knots and *Guppy* is surfing way too fast through the waves. She broaches dangerously, turning beam-on to the oncoming breakers. Poor *Guppy* only just manages not to capsize. Dad had, of course, seen this coming for some time, but had thought: let it happen and she'll see. He thinks that the best lessons are learnt from experience, and now he also knows that *Guppy* can take it. I hurry to drop the double-reefed mainsail, and *Guppy* is now sailing under a half-reefed jib at a speed of 8 knots. I can feel that the windpilot now has her well under control. Dad says I'm pretty stubborn, but from now on I'll reduce sail a little sooner. I promise, Dad, honestly ...

DAY 10: *14 August*

After nearly two weeks at sea, we're finally there. We aren't taking any chances with the Lisbon harbour authorities, and have sailed past this port for fear of them stopping us. Lisbon is the harbour from which I was meant to start my journey, according to media reports, and we are worried that the Dutch authorities may have informed their counterparts in Portugal that I'm sailing in European waters without a skipper's ticket. This could be the last trump they might play to stop my voyage. Outside the 12-mile zone you don't need any papers as you are surrounded only by water and nothing much can happen. Closer to land you need more sailing knowledge and experience, which is why a licence is compulsory within this zone. I had passed my Yachtmaster's Offshore Certificate exam at the age of 13, but then received a letter saying that, although I had passed, I wouldn't be issued a licence because I was a minor!

At night we sail into the harbour of Portimão in the south of Portugal, a few hundred miles further down the coast. It's almost calm. I sail *Guppy* past a few rocks and can smell land. It's weird how strong everything smells once you've been at sea for two weeks. I smell the scent of flowers, plants and the city. Close to the harbour, I wake up my crew.

'Dad,' I shout, 'we've arrived!'

When he surfaces, still blurry from sleep, I throw a couple of fenders into his arms. I'm making the most of his help while he's still on board. *Guppy* is allowed to tie up for free at the Portimão marina. We'd been told to go to Box O64, but it doesn't seem to exist. This we only discovered after having sailed around the harbour four times in the dark. We eventually tie up alongside a jetty near what we presume to be the arrival jetty.

Portugal, Portimão

In the morning, we realise that it's not the arrival jetty but the VIP jetty, as we are surrounded by mega-yachts. Oops! We move to the correct jetty and are finally allocated a box that actually does exist. I go to the authorities to register while Dad continues to check the last of the equipment and solve the remaining problems on *Gup*. I'm able to get clearance for *Guppy*, which is registered in my name, without a hitch. I walk back to *Guppy* in a good mood, take a shower and do the laundry. We have three whole loads! The bad weather we had getting here ensured that all our clothes and bed linen were covered in salt. We give *Guppy* a good wash, both inside and out, to get all the salt off her, too. By evening everything is shipshape again.

It's incredibly hot here and I have exchanged the winter coat that I wore for most of the way for a T-shirt and a pair of shorts. Luckily there's a bit of wind to make the heat bearable. We continue to work hard on *Guppy* for the next few days, because I want to leave as soon as possible.

We go to the water sports centre to buy the necessary parts, but they don't have what we need and we decide to go into town. After a long barefoot walk — having forgotten to put on my shoes — an ice-cream and a dip in a fountain, we get back to *Guppy*. The media have found us and there's a camera focused on *Guppy* from behind every shrub. That's bad news, because now the Netherlands will know where we are.

I hear someone knocking on the hull. It has been dark for a while, and besides Dad, who is working in the engine compartment, there is no one here. I step outside and see two men in police uniform standing in the dim light. As soon as I appear, they turn their heads my way and ask, gruffly, if I'm the captain.

'I am,' I confirm after some hesitation.

'We would like to see your skipper's ticket' is the demand that immediately follows.

All sorts of thoughts flash through my head while I sum up these men, but I keep calm and tell them that I passed my Yachtmaster's Offshore Certificate exams the previous year and that this permits me to sail in these waters. The Dutch authorities, however, had not issued me with the

30

official certificate. I show them the document that says that I passed my exams. Dad now emerges from the engine room and, after sizing up the situation, says that he's presently the captain and shows them his certificate. After a short discussion, the two of them recede into the dark. We look at one another and understand exactly what has just happened.

The next morning we walk to see the harbour police for an explanation. They have just heard about last night's visit and say they were given an order by the powers-that-be that I am not to sail out of the harbour. The Customs officials are apologetic about it, but say they have no choice. Damn, when are they going to give up hounding me like they did in the Netherlands? This means I won't be able to sail single-handedly through the 12-mile zone from here to start my voyage. As long as Dad is on board with his skipper's ticket, they can't touch us. We decide to sail to Gibraltar the next day on Dad's certificate. We had thought of Gibraltar earlier, as this former British colony keeps itself apart from Europe and doesn't require you to have this certificate. The chances of the Netherlands being able to reach us there in the short term can't be that big. To minimise the risk, I'll stay there for a few days before starting out on my own. But what if the media get to learn about our whereabouts? We decide not to take the risk and tell no one of our intentions; especially not the media. It's my last hope of ever starting on my solo voyage.

Portugal, Portimão–Gibraltar: 200 nautical miles

DAY 1: *18 August*

Less than half an hour after our departure from the harbour of Portimão, the Military Police come alongside *Guppy* wanting to know where we are going, whether we are leaving Portugal, and who is on board. These may have been standard queries, but had I been on my own I am sure they would have taken me straight back to the harbour. When asked where we are going, we tell them we're doing a trial run and keep quiet about going to Gibraltar. Nobody knows this; not even my grandparents, mum or friends. I've worked so hard to make a start that I'm dead scared that the media will get to know about it and, once more, ruin my chances. The media think I'm in Portugal and will wait there for our expected return. After all the incidents of the past year, I really need a break and I'm looking forward to seeing the famous British peninsula with its monkey rock.

Towards evening we experience a headwind and start the engine. We want to get to Gibraltar as soon as possible to prevent anyone from finding out that I might start from this 'free state'. That night I lie in my cockpit looking at *Guppy*'s swaying mast and the beautiful starlit sky while Dad is sleeping. As the Strait of Gibraltar nears, the wind shifts and gathers momentum, urging *Guppy* to take advantage under full sail. She's having a whale of a time!

DAY 2: *19 August*

In the Strait of Gibraltar, I have a wonderful view of the coastlines of both Morocco and Spain. There are high mountains on either side of the strait, which is far narrower than I expected. Halfway through, I'm tempted to sail through the whirlpool that is marked on the chart. Dad doesn't think it's a good idea, but, after some persuasion and my query about what might happen, he says: 'Well, it may be possible, but you could sail around it.'

The whirlpool can be seen from a distance but, before I know what's happening, *Gup* is drawn into the current and big splashes half-fill the cockpit.

'Yes, Dad, I know I'm stubborn,' I acknowledge, 'but that was so cool!'

At about 18.00, I sail *Guppy* through the harbour entrance of Gibraltar.

Gibraltar

They don't recognise me at the harbour office, but the crew on the neighbouring boat recognises *Guppy* and me immediately. I clear *Guppy* in again without any problems, and that evening we enjoy a pizza on the quayside. There are just a few chores to do before I can set off. Topping up the water and diesel tanks are two of the minor ones. Dad is still busy fixing the last of the equipment — work held up by all the distractions. We need to fix the sticker of a new sponsor on the boat, but this turns out to be a disaster. The sticker is much too thin and the heat turns it into a sort of chewing gum. There's nothing much we can do about it and we leave it as it is.

We enjoy another delicious pizza the next afternoon, and then take a rental car into the mountains to visit the famous monkeys. Within minutes there's one on top of the car, one on the inside and many more around us. It's really funny to see them this close; so different to a zoo. After this, I insist on seeing the other side of the mountain, so we try to get as high as possible by car and walk the last bit. There's a huge drop on the other side and we have a magnificent view. I'll approach the Rock of Gibraltar from this side when I return, I think, while looking out over the Mediterranean. The Atlantic Ocean on the other side is where I'll start my voyage the next day. We have carried out lots of improvements on *Guppy* over the past weeks and she should be ready now. I will say farewell to Dad in the morning.

Gibraltar–Canary Islands: 650 nautical miles

DAY 1: *21 August*

I'm on my way at last! Cleared out without a hitch and really on my way ... Here I go, 14 years old and heading for who knows where. A trip around the world. Fantastic! But first I need to get clear of the 12-mile zone in European waters; only then do all the papers and rules cease to count. Even a toddler is allowed to sail a boat in international waters. My throat is tight with tension. I reach the 12-mile limit and I'm free. At least until the Canary Islands, where there may be tension once again. With my stereo playing full blast, *Guppy* surges westward at top speed. I'm standing on the bow and feel the tension ebbing bit by bit. Nothing and no one can snatch my dream away from me now!

There's a following wind of some 20 knots; the genoa is fully boomed out and *Guppy* is running at 7 knots. Once I've left the busy Strait of Gibraltar I'm able to take a break, but I've a strange feeling in my tummy. Although I'm really happy that I'm finally on my way, I'm now apprehensive about what's in store for me once I arrive in the Canary Islands. Do the Dutch authorities have any influence there? I reassure myself that that would really be taking things too far.

I warm up two sausage rolls and try to get some food inside me, but I'm not that hungry and only manage to eat one of them. I'm feeling so weak; maybe a Coke will help, but nothing changes the strange feeling I have in my tummy. I know that many seafarers feel a little nauseous at the start of their voyage, but this is different. Tension maybe? It has been such a difficult time.

It's not that warm. I put on a jersey and try to find a dry spot on *Guppy* that's sunny. Slowly a huge smile spreads over my face and I try to calculate how much further I need to travel on this stage of the voyage. If *Guppy* maintains her present speed, I'll be there in six days. A huge cargo ship passes me at full throttle, and then gradually the first day disappears beyond the horizon as night falls over me like a blanket.

The first night I'm on full alert with numerous fishing boats close by and hardly manage to shut an eye. Although I should be able to sleep, I realise how difficult it is even though I am dead tired. The tension I've experienced over the past year has taken its toll, and the idea that I'm now below deck in my bunk while no one is on watch keeps me wide awake. There isn't a ship in sight, however; not even on the radar. The alarm will wake me every 20 minutes, but it's my first night and I get up every five minutes to take a look. Once I've convinced myself that I can shut my eyes for 20 minutes, I succeed in staying in my bunk for only 10. It's strange that, with all my sailing experience, this is still a new situation for me. When I was 11, 12 and 13, I spent long stretches of time out at sea alone — up to seven weeks, sometimes.

DAY 2: *22 August*

While I look out over the ocean, I become aware of a feeling of loneliness. It's been such a strange time. After working quietly on my own to get things ready for my voyage, I was suddenly engulfed in such media hype, intrigue and false reports that I was almost never alone. It had been really hard to handle, and now that I've finally found some peace everything feels different. It feels like a lifetime has passed me by; as if there's an entirely different girl on this boat. And all that thanks to a year of strife with the authorities. I'm fully convinced that I wouldn't have had the slightest problem with either loneliness or appetite loss if I'd been allowed to leave a year ago. Fortunately, the feeling of being lonely evaporates swiftly. It's something that I've never really known, but then I suppose there's a first time for everything … Loneliness and sailing around the world.

DAY 3: *23 August*

I'm still struggling to eat. It took me a whole night to get a puffed rice cake inside me. All I've managed to eat since my departure from Gibraltar has been a few bites of *ontbijtkoek* (Dutch spice cake) and a cup of tea. I'm too nervous about what lies ahead; will the police try to arrest me again?

The sailing goes as usual. I spend the whole day adjusting and trimming the sails and checking my course. If there's time left over, I try to eat something and catch some sleep. It can be a bit dull sometimes, especially when all the really simple chores become a real challenge, such as making a cup of tea or going to the toilet.

I'm having a little trouble being on my own. I'd love to be on the phone to Dad the whole day, but that's not possible. I have a satellite phone on board, but calls are expensive, so it's only there for emergency situations. I have a tracker on board with a satellite system, and Dad is able to follow me on his laptop. He can see exactly where I am and at what speed I'm sailing.

The sun is out today and I see a ship for the first time in 36 hours. I still have 310 miles to cover to reach my first destination. The genoa is boomed out and *Guppy* is running at about 6 knots. It's really going well and I'm feeling better with each mile. I've just gobbled up an entire pot of apple sauce and I'm suddenly ravenous. Yippee!

DAY 4: *24 August*

With a following wind of 25 knots and an average speed of 6.5 knots, *Guppy* flies towards Lanzarote. It's still slightly overcast, but the sun comes through from time to time. At 09.56, to be precise, I have a yacht behind me. It's also a two-master that's sailing a little higher than me. I think he's on his way to Las Palmas. The clouds suddenly disappear and I decide to open a packet of crisps in the cockpit. The crisps are devoured in minutes and I try to take a nap. When I don't succeed, I go into the cabin and continue to read Joshua Slocum's book *Sailing Alone Around the World*. (Slocum was the world's first solo circumnavigator.)

I have been at sea for four days and am feeling better each day. At last I've found my peace and have my rhythm back, and I'm in my element. During the night another yacht crosses my path and I'm accompanied by dolphins for a while. Another 110 miles to Marina Rubicon, the harbour at Lanzarote where I'm going to moor. I call my mum for a few minutes via the satellite phone and it's good to hear her voice.

DAY 5: *25 August*

Today I've set the alarm on the chart plotter as I've managed to sleep through the alarm clock in the galley before, and now that I'm approaching land I don't want that to happen again. The radar also sounds an alarm when it receives a land echo, but better safe than sorry. In the morning, my navigation tells me that I'm about 10 miles from the coast. I strain to see land, but can see nothing. That's when I realise how foggy it's become. Twenty minutes ago it was entirely clear and now I'm surrounded by a thick, white mass. My mobile phone now has reception, which also confirms that we are close to shore. I see the contours of Lanzarote on the radar and, although I'd like to sleep a little longer, my last nap is now well and truly over. I don't dare to keep my eyes shut this close to land. *Guppy* is rolling heavily and I have difficulty writing this.

It's 09.00 in the morning when I finally see a few mountain peaks jutting through the clouds above Lanzarote. About time, as I'm a mere three miles from shore. It's another 24 miles to the marina and *Guppy* surges ahead at 7 knots. Hopefully the mist will recede so that I can see more of my first island. My wish is fulfilled; the mist disappears and it's suddenly very hot. I've hardly seen the sun during my crossing as it hid behind the clouds, and now it's suddenly burning my skin. The wind falls away and I stay in the shade of the bimini top. I'm slowly approaching my first destination. The wind slowly dies behind the mountains on the last mile. I lower the mainsail and start the engine to cruise the rest of the way. I've lost that feeling of loneliness. How I would have liked to sail on now that I have found my rhythm!

When I pass a restaurant on my entry into the harbour and see all the guests look my way simultaneously, I know that I have been recognised ... Seconds later all cameras are pointed my way, and to my utter dismay the arrival jetty lies directly in front of the restaurant. I moor *Guppy* alongside, ignore the frantic tourists who want to photograph me, and walk to the harbour office with my papers, in a bit of a daze. There is also a boat full of tourists who seem to know who I am. I decide not to let them annoy me, and greet them. I do, however, ask the port authorities for the quietest spot in the harbour, away from prying eyes, when they enquire where I wish to moor *Guppy*.

So there *Guppy* lies, at the rear end of Marina Rubicon in Lanzarote. The first stage of the voyage has been a success and I'm looking forward to the next. It's certainly a quiet spot and I'm not bothered much in the days that follow. Luckily, it was only a single incident, as I'm sick and tired of all the attention I've been getting.

Lanzarote

On my first day, I meet a woman who is also called Laura; she works at the harbour office and was born on Lanzarote. My English is immediately put to the test and I find I'm learning new words fast. Phoning the Netherlands is very expensive and I decide to buy a Spanish SIM-card for my mobile phone. It's incredibly hot today without a breath of wind, and I have to tear myself away from under the shady bimini to walk towards the harbour office. That's where I meet Laura, who tells me that I'll be able to find a SIM-card at Playa Blanca, which is about a 20-minute walk away. Not much fun in this heat, and luckily she reads my thoughts and offers to take me there and back by car.

'I need to go to the post office anyway, and that's just opposite it,' she explains.

I eagerly accept her offer, and within five minutes I'm sitting in a bright-red car on my way to Playa Blanca. It's the first time I've ventured outside the harbour. Amazed, I look around me. The island is rather bare. Some planted palm trees, which need to be irrigated, and some cacti make up the total vegetation of the island. The rest is one black mass of lava stone and volcanoes.

Playa Blanca is very touristy and finding a spot to park the car is an issue — yes, even here! We walk to the shop only to find that it has run out of SIM-cards, but they tell us they will be receiving new stock at six. I'm lucky that Laura is willing to run me back to this shop again. Ten minutes after six and €12 poorer, I'm the owner of a Spanish SIM-card. The €15 call credit on it is used up in no time and I resolve not to buy new credit. People can phone me if they need to. This is one of the better decisions I make. If people ask me why they haven't heard from me, I just tell them I've no more call credit — the best excuse ever. I've also just discovered that it's an hour earlier here than in the Netherlands.

After trying to access my email from *Guppy* without any luck, I walk to the harbour office in the hope of finding an internet connection. Laura is still in the office and I'm able to use my own laptop to check my email. The WiFi here is perfect, even if the internet is very slow, but at least I can answer the concerned emails from my parents, grandparents and other family members and read the messages sent by friends who tell me that they miss me and want to know how I am. After this, I tackle the enormous load of entries on the guest-book page of my website. They're great to read and it's amazing how many people follow my blog and are supportive. This is why I'm so dependent on the internet. But there are often messages from the media and other people who seek to exploit their association with me. Luckily to a lesser degree than in the Netherlands, but it's still annoying. When will they ever leave me alone?

When Laura goes home, I walk back to *Guppy* and immediately fall asleep. It's wonderful to sleep through the night, although I'm beginning to long for the sea again. It may, however, be a while before the hurricane season is over and I can cross the Atlantic Ocean safely, which gives me time to explore the Canary Islands.

With the exception of the odd squall, it's almost always calm and incredibly hot. I do my schoolwork in the mornings, go for a walk and spend the afternoons doing some chores on *Guppy*, or just read until the worst of the heat has passed.

It's market day on Wednesday and I decide to take a look. Unfortunately, it caters for the tourists and I quickly return to *Guppy*. Besides Laura from the harbour office, I don't know any other people yet, but I have no problem being on my own.

My dinner tonight will consist of mashed potatoes and green beans. Not having read the cooking instructions correctly, the mashed potatoes turn out more like soup. I chuck in the green beans for good measure and it doesn't taste too bad. I'm often asked what it's like cooking and eating on board. I've been able to cook for myself since about the age of six and, to be honest, it began with microwave meals. Dad had his own business and, however hard he tried to get home early, he was often away from home from early in the morning till late at night; which meant cooking my own breakfast and dinner.

The 3-kilometre cycle to school was something I'd done since I was six, but only after Dad had shown me how to cross the more difficult intersections. Other parents frowned at this and we were looked upon with some disapproval. Dad didn't like the situation at home either, and for years he worked extra hard to ensure that he was home earlier for me, but this only resulted in a burnout which forced him to give up his business. In the years that followed we had precious little to live on. After school, I'd use the scant money we had to buy some food. But I remember it as a good time, because from that moment Dad was always at home for me, and would be awaiting my return from school with a cup of tea in the shed next to the boat he was building. The shed was our home and I appreciated the fact that he was there for me, and in this way we managed to bolster one another.

At first, I didn't really understand what the problem was; he was often so down-hearted and angry at the slightest thing. Later he explained it all to me and apologised for his behaviour. I learnt to cope with the situation and helped where I could. In spite of all this, I managed to have a really good youth. If he had continued to work, I might have been one of those kids who only sees her parents for an hour before they go to bed. There wasn't much money in our household, but Dad was always there for me. After a while, he did some work for the wharf where our boat was berthed. It was a great place to grow up as a kid. I could sail, build huts, climb trees and all sorts of other things.

Now back to cooking. I could cook whole meals from the age of eight. I started with spaghetti and macaroni, and then ventured on to potatoes, vegetables and meat. I can now cook up a storm. It's mostly common sense and easy if you follow the instructions on the packet. Not that that's my strong point. I've had quite a number of 'burning' incidents in the kitchen I could tell you about. One of them happened on a holiday I went on with the previous *Guppy* in Friesland in the north of the Netherlands when I was 10. It involved making popcorn. I had the corn but didn't realise that you needed to warm up some oil first. So I threw the corn into a dry pot, put the lid on it and went up on deck. Within minutes there were clouds of black smoke billowing from the galley. I covered my face with a towel and ran to turn off the gas. The pot was pitch black and remained that way for years. The burnt corn flew everywhere and little *Guppy* smelled bad for another three weeks — which was the worst part of it, but it was a good lesson for me.

Cooking on board is much more of a challenge than it is on land. I have a cardanic gas stove with an oven. It's suspended in such a way that it remains horizontal at all times and doesn't follow the motion of the boat. It means that even when *Guppy* tilts on her side, the pots stay upright — with the macaroni inside them and not on the ceiling. Although I'm not a bad cook, I don't enjoy cooking. When I'm in a harbour, as I am now, I can use my fridge and make elaborate meals with meat and vegetables, but to be honest I'm a little lazy when it comes to cooking. I usually make easy meals that are quick to prepare. At sea, however, I have all the time, but little variety. Under the bunks in the cabin there are dozens of tins that will keep for ages with a range of meals from chicken in satay sauce to all sorts of vegetables; bags of rice and … hmm … today, mashed potato soup!

Sitting in the cockpit on a warm evening, I'm casually fiddling with the helm when I feel some resistance. Alarmed, I dive into the aft compartment to see if there's anything obstructing the rudder head or whether one of the steering cables has worked loose. So far as I can see, there's nothing wrong. I decide to check the entire compartment and all the steering cable rollers. When I have finally moved everything out of the compartment and into the cockpit, I come to the conclusion that the hitch lies elsewhere. I sleep on it for a night and then continue my search for the problem the next day. It seems as if the faulty rudder is getting worse.

I can't stand the fact that I can't even locate the problem, never mind solve it. At noon, I decide to stop looking for it because I've promised to go to the beach with Laura from the harbour office. She fetches me and we drive past some villages and over some pretty high mountains. While we are driving, she tells me more about the island. I hear about the pirates who occupied Lanzarote centuries ago and about the volcanic eruption that created the islands in the distant past. This island has many small volcanoes, some of them still active, and I tell Laura that I've never seen a volcano in my life.

'No? Then I will take you to see one,' she insists.

After a few hours on the beach and in the sea at Famara, some of Laura's friends join us. Amongst them are a man and his daughter who is a little younger than me and speaks German. That's not a problem; my mum is German and we always watched German television at home because it was free. The girl has a body board and I borrow it to try to surf the waves. At first it's tricky, but I soon get the hang of it. My experienced nine-year-old instructor shouts her encouragement: 'Yes, yes, yes, catch it now!'

She's been living on Lanzarote for a few years and has the advantage. When we've finished swimming, we join a party in the village of Famara, but the party seems to be dispersing. We hear some loud music coming from another spot in the village and follow our ears. We land up at another party and amuse ourselves watching the tipsy locals. Afterwards, we say farewell and pass a few small volcanoes on our way back to Marina Rubicon. At 19.00 I'm back on *Guppy* and have to face the fact that there really is something wrong with the rudder; I'd been able to forget about it for a few hours. It was going to be difficult to sail with it in this condition. I decide to phone Dad and ask his advice. He says he needs to think about it for a while and I realise that tomorrow is another day.

How time flies. I can't believe I left the Netherlands 27 days ago. Seriously, I haven't missed it for a minute! I do miss my parents, sister and friends, of course, but much less than I expected. I'm experiencing so much that's new to me.

This morning, I started with my schoolwork. I do it because I want to pass my exams, but can't really see much fun in it otherwise. I think about all my friends who are forced to attend school every day, and this soon motivates me to complete my assigned task. I'm thankful that I can devote two to three hours a day to my schoolwork and not have to spend every day in a boring classroom. The way I'm living now is much more educational than spending a few years at school.

Once I've finished my schoolwork, I start on the problem with the helm again. Sigh. It really is incredibly hot, and, after having polished off a carton of iced tea, I make my way to the aft compartment with new resolve to find the fault. I have armed myself with the tools to remove the cables from the steering quadrant. If the helm refuses to move from side to side, I really have a problem. After a while I manage to remove the cables and I crawl out of the compartment with grease-blackened hands. I say a quick prayer before testing the rudder: 'Please God, let me be able to move the rudder with ease!'

If this isn't possible, it could be something in the watertight joint or the rudder head. There could be a leak in the packing and, as the rudder stock is made of steel, it may well have rusted and jammed because it hasn't been used for a while. If this is so, *Guppy* will have to be hoisted out of the water. I don't want *Guppy* on land, so here goes. I take the tiller in my hand and push. A little harder this time, but still no movement. Shit! Defeated, I move to the cockpit to think about what the cause could be. I eventually phone Dad and tell him the news. He isn't happy about it either.

'Well, Laura, *Guppy* will have to come out of the water. That means I'll have to come over because you won't be able to solve the problem with the tools you have on board,' he explains.

Thanks, I think, as if I can't cope; but I do realise that this is a problem I'll need some help with. The only thing I can do at the moment is try to get some movement in the rudder by squeezing in some grease. I hang on to the helm with all my weight and manage

42

to get some play in it, but this doesn't solve the problem, of course. Fortunately, it's possible to get *Gup* hoisted out of the water here, but this is certainly not a good start to my voyage.

Yesterday, Sylvia, who works at the harbour office with Laura, asked me if I would like to sail along with the kids from the sailing school, just for fun. Well, I wouldn't be Laura if I didn't jump at the chance. I had to be there at ten the next morning, so I got up at, hmm, a quarter past ten … fairly punctual for me. None of the five boys in the group speak a word of English; not even the instructor. So it's a case of communicating with my hands and feet and it seems to work. I get the oldest and most neglected Laser with a worn-out sail minus battens. The others take all the best boats for themselves. Thank you, I think. They're either worried about losing against me or think that I can't sail. This is obviously not the case, as nobody seems surprised when I manage to get the boat safely down a slippery slope and into the metre-high swell.

At sea, we compete in a few races, and after winning two of the six it's clear why I'd been allocated this rotten boat, but it doesn't worry me and I have a great time. As they say, don't look a gift horse in the mouth. I recently read that since the news of my plans to sail around the world went worldwide, more kids' have been joining sailing clubs. Good to know.

When everyone has stopped sailing, I continue for a little longer. The wind picks up and I'm able to plane the Laser over the azure sea from one end of the bay to the other. When I eventually get back to shore, I'm soaked to the bone and thoroughly windswept. After a shower, I go back to *Guppy* to check my email. There's one from Dad, telling me that he'll be arriving on Thursday. I'm happy because I'm crazy about my dad; but at the same time, I'm only just getting used to living on my own and he could have stayed at home a little longer as far as I'm concerned.

The next morning I test the rudder again and the problem is still there, so it's really important that Dad comes over with the right tools and materials. He thinks there's a chance we may not need to take *Guppy* out of the water after all. I dance for joy and tell *Guppy* the good news.

'You don't have to come out of the water, *Guppy*!' I confide to my gently swaying home.

After a week in Lanzarote I couldn't have imagined how different my life would be over here. In the Netherlands I'd get up at six every day to take Spot for a walk before cycling 12 kilometres to school in the dark; sometimes in the rain and snow. Now I wake up at eight, climb out of my bunk and simply start my schoolwork. Sleeping in longer doesn't work, though, as the heat is too intense. Temperatures reached 48 degrees Celsius this week!

I follow a teaching roster from the *Wereldschool*, and the lessons I would normally get from a teacher are on paper. The schoolwork is actually the same. For chemistry and biology I need to do practical exercises and have brought along some substances and test-tubes for this purpose. I have access to teachers via the internet to answer any questions I may have, but this hasn't been necessary so far. I'm way ahead of schedule for maths and I have my first test next week. The tests are on a CD. I could do them with my books open, which is what I used to do at school, but cribbing is no fun this way.

Funny that I used to spend all day at school until four in the afternoon and now finish my schoolwork in two hours. It's ten to eight in the morning and I'm busy with geography. Dad is scheduled to land in about an hour's time. He arrives while I'm still buried in my school books. I fly into his arms. It's so good to see him again.

'Goodness, Laura, you're so tanned!' he exclaims and dives straight into the aft compartment to establish what the problem is with the rudder without pausing for breath.

'Hey, Dad, would you like anything to eat or drink?'

'Later' is his off-hand reply. 'Can you pass me wrench 19?'

Back home, we'd often forget to eat when we were tinkering with my boat or Dad's boat. Ten minutes later, we take a break, have something to drink and catch up on the news from the home front. I, in turn, tell him all about the experiences I've had while at sea and here on the island. After a while we get back to the work plan to get the rudder moving again. One solution is for me to start sailing non-stop, Dad jokes. And the other? Well, Dad has brought along a new grease injector. We'll replace the old stuffing box. We seal it off with fresh packing, fit a nipple and fill it with grease but, once this is done, it looks like the new grease injector is leaking. Just our luck. We put back the old stuffing box. Now we try to squeeze as much grease as possible into the rudderstock bearings, hoping this will stop the leak and force as much of the water out as possible. While Dad works below, I'm up on deck moving the tiller from port to starboard for all I'm worth. The jammed rudder seems to be easing up a little.

There's a chandlery in the harbour and we go and see if they have a better grease injector in stock. Unfortunately, that's not the case. We walk on to talk to Cecile, a Dutch woman who's been living on the island for some time and works in the harbour, to find out if she knows where we can find a grease injector.

'You'll probably find one at the hardware store at Playa Blanca,' she says.

'Right, and where is that?'

'Do you intend walking there?' she asks.

'Yes, of course,' we answer.

How else were we to get there? She answers that it's really far and that she'll take us there by car when she knocks off work. I actually hate walking, so I immediately accept her offer. Dad is too polite and tells her not to worry. OMG, I think. Fortunately, she insists and we agree to meet at the harbour office at six. We also meet Sylvia and a couple of others and I introduce them: 'Hi. This is my dad.'

It's strange walking around with Dad when I've been here for a week and already know almost everyone. When we get to the hardware store at a quarter past six, it has what we are looking for, but this is not the Netherlands and none of the kits are complete. We finally find one that contains the parts we need, and we decide that we can build one complete grease injector from two incomplete ones, but we'll have to wait with the repairs as I have a busy social life. There's a big Dutch motor boat tied to our jetty and we've been invited over for dinner. Gerda and Willem are very hospitable and the food is delicious, which means that I eat far too much. We get back to *Guppy* at 10 and I need a couple of hours to digest my food.

We use the few days that Dad is on Lanzarote to complete a number of odd jobs on *Guppy*; such as protecting the sails where they rub against the stays and rigging with tape, as these are weak spots that tear easily. We mount some wheels on the dinghy so that I'm able to beach it easily and reduce the risk of it being swept out to sea. I also mark the anchor chain with yellow paint at 10-metre intervals. This will come in handy when I anchor offshore. When anchoring, most yachts pay out about 30 metres of chain, so that when anchored they all occupy about the same swinging room. If you let out more chain and the wind changes, then your boat will swing round over a larger area. You then run the risk of anchor chains getting tangled and, even worse, yachts colliding. If you pay out less chain, then your boat risks drifting in strong winds.

I recover my roller blades when I tidy up the aft cabin. Skating is a lot better than walking. I skate over the boulevard to the hardware store, past the tourist shops and over the hill to a busy road. I'm no longer used to skating and soon have blisters on my feet. I so detest walking that I carry on skating regardless of the pain.

We plunge into the pool at the marina between chores to cool off, and in the evenings walk along the beach to Playa Blanca. I don't mind these tourist traps just once in a while, but you don't get to see the real island that way. Exploring on your own is much more rewarding.

We eat pancakes in the town and hire a car to tour the island. The local authorities have given us free entry to all the tourist attractions. We first drive along the west coast to the north to find a cave somewhere. It's actually a lava tunnel that was created by underground streams of lava. Once inside you can see this clearly, as some of the walls have been scoured so smooth by the heat that it looks like a plastic passage. At some spots it's so sharp that you need to take care not to fall and cut yourself. There's an underground lake in the tunnel that looks just like a mirror because the water is so still and resembles a black hole. This illusion is broken when I throw a stone into it. It's amazing.

We drive on to El Mirador del Rio at the most northerly point of Lanzarote, with a beautiful view of Grazioza, an island to the north with just one village. According to my childhood television heroes, *Bassie and Adriaan*, the island resembles a fried egg. I used to watch this comic duo a lot and it's so special to see the real thing now. Countless birds hover above me and I feel as though I'm one of them, free as a bird. It's great to be able to see the entire island below us in this way;

just like standing on *Guppy*'s bow and looking out over the endless sea up to the horizon. A few geography lessons richer, we return to *Guppy*, who has been waiting for her owner patiently all the while.

Now and then I join the Laser group for some sailing, just to be on the water again. I meet all sorts of interesting people, and one of them is José, an older, well-known islander who earns his living with tourists. One of his ventures is canoeing at full moon. He tells me an adventurous story about his sixtieth birthday when he, together with a friend and his dog, surfed on a duo surfboard non-stop for 60 nautical miles.

The time flies and Dad needs to go home again. We check the rudder once more, and he reminds me for the hundredth time that I need to grease it regularly.

'Yes, Dad, of course,' I respond each time.

'And look out for this and don't forget that,' he continues.

'Yes, Dad, sure I will.' Parents!

I'm woken up by a soft tapping noise. It takes a couple of seconds before I realise that it's rain. Rain? Although I always close all the hatches at night and don't leave anything valuable on deck, I get out of bed to check that everything is OK. Now that I'm up, I stay on deck. It's still very early, but I see several other people shutting hatches and bringing in the washing.

Once I've finished my schoolwork, I go outside and try to get onto the internet on my laptop. It's a lot of trouble and I sometimes succeed, but it's still raining fairly hard so I go back inside before my laptop drowns. Once inside I see a heap of washing, decide to do something about it and get a token from the harbour office so that I can do the washing and hang it outdoors when the sun comes out tomorrow. It's still drizzling, and at sunset the puddles turn to gold as they reflect the dying rays of the sun.

The next morning I'm woken at eight by the broiling sun. I get up and am annoyed to discover that there's no bread. That's because it rained yesterday and I forgot to get some. Well, that's what I tell myself. I simply hate muesli, but force it down with a cup of chocolate milk while I do my schoolwork. Once that is done, I haul my dirty washing to the laundrette. When I get back, I hang it neatly over the railing and go to sit in the cockpit. It's been years since I've done the washing in a washing machine. I managed to blow the washing machine at home up a couple of years ago. All I did was fill it with washing, press 'start' and after five minutes it just went *bang* and jumped more than a metre from where it stood! When Dad got home and checked it, he wasn't amused. Somehow the heating element had got twisted around the tub of the machine. The whole thing had literally fallen apart, all because I'd forgotten to close the lid of the top-loader properly. I give the washing machine at the laundrette a close inspection before pressing 'start', and listen for any odd sounds for about 10 minutes before I'm convinced that this will end well.

Mum phoned this afternoon. It's cold and wet in the Netherlands, she tells me, and she's got a bad cold. She, my sister and my stepfather have all been ill. Mum doesn't have too much time to talk. She needs to accompany Kim to a tailor in Almere for costumes for her performance in Geneva at the end of November. My sister is made of rubber and she's going to perform in a big circus. She'll be doing a trapeze act with a boy, and it's going to be broadcast on television.

It's still boiling hot, but the wind has picked up and it's overcast. Pleasant weather, you'd think, but I'm sitting in the cabin to avoid getting a mouthful of the desert sand that's being carried by the wind from the Sahara. I've been on Lanzarote for quite some time now and want to leave on Monday. I keep thinking that there's something happening on Monday and can't figure out what, until it dawns on me that it's my birthday! OK, so I'll have to plan my departure for Tuesday afternoon then and hope to reach Gran Canaria by the following afternoon. I've been offered a mooring there at the Pasito Blanco marina for two weeks.

In the evening I have dinner on board a Dutch yacht, *Luna Verde*, a Contest 50. Wilma and Thijs Viegers want to take three to four years to sail around the world. Their children and grandchildren are there, too. The food is delicious and we talk about all sorts of things ... About boats and sailing, of course, but loads of other stuff while the kids romp around with a piece of rope they have found, making it impossible to move and finally getting totally tangled in it themselves.

It's still early when I hear lots of voices and see a large number of big-game fishing boats leave the harbour. There are fishing competitions taking place this weekend. It's not really my thing to murder innocent fish with fishing rods and hooks. Luckily, they aren't allowed to bring their catch back to the harbour. Competitors need to take photographs of their catches and then release them. As I said, not my game. But the long line of boats leaving the harbour does look very festive.

There's a big party in the harbour tonight with lots of performances. There are acrobats and a big band with drums. Cecile is there, too, and asks me if I would like to join the boat that will fire the starting gun. I think it might be fun. The committee boat, which belongs to the new, lightweight, faster class of boats, is slightly bigger than *Guppy*. I've only just boarded when I'm asked to take the helm. It seems I'm the first woman ever to be given this honour. Slowly I manoeuvre the expensive yacht out of the harbour and cruise to where the race begins. The captain then blows the horn and a fleet of who knows how many boats dashes off to who knows where. Once I have reversed the boat — which handles quite differently to my heavier *Guppy* — neatly into its berth box, I walk back to my own boat. I check my email, read a book, feed myself and fall asleep contentedly.

When I finally open my eyes, I see a huge mess before me and decide it's time for a spring clean, but where to start? I take a deep breath and decide to tackle the kitchen.

Willem pops in that afternoon and asks whether I'd like to go along for a volcano hike. I accept, and at about five that afternoon walk towards their motor boat that's tied up to the same jetty. The four of us, Willem, his sister Loet, Gerda and I, visit an extinct volcano that is really impressive. It's entirely black and I manage to find a rock with a sort of precious-looking green stone embedded in it. It's an olivine according to Willem, but, unfortunately, not worth much.

After our hike, we go to Thao, a fish restaurant. I try some squid for the first time in my life and am not mad about it. I manage to stomach the rest of the meal, which includes bread and a variety of fish. I'm not really a seafood lover and that hasn't changed, but I pretend to enjoy it. We then drive home past quiet villages that twinkle in the dark.

It's 20 September — MY BIRTHDAY!!! I wake up cheerfully and immediately feel it. I've turned 15! I bounce out of my bunk and help myself to a slice of birthday cake … Ha, ha, in my dreams! In fact, it doesn't happen quite like that. I'm still half asleep when the phone goes.

I answer and a loud 'Happy Birthday' thunders in my ear. It's my mum and sister. My mum has to go to work and my sister is off to school, which is why they have called so early.

'We just wanted to make sure we were the first,' my mum says proudly.

Well, they certainly succeeded on that score. At ten past seven local time, someone from the Belgian Radio phones and then it's Dad. And all this before eight in the morning. I'm just climbing out of my bunk when my gran and granddad phone. Now I've had them all, I think, and start on my schoolwork. Just before I'm finished, Thijs and Wilma from the *Luna Verde* come by. They've brought presents for me. Shower gel, sweets and a lovely photograph taken at a dinner on their boat. How sweet of them to have remembered my birthday!

At half past 11, Sylvia arrives with the local media; something we had agreed on beforehand. She's brought along a birthday cake, too. After a short chat and photo session with the paparazzi (they never seem to have enough), they all depart. In the meantime, Loet has arrived. She is off to Playa Papagayo today to do some snorkelling and invites me to come along. I quickly grab my things, and we drive to a beautiful beach that's surrounded on three sides by cliffs. We walk down a steep set of steps to a nice spot. I immediately dive in and am enchanted as beautifully coloured fish shoot past the rocks underwater.

While we are on the beach enjoying the sun, Loet has an idea and invites me to come and cook in her apartment. Yeah, why not? At the Hyperdino, the local supermarket, we buy steak, veggies and potatoes, and cook a delicious meal. When Loet takes me back to *Guppy* at about 10, we decide to sneak into a five-star hotel just to take a look. It's incredibly posh, with a number of swimming pools set in what looks like a jungle. The glass revolving doors are so clean that I accidentally walk into one. Ouch!

I get up at 07.00. I will be leaving Lanzarote today, but still have a few things to do; such as writing up my blog, emailing the marina at Pasito Blanco and, of course, saying goodbye to everyone here. It will take only 24 hours to sail to Gran Canaria, and all I need to do in terms of preparation is to check the rigging and see that all the valves and hatches are closed securely. Most importantly, I mustn't forget to put the plug in the sink. If you fail to do this and the boat starts to roll, you have a good chance of a saltwater bed. This happened to me when I made the crossing to England for the first time on little *Guppy*, and I've learnt my lesson.

Two hours later I'm ready to cast off the mooring lines. I cruise out of the Marina Rubicon and say farewell to Lanzarote and everyone there. It's time for new islands, new adventures and new faces. I'm ready for the next stage of my voyage.

Lanzarote–Gran Canaria: 130 nautical miles

DAY 1: *21 September*

It's great to be back on the water. It's as hot as hell today and there's almost no wind when I leave. *Guppy* is bobbing and weaving through the water at 1 knot towards Gran Canaria. Fortunately, the wind picks up steadily. I'm standing on the bow and the wind is blowing through my hair. *Guppy* shoots through the water and is soon running at around 6 knots.

That evening, *Guppy* sails across the reflection of the full moon in the water. Stunning! From a distance of 40 miles, I begin to see the lights of my next destination. There's a glare along the coast and it takes me half an hour to realise that it's a motorway. I'm sitting in the cockpit enjoying the view, when I feel a few drops of water. I ask myself if it's seawater or rain and the question is answered quickly. As soon as I move from under the bimini top, I'm soaked. I'd had a feeling that something was in store for me, and I had dropped the mizzen. I check to see that there's nothing valuable on deck, hang the transparent flap over the cabin entrance and shelter inside until the downpour is over.

It's still dark when I sail past the Maspalomas lighthouse and into the harbour of Pasito Blanco. I'm alarmed when I see that the boats are tied up bow to moorings, stern to jetty. I've never tried this before, and certainly not on my own. I can't find the arrival jetty and decide to tie up alongside a decrepit, blue catamaran that looks as though it's about to sink. It's a few hours before sunrise, so I dive into my sleeping bag and soon fall asleep.

Gran Canaria

There's a big surprise in store for me when I wake up. I arrived in the dark, but now see that I'm surrounded by tall, green mountains, totally different to the dry, black Lanzarote landscape. I call up the harbour authorities on the VHF and am instructed to sail to the other side of the harbour. The arrival jetty is a high concrete structure. I walk to the harbour office with my ship's papers and am allocated a berth. They're very friendly and help me to moor the boat. We've only just tied *Guppy* up when the heavens open. Yuck! I had wanted to explore my new surroundings, but decide to do my schoolwork instead. I do some extra work and have already completed some tests. My results include 90 per cent for German and 80 per cent for biology. Not bad, hey?

I'm busy calculating how many miles I still need to cover and what lies ahead of me, when two Dutch men arrive to paste a sticker on *Guppy*. Jongert is one of my sponsors and I'd had some problems with their sticker in Gibraltar. Together we work out how it's done, and they invite me to join them for dinner. We drive to Maspalomas, and I'm impressed by what I see on the way, although it's dark by now. Not only is it much greener than Lanzarote, but the mountains are much higher, the towns larger and it's much busier and less volcanic. It's a pleasant meal, and as they drive me back to *Guppy* I realise that I'm exhausted, having had only one hour's sleep in the past 37 hours.

By the next morning, the rain has stopped and I find a small Spar supermarket in the harbour. I'm shocked when they charge me €2,36 for a French loaf. That's way too expensive, but they don't have any other bread. They won't catch me doing that again. The French loaf is not even nice, and it's as though you're eating money.

It's hot and calm again today. I love the warmth, but it does make me feel dozy. A friend who lives close to us in the Netherlands and spends his winters on Gran Canaria, Ed Willems, is picking me up at 10 to show me a bit of the island. We drive along the coast and past some huts and villages in the mountains. We stop at a village in the middle of nowhere, have something to drink and walk to a reservoir. Unfortunately, the restaurant we were planning to stop at has just been taken over by a bunch of tourists and we make our escape.

After enjoying a Coke, we continue to climb to the top along twisting roads. Here there is another reservoir. We have something to eat and start our descent to Puerto Mogán, past mountains that are red, blue, purple, yellow and orange. An unbelievable sight! It looks like they've let a child loose with a box of crayons, but in fact it's the minerals — phosphorus, iron and others — in the rocks that give them their tints.

Virtually everything is new to me; the heat, the traditions, the palm trees. Lanzarote had its own beauty, but Gran Canaria is much prettier with its tall, rugged mountains, green valleys and small Spanish villages.

A few days later I'm climbing along winding roads again with a friend. After a stop to go to the toilet at a messy pub, we arrive at the highest village on Gran Canaria. Artenara lies at an altitude of 1270 metres, and most of the houses are half built into the mountain. It even has a swimming pool and football field. We carry on driving along the endless mountain roads through a rugged landscape.

After passing many tiny villages tucked into the mountains, we eventually get to an old, deep volcanic crater. I run up the slope to the top in my flip-flops and it feels great to be standing there on my own. I have a view of the whole island and even manage to see the Teide, a mountain on Tenerife that's always topped with snow. While I'm standing there, I realise that I'm finally beginning to feel myself again. It's taken some time, but I'd had so much to contend with in the Netherlands. The authorities, organisations that distorted the truth in their reports, journalists who blithely accepted the lies from the authorities, hearings behind closed doors after which a totally different version was brought out. All this while I exerted myself day and night to get everything organised for my voyage. Sponsors that quit because of all the commotion that had been created, and of course I needed to continue going to school. And then, suddenly, I found myself sailing from Gibraltar and I was finally on my own — something I had to get used to at first. I'd even felt a little lonely, which was new for me. It all went so fast; one moment I was in the midst of a crowd all talking to me at the same time and the next — *whoosh* — I was transported to a jungle in another part of the world. I feel the anxiety ebbing away quickly, and it leaves me feeling terrific.

The harbour where I'm moored is fairly quiet, remote and secure. It's only really busy in the weekends. At night, I enjoy *Guppy*'s gentle swaying, the soft sound of the wind and the stars that are so much brighter than in the Netherlands. If I need to, I can contact Dad and my friends within seconds. It's funny, but I'm never really bored on my own. There's always something to do; reading, taking photographs, swimming, repairs, schoolwork, cooking and cleaning *Guppy*. These sorts of things don't feel like duties; they're just part of life.

It's 26 September. I call Mum in the morning because she turns 50 today. I then tidy *Guppy*, answer my emails and receive all sorts of gifts from strangers who seem to like the fact that I'm in the harbour in Pasito Blanco; a bracelet, a packet of sweets, some newspapers and later an ice cream and some chocolates. It's amazing really, I'm in a closed, guarded harbour and still people manage to find me. It often reassures me, but also makes me uneasy at times. I even find a book wrapped up in plastic on the jetty one day. There's no one around, so I take it inside; it's a book about sailing written by Connor O'Brien. Later, when I read my blog's guest book, I see that it's meant for me.

Just then, I hear my name being called. It's the De Bruyn family. A Dutch family who moved here a couple of years ago. Mrs De Bruyn works on a dolphin boat for tourists, and they had sent me an email asking me whether I would like to make contact. The whole family is present; Reggy, Antonio and their 16- and 17-year-old sons, Didier and Beau, who are so shy that they don't utter a word during the entire visit. The captain of the *Spirit of the Sea*, the dolphin boat, has also come along and I'm invited to go on a trip to view the dolphins. That should be fun!

The first book about me, written by my gran, has just been published and I've received a copy. At the time she was writing it, I didn't really appreciate what she was doing for me; I just wanted to sail, but now I'm very grateful that she went to so much trouble to describe some of the behaviour of the Dutch authorities. She writes about the actions that were all intended to prohibit me from sailing.

Unfortunately, the book doesn't record the worst incidents because we were still involved in various court cases at the time of publishing.

When I wake up at eight, I lie in a little. I then tackle my schoolwork; there's a lot to cover because I do yesterday's homework and tomorrow's too. Then the phone starts to ring. It takes me a while before I understand what Grimanesa, a woman on the island who works for a jeweller, is trying to tell me. From her 'Spanglish', I manage to understand the words 'bananas' and 'Spar'. Do they want to bring bananas? Yes, that's it. Within 15 minutes, there's a big bunch of bananas and a box of fruit in the cockpit. Totally amazed and wondering what to do with all this fruit, I sit next to a bunch of bananas that's as big as I am. I decided to hang the green bunch of bananas on the solar panel rack. It's quite a struggle and some of the bananas don't survive the onslaught. An hour later, I proudly survey the bunch that's now suspended from the rack, and start thinking what I'll do with them when they all ripen at the same time.

I wake up the following morning shocked to see that it's already half past eight. HALF PAST EIGHT! Shit, I have to be at the gateway by nine for the dolphin boat trip! What I actually feel like doing at this point is eating something and checking my emails in peace. But that's not to be. Getting anywhere on time still isn't one of my strong points. I hastily gobble down a sandwich and start to walk to the boom where Antonio and Beau are waiting for me in the most rickety Renault I have ever seen.

'Yes, it makes a bit of a racket. Take no notice. You can't use the safety belts either. That's because the sun has weathered them.'

Right, I think to myself, as we start our journey along the coastal road to Puerto Rico. There we board the *Spirit of the Sea* where Reggy works. After having a photograph taken with the whole crew, we depart with a half-full boat. Gran Canaria becomes smaller and smaller as we cruise out to sea, and after about an hour and a half we are relayed the position of some dolphins. There are just two of them and they don't surface very often. The rest of the time I sit on the bow with Beau who is still very shy but a little more talkative than before, even though I have to drag every word out of him. We have more luck on the second round and see a pod of five dolphins playing in the sea.

When we return to the harbour at about three that afternoon and the tourists have disembarked, we drive to the De Bruyn family home. I say hello to their third son, who lives in the Netherlands, via Skype. It's hot here with no wind, unlike the boat, and I need to get used to the heat. We eat genuine Canary Island potatoes, cooked in their skins, and a 'mojo' dip (a sweetish, red sauce made locally) and Canary Island chicken. It's simply delicious and the company is great. They also invite me to tie *Guppy* up at one of their moorings once I have to move from the sponsored berth at the marina. That's really cool, as I can't afford to pay for the marina.

Bang, clatter, splash! WTF! I shoot upright, banging my head against the ceiling of the bunk and run outside only half awake. The heavy bunch of bananas has come loose and is now lying in the water behind *Guppy*. I struggle to haul it back on board and leave this menace on the afterdeck for the time being.

At half past 10, Ido van Oost comes to fetch me. He's a Dutchman who has lived on the island for years and wants to meet me, so no time for schoolwork today. Not such a disaster as it's Sunday. Together with Ido and his wife, Dedy, we first visit friends of theirs and then go on to Cita, a local shopping mall. Here we have a feast of herring, white bread and *hutspot* (a traditional Dutch dish made from mashed potatoes, carrots and onions with gravy) with 75 members of the Dutch community on the island. It's in honour of the *Leids Ontzet* (the Relief of Leiden — celebrating the end of the siege of this Dutch city by the Spanish in 1575 during the Eighty Year War). It feels really strange to be celebrating this in temperatures of 25 degrees Celsius. It's also strange to hear that Gran Canaria once belonged to the Netherlands for exactly one week in the distant past.

During this gathering of the *Nederlandse Vereniging* (Dutch Association), I meet Thomas and his wife. I feel I know them from somewhere … After a while the penny drops and I remember that I met them on one of my solo-sailing holidays when I was 11. That was four years ago when I was on little *Guppy*. What a coincidence! I must have made an impression at the time because they could recall our meeting vividly.

At about six, I'm back on *Gup* and she's still a mess. I decide to do the dishes, tidy up, vacuum clean and try to solve my electrical problem.

Through my own fault, the cable got jammed between the boat and the jetty and has torn. I'm going to have to shorten the cable and put a new plug on the end of it. I don't have one in stock, of course, so I ask my French neighbours if they have a spare and they give me one. It's fixed within minutes and — *voilà* — I once again have power.

It's half past one, and Grimanesa and a few of her colleagues from the jewellery store, Joy Artesana, should be arriving at any moment. They've invited me to go for a meal with all the staff and they arrive at two. I show them *Guppy*, and we drive to a restaurant that resembles what would be called a shed in the Netherlands. We are surrounded by feral cats begging for food. They seem to be successful, as none of them look underfed.

We once again eat Canary Island potatoes with 'mojo' sauce; I love them. We also have a messy grilled fish complete with tail and eyes, and once again I'm faced with squid — this time in a macaroni dish. I carefully sift out the macaroni and leave the squid for the rest to eat. When we have finished the meal, I receive a gift: it's a necklace they've made especially for me. I'm totally overwhelmed. It has a pendant with the *Guppy* emblem on it. I've never seen anything so lovely. I thank them a hundred times and can't get over the fact that it was made especially for me. Most of the staff go back to work, and I proudly show *Guppy* my new necklace when I get back.

When I step on deck, I find a note from a diving school, Let's Go Diving: *Hello Laura, I have a diving school in Pasito Blanco. If you'd like, I'm happy to offer you a dive, free of charge. Just give me a call.* Great! That's going to be so cool. I phone them immediately.

'If you want, you can come tomorrow,' he says.

'OK, awesome!'

'At two at our boat?'

'Sure, I'll be there!'

Totally excited, I hang up and tell Dad all about it on Skype a little later. He ends up giving me a long explanation about how to dive and tells me to keep my wits about me. Mum and Dad did a lot of diving on their voyage around the world and know all about the potential dangers. I promise to take care and not do anything stupid.

The next afternoon we go out to sea and I have my first diving lesson with my instructor. It's so beautiful underwater, and totally different to the dark, muddy waters in the Netherlands. I see the living versions of what I've been eating; an octopus with tentacles covered in little suction cups and a number of squid. Looking at these pretty and intelligent creatures, I resolve never to eat one again. But then I'd already decided that after my first bite because I really didn't enjoy it. When we get back, I decide that I'm going to go for my diving certificate, and now regularly sit and read all about diving from an instruction CD on my laptop.

I'm on my way to Las Palmas to go to the airport with Ido again. This time Dad is coming over to install some new gadgets. The plane has already landed when we arrive, and a stream of pale Dutch tourists come through the arrival gates with all their luggage, but there's no sign of Dad. We wait, and wait, and wait. He eventually emerges as one of the last passengers. It's taken so long because he's brought so much baggage, including a new radar. The old radar on *Guppy* still wasn't working as it should, and the local agent couldn't solve the problem. This needs to be solved before I can continue, as it's no fun sailing without one. The alarm should give me warning about oncoming ships and it wasn't doing so. So Dad has bought a brand-new radar which we're going to install on *Guppy*.

It's beginning to get hot as we drag the supplies on board. I can't wait to open all the presents that Dad has brought: a brightly coloured code zero sail, a plotter and masses of cables, flex and — wow — a new rudder blade for the windvane and two spare blades. The cockpit is full of gadgets — and not only the cockpit. Once Dad has gone inside, there's no way I can follow him for all the clutter. Just when I've taken so much trouble to tidy everything!

Dad only has three days, so we work hard to get things done. We install the new radar in the mast and its cables, fit a stainless-steel strip on the bow and fit a new anchor-chain roller. We add blocks in the mast for the new code zero, to help me hoist the sail if necessary. After three days of non-stop work, I survey all of *Guppy*'s new gadgets and smile. Everything is shipshape and I can't thank Dad enough when I accompany him back to the airport with Ido.

'So when are you starting off again?' is the question the landlubbers ask me often. I can only make the crossing at the end of November when the hurricane season has ended. Many people are under the impression that the most dangerous part of my journey is crossing the Atlantic Ocean. They don't realise that sailing along coastlines, islands with their rocks, reefs and currents, busy shipping routes and entering unknown harbours is all far more hazardous than the open sea.

I have chosen a route around the world that's much more difficult than a non-stop voyage across the oceans, and in this way I'm going to be seeing much more of the world. I have two years in which to complete my voyage, so I'm not in a hurry and am certainly not going to risk a hurricane. The advantage is that I now have plenty of time on Gran Canaria and can get ahead of my schoolwork schedule, take diving lessons and, as I'm planning to do today, go on a hike into the mountains.

I'm ready by half past eight. The hiking enthusiasts have gathered in the parking area and I'm sure it's going to be a lot of fun. We drive up the mountains and then hike around Roque Nublo. I'm not fond of walking, but it's very beautiful. Gran Canaria continues to surprise me. One moment you're in a desert landscape that looks like the Sahara, and the next you arrive at a lake in a pine forest. Even at these altitudes, I'm recognised by passing tourists. Hmm …

In exchange for having had a free berth in the harbour of Pasito Blanco, I have agreed to talk to some local journalists on my last day here. After a few interviews, I sail *Guppy* to Anfi, where Reggy, Beau and the captain of the *Spirit of the Sea* are waiting for me in their dinghy to point out the mooring they have offered me.

I wake up at seven the next morning, and by eight o'clock decide to get up as it's Saturday and the locals take to the water in anything that floats. They seem to have just discovered *Guppy* … Spanish boats pass me regularly and their occupants cheerfully start talking to me in Spanish, of which I don't understand a word, and then take photos before moving on. There's also a Belgian film crew that's interested in doing some filming and, as this has been set up beforehand, I help them to load everything on *Guppy*. I'm not happy when they ask me to sail for 20 minutes as it means raising the anchor, which I certainly don't feel like doing, but then they offer to help and I give in.

That evening we have a meal on the boulevard and I bump into my friends Beau and Didier, as I often do at spots on the beach where there's good WiFi reception from a hotel. The beach is long and white, which is seldom the case on the Canary Islands, as most of the beaches have black lava sand. The big Hotel Anfi had hoped to create its own white, private beach by shipping over tons of white sand from the Caribbean. Unfortunately for the hotel, the beaches here are all public beaches, so even if they've created it themselves, everyone has access to it and is able to enjoy this long, white beach.

Early the next morning, I'm fetched for my diving exam. After a few beautiful dives, including a dive down to a wreck, I pass my exam and am now certified to dive anywhere in the world.

Now and again, the De Bruyn family ask me for dinner and slowly Beau and Didier lose their reserve and talk to me. In the beginning they looked at me as though I was some rare creature …

After being anchored at Anfi for some time, I'm offered a sponsored spot in the Puerto de Mogán harbour; a beautiful, less touristy harbour situated amongst the mountains. I'm allowed to stay here for 10 days to attract publicity for this harbour, and that works out well for me. My mum and sister, Kim, who weren't able to say farewell to me before my departure, are arriving the following day. They were away on holiday when I left and now want to see me before I leave Gran Canaria. It's much easier for them to come on board if I'm in a harbour.

I'm impressed when the management welcomes me at the marina and shows me to a quiet spot far from the tourist shops. I moor *Guppy* between two other boats with her stern to the jetty and the bow to a mooring. Close to me is the yacht of a Dutch couple who are on the point of going out for a pizza. They ask me to join them. Despite having enjoyed a pizza the day before, I jump at the chance and it's a lively meal.

The manager of the hotel across from *Guppy* comes by and invites me to use their swimming pool and also take breakfast at the hotel. This is so cool! Fresh eggs and croissants every morning, yum! Although I've just arrived at Puerto de Mogán, I go back to Anfi at about noon. Not with *Guppy* this time, but by the ferry that cruises along the coast. In Anfi, I go swimming with Beau, and that evening we all watch television at his home. It's good to find myself in the heart of a family again. That's something I sometimes miss on *Guppy*; enjoying meals together, watching television, talking and having a good discussion.

My mum and sister arrive today and I wait for them at the airport. I haven't seen them for half a year, but they haven't changed a bit. Kim's hair is longer and it suits her, and my mum is just as clumsy as ever. I advise her to rent a car. In fact, I had suggested we do so in the emails we exchanged the previous week, so I'm totally surprised when she tells me she may not have her driver's licence on her. We empty half her handbag at the airport and manage to find it, or what's left of it. Sigh. Nothing has changed. We manage to rent a little black car and head for Puerto de Mogán. It's a journey of more than an hour and they hadn't expected that, so I'm constantly hearing: 'Are we almost there?' And at almost every harbour: 'Isn't that *Guppy*?'

As we approach the last harbour, Kim cheers: 'Hey, that really is *Guppy*! We're there!'

I'm crazy about my little sister and we do a lot of things together. My mother brightens up considerably in the warm climate and she loves the life on board. It reminds her of her seven-year world voyage on board *Diario* with Dad. She's constantly telling me how they did things back then; the washing, the cleaning, et cetera.

My mum, Kim and I have been invited by the hotel-with-the-pool-and-the-free-breakfasts for a meal with the manager, mayor and other VIPs. This could be a trial ... There is rice with squid and lobster on the menu; all the things I really don't enjoy, but of course I can't say so. I see that Kim and my mum are also looking at the dishes with suspicion. One of the guests, whom I later discover is actually the mayor, shows me how to open the lobster and points out the edible parts. I subtly arrange everything on my plate to look as though I've eaten a good portion.

Kim and I have a lot of fun together, and I'm really glad that we are together again. I go diving with my mum on one occasion, and we go swimming often as there's a heat wave that week. We visit Puerto de Mogán dozens of times and Mum soon makes some friends. She's constantly fantasising about emigrating to Gran Canaria. If she continues doing this long enough, it may just happen.

There are another two Dutch yachts moored to the same jetty as *Guppy*. One of them has a washing machine and Mum thinks this is terrific. It's not much fun trying to wash your bedding in the basin. We make contact with the crew of *Tante Rietje* from Enkhuizen in the

Netherlands. They ask us to join them for dinner that evening. Great! We eat *piepertjes* (new potatoes) and hamburgers. My mum, who is of German origin, has never heard the Dutch word *piepertjes* before and says it sounds wonderful; so wonderful that she repeats the word all night long.

At six in the morning we are woken up by the noise of metal poles clattering to the ground and banging against each other. They are busy setting up the market. Half asleep, I crawl out of the bunk that I'm sharing with a restless Kim. I eventually crawl back in and manage to sleep despite the noise from the market. I wake up at about nine. Mum is already up and I pull Kim out of bed. Luckily it's market day today and the word *piepertjes* is soon forgotten.

We wander around the market with the pocket money Mum has given us. I buy two pairs of shorts and a T-shirt. It really is a big market, but by the afternoon it's too hot to walk around and we decide to cool off in the pool.

We've arranged to visit the De Bruyn family at four o'clock because Mum wants to meet 'that boy and his family'. We walk towards the spot where the car was parked, but it seems to have disappeared into thin air. Oh shit! I ask some people at one of the stalls if they know what's happened to our car. They tell me that it's probably been towed away and that we should go to the police to enquire. They say the police station is 8 kilometres away and, seeing that we no longer have a car, it means we will have to walk.

We decide to go to some people Mum met yesterday and ask if they can help us. Of course they will! We all climb into their car, but it doesn't want to start. Someone has left the car lights on all night and the battery is flat. Eventually someone from the village helps us, but when we've driven quite a bit more than 8 kilometres to the station, there's no sign of our car … The policeman tells us to go back to the parking area outside the Spar and look for it there.

We drive all the way back and, indeed, there's our little black car with a notice written in Spanish on the windscreen. It's probably a long explanation about moving the car but none of us can read it. We step in and drive to Anfi but don't get there at four as promised. Fortunately, this isn't a problem. I introduce my mum to Beau, Didier, Antonio and Reggy. Beau, Kim and I go swimming. Kim has forgotten to bring her swimsuit and is asking herself if she should swim in her underwear. I help her to make up her mind by giving her a little shove into the water.

She leaves the pool earlier than the rest of us, and when we get back I find that she has accused me of throwing her into the water. Sisters! Oh well … We eat all sorts of things and eventually also a potato tart which my mum immediately renames *piepertjes* tart. I suspect we are going to hear about *piepertjes* for some time …

The next morning Mum and Kim get ready to go back to the Netherlands; their holiday has come to an end.

The 10 days of luxury at Puerto de Mogán are also over, and I sail back to Anfi together with Beau. I now spend most of my time getting *Guppy* ready for our voyage. She has to be in good shape before I cross the Atlantic. I make one more trip with Beau to Puerto Rico to fill up with diesel and we load all the groceries on board. When I have everything that will sustain me until I get to the Caribbean, we sail back. There's a lovely breeze, and because Beau has never sailed before, we go for a little excursion. We're still about four miles from the coast when the sun sets. We decide to pump up the dinghy in the meantime, but can't find the tube of the foot pump we need for this amongst the mess in the aft cabin. We eventually just use our lungs. Half an hour later we are dizzy from the effort, but the dinghy is inflated. It's pitch dark as we near Anfi, and we decide to use only the mooring without dropping anchor. No wind is forecast and I now trust this mooring. Once *Guppy* is moored, we get in the dinghy, which is the size of a liferaft according to Beau, and paddle to the beach. We have forgotten our flip-flops, but decide not to go back for them. Dinner has been waiting for us for some time when we enter on our bare feet.

Later we take their dog, Boss, for a walk and it reminds me of my loyal friend, Spot. It has been a long time since I walked a dog and I lose myself in happy nostalgia. On the sledge, in the snow, on the boat, in bed with his muddy paws; having rolled in stinking fish, bowling me over in his enthusiasm. Spot features in all the memories of my youth. I miss my life with my loyal old Spot. He's now with Dad, and I don't think the long crossings I'm about to venture on would have suited him. I need to do this on my own, however tempting the idea of having him with me may be.

While I really want to do some proper sailing again, I'm going to miss the life that I've built up for myself here and the people I've come to know. I feel at home here and everyone is so friendly. It still upsets me to think back on everything that the Dutch authorities put me through in the past year before my departure. I try to suppress these thoughts, but they continue to surface from time to time. It is and remains a part of my life, but now I have left and have what I really wanted. I'm living the way I dreamt and fantasised about as an eight-year-old. The freedom is wonderful. I enjoy every day, every hour, every minute of this experience, and it seems as if I'm part of a dream; as if it's not quite real. It's weird to think that I jumped from the hell that the Dutch authorities had turned my life into, to this heaven that I'd only dreamt of; from that dark place to this warm light. I'm so glad I've persevered and that Dad supported me at all times.

But everything is not always sunshine and roses. I've had a bad earache for a couple of days and have decided to see a doctor. He diagnoses an ear infection and gives me an injection in my backside. Now I have more pain from the injection than my ear! I also get some pills and eardrops. I hate taking medicine, but by the end of the day my earache is a little better so it hasn't all been for nothing.

I pack the most into my last days on the island. I have a fun day at the Palmitos Park with Ido and Dedy. The Palmitos Park is a zoo with dolphins, and we have a great time. But the hurricane season is coming to an end, and the day soon arrives when I decide to move on. That afternoon *Guppy* and I say farewell to all the kind people on this wonderful island.

Gran Canaria–Cape Verde Islands: 780 nautical miles

DAY 1: *10 November*

Guppy and I are on our way to the Cape Verde Islands. I've prepared well for this voyage but soon realise that the batteries are almost empty. It's probably because I left the fridge on while *Guppy* lay at anchor.

Stupid! The solar panels just aren't able to supply enough power for the fridge in this heat.

The route I'm following is calm and I don't expect to see any other sailors on my way to the Cape Verde Islands. It's great to be sailing again, but I also have a lump in my throat as I watch the coastline receding slowly. I have been on Gran Canaria for two months and the past few weeks have been amazing. Saying farewell to the island and the many people I met there was really difficult; more difficult than I'd ever have imagined. It feels strange to be on my own again after such a busy time and to have no one around to talk to, but the dolphins playing around *Guppy*'s bow soon make me forget my sadness as we sail into the sunset.

DAY 2: *11 November*

Wow, it's a hundred days since I left the Netherlands. A wind has sprung up and it's coming from just the right direction. It still feels a little weird to be on my own, but familiar at the same time. When I look back, I have a problem letting go of that thin strip of land I called 'home' for a while. This morning I saw the last of the mountain peaks on Gran Canaria disappear. There are a few clouds on the horizon, but the morning sun is nice and warm. *Guppy* is sailing at 5.5 knots after a night of little wind. The windvane steers *Guppy* and I can sit and enjoy the view over the endless expanse of undulating blue waves. I pass two cargo ships sailing in opposite directions. The increasingly high temperatures are an indication that we are nearing the Equator.

DAY 3: *12 November*

There's a strong wind blowing and *Guppy* is running at 7 knots with the occasional 8 knots. Last night I passed another ship. It's still a bit cloudy and fairly cool. If *Guppy* continues at this speed, I should get to the island of Sal in four days' time. It's great to feel the wind in my hair and to see *Guppy* cutting through the waves ... *Guppy* and I are a team chasing the horizon. It's 13.30, ship in sight; 231 miles sailed and another 536 to go. Today we completed 131 miles. I lower the foresail and we are now sailing only on the jib and reefed mainsail.

DAY 4: *13 November*

Yuck, it's really overcast today. The radar and even the Echomax, my active radar-reflector, don't give any sign of ships. I switch off the radar and switch on the Echomax alarm. I'm going to stay in bed until the sun comes up, I tell myself. The sun stays hidden and, after checking that all is well on deck, I go back inside to lie and read on the couch. This sombre weather always makes me a bit grumpy. My thoughts drift back to the awful year I had when I was under the supervision of the state and it upsets me all over again. I try to read some more, but my thoughts are somewhere else. Better catch up with my schoolwork because I'm falling a little behind on that score.

It's 17.15 and I feel we've achieved something. *Guppy* and I have completed 400 miles and have another 380 to go; that's well past the halfway mark. The sun has started to shine and the wind has dropped a little, which means that the cockpit remains fairly dry now. Guppy is now sailing with mainsail, mizzen, flying jib and genoa, averaging 6 knots. It's going well and I'm feeling a little better.

I've just had some ravioli on deck and succeeded in getting most of it into my tummy instead of on the cockpit floor, so all is well. Now to write up my blog and send the text to Dad via the satellite phone which he'll then place on my website. Back in the Netherlands I'd wanted to install an SSB radio with an email facility on *Guppy*, but this wasn't possible as you need a special licence to own a radio with such a high transmission power. They thwarted every attempt I made to get one and I ended up leaving without one. So the only means of communication at sea is via the satellite telephone. I still hope to buy an SSB radio somewhere along my route so that I can send my emails and also receive weather charts.

DAY 5: *14 November*

What a feeling! I managed to sleep well last night; an hour at a time. *Guppy*'s speed has dropped a little and we are now making headway at 4.5 knots. If we continue at this speed we should arrive on the night of Tuesday going into Wednesday, but I'd rather not approach an unknown harbour in the dark. *Guppy* is sailing gently and I have to accept that we won't be going at top speeds for a while.

Compared with yesterday's blues, I'm feeling really well today. The sun shines almost constantly and *Guppy* is under full sail with flying jib, jib, mainsail and mizzen. I've started reading *Vrijheid en Eenvoud* (*Freedom and Simplicity*) by Ben Hoekendijk. He sailed around the Atlantic, but the old man wrote a little too much about religion for my taste.

I keep hoping that *Guppy*'s speed picks up so that I can reach the Cape Verde Islands by Tuesday evening. A little later, my wish is fulfilled and *Guppy* is sailing at 6 knots in the sunshine. I'm enjoying her motion and am proud of her. She's brought me this far and will bring me to many more places on this earth. I look out over the endless sea contentedly while *Guppy* ploughs through the infinite salty water to show me a new island. I ask myself if *Guppy* has seen any of these harbours before. Who knows where she's been in the past 33 years of her life. I wish she could speak and tell me all about her travels … Instead, she plunges into the next wave wearing a white foam moustache. This is an absolute 'top of the world' feeling. How often had I been able to feel this wonderful warmth and exhilaration in that now far-off, sombre country, the Netherlands? *Guppy* has covered 500 miles and there are 280 to go.

DAY 6: *15 November*

It's 02.30 and — argh — what a night! I can't sleep and am playing on my portable PlayStation in order to get through the night. The sky is pitch black and while I'm looking at it, it suddenly begins to pour. This is followed by an unexpected squall and then the wind drops again … All very annoying, but the sky behind me begins to clear. I try to catch up on some sleep, and two hours later I wake up fairly refreshed.

With 635 miles now completed, there are 140 to go. During the last 24 hours, *Guppy* has managed to cover 135 miles, despite the unhelpful winds last night. If I maintain a speed of more than 5.5 knots, I should reach Palmera, the capital and only harbour on Sal, by daylight, so let's hope the wind doesn't drop. I see flying fish for the first time on this voyage, some 30 of them in total and they certainly are strange creatures.

It's almost 18.30 and time to write up my blog, struggle with the satellite phone and send my message in one go. In the evening, the wind drops and I try to hoist the code zero. In the process I knock my little toe. Oh well, let's put a plaster on it. While I'm fixing up the code zero, I find two dead flying fish on deck. I know they are edible but choose to give them a burial at sea. *Guppy* is actually running a little too much before the wind for the code zero, but she's moving in the right direction at a speed of 6 knots.

DAY 7: *16 November*

During the night the wind drops gradually, and at 03.00 I start the engine. There's no chance of sleeping with this noise. The engine is also making an irritating squeal because of the alarm signal that goes off when the voltage is too low in the almost-empty batteries. *Guppy* has a huge battery capacity, but when they're all flat even the 110-amp alternator on the Volvo can't get the voltage up quickly enough for the alarm not to go off. In total, I manage to get less than two and a half hours' sleep.

The wind picks up a little as the sun rises and I'm thrilled to cut the noisy engine. *Guppy* is soon sailing at about 6 knots under full sail with mizzen, mainsail and code zero. Awesome! I've spotted a yacht on the horizon. It's a small white dot and I leave it at that. I've managed to bump my toe again and it's bleeding.

10.45 hours: Land in sight! The island of Sal is appearing on the horizon and it looks like an egg-shaped sand hill. Hmm.

13.34 hours: There are now three sand hills in sight. Why does it always take so long before you actually arrive? I'll probably only reach land by 16.30 and then it will take another two hours to the harbour of Palmera. I hope there'll be enough daylight.

Late in the afternoon the three sand hills are now connected and slowly houses and more land emerge. I'm nearing my goal. On closer inspection, the island doesn't look very promising. I see a few square concrete houses, an old cargo ship and some gas reservoirs. I'm wondering if there's another yacht in the area, but as soon as *Guppy* turns into the bay, I see dozens of them.

It's wonderful to be out of the wind, but I have trouble finding a place to anchor. A cheerful Cape Verdean approaches me.

'I you help,' he says in broken English.

He ties his boat — a wonder that this contraption still floats — alongside *Guppy*, climbs onto the foredeck and gestures.

'OK, this way', and then 'that way', he says, leading me closer and closer to the beach. Worried about running aground, I tell him that *Guppy* is 2 metres deep. He assures me that all this is 'no problem'. He eventually points out a good spot where he drops the anchor for me. Great, it means I don't have to exert myself! I ask him if he knows Carlos, a man who works for Trans-Ocean.

'Yes, of course,' he says, and tells me he'll take me to him.

I've once again inflated the dinghy by mouth (I still haven't found the tube for the pump), and paddle after the wooden contraption in my little red dinghy to step onto Cape Verdean soil.

Sal

This place is unbelievable! The crooked streets are full of well-fed dogs and Cape Verdeans who just sit and talk as I pass. What a wonderful, relaxed atmosphere! Strains of reggae music echo through the unpainted, broken-down concrete homes. Most of the doors — and not all the houses have doors — consist of a mere piece of wood. It's pretty primitive here.

Carlos isn't at home, and so my friendly helper, whose name I've managed to forget again, takes me to the Customs office — a yellow building containing one desk and one Cape Verdean. It takes him 45 minutes to make a copy of my passport and to fill in a short form. Then I need to go to the Harbour Police. In this derelict, unpainted concrete hovel, there's a table, a chair and an antique television. All they have to do is stamp my passport, but it takes them more than an hour to do so due to the fact that the four of them can't tear themselves away from the television.

On my way back to *Guppy* I meet Carlos, who runs the Trans-Ocean sailors' support station. I drink some water and chat to some Dutch people who run a charter business here, and they invite me to join them for a meal on the wharf at 19.15 that evening.

'And what's the time over here right now?' I ask.

They tell me that it's an hour earlier than on the Canary Islands. That's two hours earlier than in the Netherlands. At 19.00, I paddle to the wharf with the bar where the crew has gathered. We go to an Italian restaurant that doesn't have pizzas, but we're served all kinds of fish followed by spaghetti. It's great to be able to talk Dutch again. It's now 21.30 Cape Verdean time, and time for me to catch up on some sleep as I've quite a bit to do tomorrow.

I set the alarm and am rudely awakened at seven in the morning. I feel I could still sleep for hours; just sleep without interruptions from waves, wind or passing ships. I get up anyway. Still half asleep, I eat a sandwich and then go to check up on the engines; the oil, coolant, filters and V-belt. The V-belt needs to be tightened after all the hours of heavy duty trying to get the batteries charged, but otherwise everything seems to be in order.

I then decide to tidy up and empty the last box of provisions. While I'm stowing these supplies away under the bunks, I come across a bag of rotten potatoes that has been lying there for some time. I lift the bag and it's followed by a swarm of flies and other crap. I clear the entire storage space, clean it and then pack everything back again. I'm not fond of cleaning work and enough is enough. Time for some schoolwork now.

In between these chores, I paddle back to the wharf for my last stamp at the Clearance Office. At three o'clock, I drag my dinghy onto the foredeck. Zidane, the cheerful Cape Verdean whose name I now remember, insists on helping me heave up the heavy anchor and takes all my refuse and empty boxes with him. I show my appreciation by giving him a large packet of liquorice sweets.

Sal–São Nicolao: 85 nautical miles

DAY 1: *17 November*

When it starts to get dark, I steer *Guppy* seawards again for the 85-mile voyage to São Nicolau. There's a strong beam wind, and the waves frequently throw *Guppy* heavily onto her side. The wind comes and goes throughout the night.

DAY 2: *18 November*

At daybreak, we are 15 miles from our destination and I can see the contours of the island. São Nicolau has enormous mountains covered by a green haze. I'm hoping to anchor *Guppy* off the village of Tarrafal in a few hours. Although I'm miles from home, it doesn't always feel like it. That's because of the communication systems I have on board, such as the satellite phone and VHF. You don't often come across another ship at sea, but when you do it's nice to have a chat. At most harbours, I usually have a fairly good internet connection. I email and Skype and manage to see my dog, Spot, on the screen a few times. He barks when he hears my voice, looks for me behind the PC screen and then whines softly when he can't figure out where I am. I feel guilty about having abandoned my faithful friend. I have so much to thank him for.

Thanks to Spot, Dad let me go on the first holiday on my own for six weeks when I was 10. Spot protected me and was always at my side. He was my shadow. If anyone dared to even point at me, Spot would immediately jump between us. We did everything together; sail, swim, build huts, and he always knew when I would be back from school. He would be there waiting for me and would run to greet me. Spot has a good life with Dad, but it feels as if I've disappointed a very good friend who's been at my side since the age of six.

When it comes to communication, I realise that I have a far easier time than my parents had on their world voyage. They'd have to write lengthy letters that would take weeks to arrive and would have to dive into a telephone booth as soon as they came on shore. It may be easier now, but it can also be annoying for people to be able to reach you day and night. Now that the internet is available, I'm able to look into people's living rooms via Skype, just as if I were there. Sometimes that gives me a feeling of not really having left. I certainly haven't had the wish to step through the screen and back into the Netherlands; especially now that it's so cold and wet there ... Brr! *Viva* Africa!

A beautiful, rugged, mountainous landscape is unfolding before me. I spot some yachts and it gradually grows warmer. The VHF is on and I hear the German Trans-Ocean sailors' support station's contact person on São Nicolau. I peer through my binoculars but can't see their office. Once I've moored, they call again. They're coming over by boat. When I've checked and closed up everything, I go and have my clearance stamp checked by the police on shore.

São Nicolau

We walk to the office-cum-guest-house that's right on the shore. Many seafarers make use of its services and I'm able to take a shower here. Alas, no hot water, but after seven days of saltwater this doesn't worry me in the least. While I'm sitting on a bench, some Dutch sailors arrive from a yacht called *Mirus* that's anchored close to *Guppy*. We arrange to go for a walk the next day, then return to where our dinghies are beached and they tow me back to *Guppy*. It's not possible to fix my outboard motor to the dinghy I'm using now, so I appreciate their help. Back on deck, I slide the covers over the sails to protect them from the sun and sit and enjoy the view. São Nicolau is a beautiful island, much prettier than Sal, with tall mountains and much more vegetation.

After a night of unbroken sleep, I face a busy day. The alarm goes off at eight. I eat, drink, pack my bag, and, just as I've finished, Henk and Miranda Wallet from *Mirus* arrive in their tender. We're going on a mountain hike today with another German woman and two Frenchmen. We're squeezed into a small bus and taken along winding gravel roads to a village from which we can only walk. It's a small, pretty village with gravel roads. While we're in the village, a bunch of inquisitive kids on their way home from school offers to show us the best spot to cross the river. Two kilometres further on, they jump into a lake with a beautiful waterfall and carry on up the mountain. We walk past donkeys that are grazing, small houses and women who are cooking outdoors while trying to keep children, goats, pigs and chickens under control. We begin the real hike up the mountain at the start of a valley surrounded by high cliffs. The heat makes it quite a task, and each time we think we are nearly there, it continues to rise until we finally reach the summit after about three hours. Our hard work is rewarded with a magnificent view of the entire valley.

Finally we start on the next part of the hike. We fill our water bottles at a waterfall high in the mountains where a man lives on his own, and begin the next ascent. When we reach the top, we find a beautiful forest. The light begins to fade a little when we emerge from the forest, and we make a steep descent until we see our village and a car and walk the last bit in good spirits. Exhausted, we sit on the roadside while our Cape Verdean guide looks for a taxi. A little later a pickup arrives with wooden seats in the back. We all find a place to sit and wind our way back to Tarrafal at 70 kilometres an hour as the sun sets.

Tarrafal is one of the biggest villages on São Nicolau. The streets are pitted with potholes and the houses are made of concrete blocks, often without doors or windows. If you want to buy something, you really need to know where to go as there are no signposts or names on shops or streets. This may look like a developing country, but there are phones, internet, football fields and other Western elements that look out of place here. The people seem to be outdoors all the time and laugh a lot. When I ask them if they'd rather live in Europe, I get a steadfast 'no way'.

The island is beautiful. I accompany a taxi driver to the airport with five hotel guests, just for the ride, and manage to see some of the island in this way. We drive past lovely valleys and green mountains that rise along the roadside. After an hour of travelling along narrow, often gravel roads, through villages and across streams, we arrive at the airport. It has a small building with two doors showing two signs — *Arrivals* and *Departures* — above them. The luggage that arrives is passed to the passengers through a window. When a plane arrives, loud salsa music is played to welcome the passengers. What more could you want? They have two planes, one of which is on Sal, broken. The other plane is due to arrive at five, but according to the locals the plane is always late. They are right about this one and it gets quite tense while we wait, as the plane is unable to land in the dark. Luckily the plane lands just before dark. Back in Tarrafal, I'm dropped off at the home of a Cape Verdean family with a 15-year-old daughter. I'd met Kelly before, and she'd asked if I'd like to join her and her family for a meal. She's invited a few of her friends along, too. The girls come in one by one and serve some delicious snacks. I don't speak a word of Crioulo and they've hardly any English, but with a few words and many gestures we manage to have a great evening.

I paddle to the black beach next to the wharf where the fishermen's boats are moored a few times a day. I'm often at the Trans-Ocean support point where I can shower and make use of the internet. Guests and sailors walk in and out and I greet them all cheerfully. After having done my updates on the internet, I go to the beach. I meet Kelly there and she asks me if I'd like to play football with some of her friends. They're all about my age and most of them seem to have children who are parked on the sidelines while the game is in progress. Playing football in flip-flops isn't a success. It's really not my sport and I have trouble aiming the ball in the right direction, but it's great fun and we laugh a lot.

At 07.30 the next morning, I'm paddling to the shore again. Today I'm going on a tour of the island with Henk and Miranda from *Mirus*, Conny and Henk Werner from *Amygdala*, a man from the yacht *Deep Blue*, as well as two Dutch and two French people. Eventually all 10 of us depart in a pickup taxi. Whether you are crushed or suddenly find you have a lot of space depends on which way the road curves as the vehicle swings through the many bends. We drive over a bumpy, stony route, and after half an hour the driver makes a sharp turn over the verge and into the grass. We continue downhill, through a dry river bed, uphill, downhill again, and then he thunders down a steep drop that looks as though it ends in the sea. There are anxious looks on everyone's faces. What's he up to? Where are we going? He's still driving at full speed; another 1000, 800, 700, 600 metres to go before the edge—

Suddenly the truck grinds to a halt and we're told to get out and follow the guide. We're all pleasantly surprised when we reach some beautiful cliffs. The water has eroded the cliff face and freshwater seeps through different layers in the rock. I don't exactly understand where it comes from. At some spots the sea throws itself against these cliffs and then recedes. I could stay and watch this for hours, but we continue our tour. We drive back a short distance and decide to split up and continue in two cars. I end up with three Germans and a Frenchman in the Ford truck. We follow bumpy, winding roads to a pretty lagoon, and en route stop for some punch. Well, everyone except me; I have a Coke. Some people are very cheerful after only one glass of punch. The

Frenchman tries to make a yacht in the back of the pickup by picking up a log and pinning his T-shirt to it like a sail. Edson, the guide who's also sitting at the back of the vehicle, speaks no English, German or Dutch, and most of us don't speak any Crioulo, French, Portuguese or Italian, but by gesturing with our hands and feet we are learning a lot from each other.

The heavy rains of the past months have swept away big chunks of the only tarred road on the island. So we tell Edson that the road is kaput. In response, he looks at us and imitates a goat. In this way we learn that 'kaput' means 'goat' in Crioulo. And a *koe* — Dutch for 'cow' — means 'backside' in the local language. This I gather when I shout *koe* on seeing a cow and our guide turns to give me a strange look. And so I pick up my first words of Crioulo ... the first and the last.

The next morning, I'm up on deck early to watch the sunrise. I'm reading a book called *Her Name is Sarah*. A beautiful but sad story about a boy who is hidden in a cupboard by his sister during a *razzia* in the Second World War. The family is moved to a German concentration camp and the boy is left behind to tragically die in the cupboard.

By the time I've finished the book, it's half past four. At five I'm going to eat pizzas with Conny and Henk on board the *Amygdala*. Fortunately, my German is fair and we manage to have a good conversation. Conny is happy to hear that she isn't the only one to sometimes ask herself what on earth she's doing when she's at sea. While I can relate to books about people who complain for hours about being at sea, I personally find time on land really dreary. It's not always fun at sea, but sailing usually gives me an enormous kick. Just sighting one dolphin is enough to make my day.

At nine that evening I paddle back to *Guppy*. I want to do a little work on my own book. When I plug a USB stick containing my text into the computer, I'm distracted by all the photographs I've taken over the past year. The time of the battle with the Dutch authorities over my voyage. I see a pale, tired girl and find some lines I wrote at the time. Here are two fragments:

... My life is such a mess. I have the feeling that I've fallen into a deep abyss and don't know how to carry on with my voyage.

Just when I've met all their requirements, they go and invent
new ways to stop me. Sometimes I'm the Laura with courage
and faith who never gives up. That Laura says: Think about all
you have been through. Do you want to give the Netherlands
the satisfaction of seeing you give up? No, of course not, I
won't give them that pleasure. But I'm being harassed on
all sides, and if I don't find solutions I won't be allowed to
go. The authorities are trying to weaken my resolve. I can't
honestly remember one night when I slept well or woke up
rested. For almost a year, I've been feeling unwell, tired and
weak. What can I do? I no longer know. I'll explode soon;
that should solve the problem. HELP!!! I cry, but besides Dad
there's no one to hear me. Dad is just as depressed and doesn't
know what to do either. Now I'm sitting at home instead of
going to school. I'm feeling so weak that I think I'll fall off my
bike if I try to cycle to school. I can't even stand up properly.
I hope I'll find a way to get out of this situation. It's a good
thing I'm a fine actress, but I sometimes fear that I'll never
ever be myself again …

More than a month later, when I am tricked into losing my boat, it
really gets too much for me. Just before Christmas, I write a farewell
letter to Dad and flee to Saint Martin. This is what I write, amongst
other things:

… And now that I'm on Saint Martin my name is Jessie
Muller and I'm 17 years old. I'm almost the new owner of
the Duende, a 9-metre Dufour Arpège. Saint Martin is great;
everyone is so friendly here and the palm trees, white sands
and azure blue waters are so beautiful. In that cold, unfriendly
country, the Netherlands, this island seemed like a dream,
but it's real; it exists! It's wonderful and I love it here. In the
Netherlands it's snowing, but here it's warm and the mosquitos
are swarming around me. I've just spent a few hours on my
new boat. Tomorrow I'll clean it up inside because it really is a
mess …

When I read this text again now, it's as though it's about some other girl's life. Since my departure, I have tried not to dwell too long on my life over the past year, but now I can feel my pain and despair again in this text. When I wrote this, I couldn't have dreamt that I would ever be happy again and that I would be reading this now that it's all in the past. But it's over; thank goodness, it's over.

Quite a number of yachts have anchored in our bay over the past few days. Most of them are French. They're easy to recognise because they are usually catamarans or fast monohulls. The French aren't often that fluent in English and my French is not brilliant either, but even without conversing it can be fun being amongst them.

In another week or so I want to make the crossing from São Nicolau to Saint Martin in the Caribbean. I'm really looking forward to it. I'll be out on the ocean for three weeks. It shouldn't be that difficult with no islands, reefs, tricky harbours and little shipping traffic to contend with. Even a storm is better out at sea than close to land.

For most of the time it will be downwind sailing, which helps. There's little to do before I leave as I got all the necessary food supplies on Gran Canaria. I just need to check *Guppy* thoroughly.

There's no wind and all the boats are lying scattered across the anchorage. There's a cargo ship approaching in the distance. It's probably going to the dockside and a few of the yachts will have to move. If the captain knows how to steer, *Guppy* shouldn't be in the way. There's enough space between *Guppy* and the wharf, and so I stay where I am. I'm eating Spanish bread with Dutch *speculaas* (spicy Dutch biscuits). I've sneaked them out of the Christmas parcel that I've opened a month before I should have … Half an hour later, I get a fright when a huge wall of steel glides past *Guppy*. I look to see where the other yachts have gone and notice that they have raised their anchors and moved to a safe distance. The ship is painfully slow in passing *Guppy* and I'm tense until its stern passes and I can read PANAMA in huge letters and know that we are safe. I promise myself never to expose *Guppy* to this kind of danger again, and will be more careful about her safety from now on.

Towards evening, I paddle to shore to enjoy a meal at the Aquarium restaurant at the Trans-Ocean Sailing Association, as I often do. The food is great. Henry, the Dutch owner of the joint, was a chef and is training some of the Cape Verdeans to cook. There are now two Dutch tourists staying at the guest house. After the meal, they help me get the dinghy back in the water. Carefully I paddle back to *Guppy*, leaving a green, phosphorescent glow in my wake. It's so incredibly beautiful. I beat the water with my paddle to create more sparkle, but unfortunately half the water lands on me. Not a clever move, Laura! What a great life I have here. This is what I've always dreamt of, and it makes me happy to be here. I think of winter in the Netherlands, Spot, Dad, Kim and Mum. I really did have a great youth there. Sometimes it was difficult, but it was good too. The past year, with its six court cases, is like a black stain on my memory. I can recall every moment and every emotion. If I hadn't been able to leave, I'd have landed in a dark hole from which I'd never ever have emerged. That year had almost finished me off, and I'd escaped by the skin of my teeth. Thanks to Dad, Gran, Granddad and my lawyer, Peter de Lange, who all helped me. Now I have something that I could only have dreamt of and it's wonderful. Sometimes I still can't believe that I've really left. It still feels like a dream in which I can wake up again at any time and find myself in a courtroom across from three judges who seem to listen only to what the lawyers representing the authorities, the Child Protection and Child Care organisations have to say. The judges who didn't take the trouble to listen to what Dad and I had to say, and who rashly accepted everything the state lawyers told them. But that is all behind me now and I am free.

After getting to the beach and back by dinghy and staying dry at least 50 times, it suddenly goes wrong. I'm on my way to get my outward clearance when two big waves turn the dinghy upside-down and I land in the water. Luckily my laptop is in a waterproof bag, but I can't present myself to the officials soaking wet. Other sailors witness what has happened and feel sorry for me. I bail all the water out of the dinghy while they tow me back to *Guppy*. I then change clothes and give it another go. This time I reach land dry and walk to the Harbour Police office. After waiting for hours, I'm told that I need to go to Mindelo for the clearance outwards. No way am I going to another island for one stupid stamp! I'm sure they'll let me enter Saint Martin without the stamp and not force me to re-cross the Atlantic Ocean. At the Aquarium restaurant, I chat to Dad via Skype one last time before I start on my big ocean crossing the following day.

São Nicolau–Saint Martin: 2223 nautical miles

DAY 1: *2 December*

I get up early so that I can eat leisurely, deflate the dinghy, tidy up and pull the covers off the sails. Finally, I heave up the 30 metres of anchor chain and anchor with sweat running off my brow. There's little wind and the sun is searing hot. After completing all the hard work, I pour some water down my parched throat and continue to hoist the sails. It's not much use as there isn't much wind and it's coming from the wrong direction. That doesn't make *Gup* and me very happy. But when *Guppy* emerges from behind the islands, there's a wonderful beam wind. Yep, *Guppy* just glides away.

I'm standing on the foredeck enjoying the way she's taking on the wild sea. This is more like it! She's now sailing at about 6.5 knots and I see the Cape Verde Islands — Santa Lúcia, São Vincente and Santa Antão — disappearing on my starboard side.

I'm sitting in the cockpit enjoying everything around me. At night the starlit sky is amazing, and I spend hours looking at it. At about 11, I try to get some sleep, but it's not to be. I'm just behind the last island and the wind and sea are very variable, which means that I'm going to have to watch that *Guppy* sticks to her course. At about 04.00, I eventually allow myself some sleep and dive into my bunk.

When I wake up a little later, the wind has swung 180 degrees and *Guppy* is sailing back on her tracks. Hmm …

DAY 2: *3 December*

At daybreak the first rays of sunshine wake me and *Guppy* is still on course. There's a strong beam wind, and under full sail *Guppy* is sailing at some 7 knots. That's even better than yesterday. For the first hour I just enjoy watching *Guppy* dashing through the waves. A pod of dolphins breaks through the white horses on the sea, but they only play with *Guppy* for a short while and then quickly disappear out of sight. I play some Nirvana and go into the cabin to get some breakfast.

Towards the end of the morning, *Guppy* has sailed 123 miles and still has 2100 to go, but two hours later the wind drops and we experience light variable breezes from all points of the compass. Damn, it was too good to be true! I hoist the code zero, but even this sail collapses like a soufflé. There's nothing for it but to update my blog and send it off to the home front, but even the satellite phone is not responding. After the third 'transmission error' warning, there's a light breeze on deck. I quit updating my blog and busy myself with the sails. More sail is needed! Up goes the genoa; I think it'll help *Guppy* sail closer to the wind. As the wind continues to freshen, I decide to leave the code zero up as well. *Guppy* is now sailing well with mizzen, mainsail, jib, genoa and code zero. There's nothing more I can put up and she's going well. The speed is about 4 knots with only 10 knots of wind. I wouldn't mind going faster, but this is fine for now.

It stays a little overcast the whole day, and now that the sun is setting I'm beginning to feel cold, and that at a latitude of 17 degrees north. I certainly seem to have got used to the heat.

At night the wind falls away entirely and *Guppy* cruises on the Yanmar at about 3.5 knots. I've rolled up the genoa and jib. I hate these light winds and being becalmed, but there's nothing I can do about it. *Guppy* has covered 207 miles and we still have 2016 to go. She's done only 84 miles today. Argh, this could take some time. Damn wind, come back!

DAY 3: *4 December*

After a lovely freshwater shower from my water bottle supply, I go and read on the foredeck and gaze over the mirror-like, endless blue sea. Every now and then there's a gust of wind that I try to catch with my code zero. Due to *Guppy*'s movements, the code zero is chafing the rigging and might tear. At last there's some wind, but when it blows, it's a headwind. Nevertheless, I keep on trying. *Guppy* is still making some progress on the little Yanmar in order to avoid swaying as much as possible. Oh well, I continue to hope for wind from the right direction and carry on reading my book.

Just before dark, a lock of hair blows into my face. Wait a minute — wind! Yeah, a breath of wind. It's a headwind but better than nothing. Taking a more southerly tack, the sails fill and I can switch off the engine. It's good to see the sails doing something other than flapping listlessly to and fro. As opposed to how I felt on my previous two voyages, I'm now feeling really great and have got back into my sailing rhythm after only half a day. It's a wonderful prospect to have a few weeks of open sea and space around me and to be able to feel at one with Nature. Tonight I'm going to make rice, chicken and satay sauce. I'm feeling on top of the world.

DAY 4: *5 December*

Oh no, we're becalmed again! I must have slept in an awkward position last night because I have a stiff neck this morning. There's a crappy mega-high swell that's got *Guppy* rolling heavily. Now that I'm truly awake and sitting in the cockpit, I notice a small tear in the code zero. Shit, it's probably been flapping against the spreaders and diamond rigging half the night. Armed with some tape, thread and needle, I lower the code zero. As always, I'm attached to the lifeline, and that's certainly no luxury today. Now that the sail has been removed, *Guppy* rolls from gunnel to gunnel. This swell is really something. *Guppy* is pitching so much that I'm worried that the code zero will tear completely if I hoist it again. I decide to roll out the genoa to the point that it doesn't hit anything, and this, together with the taut mainsail in the centre, helps to steady her a little. Even so, the genoa continues to flap, but, luckily, it can take more than the code zero.

They are celebrating *Sinterklaas* in the Netherlands today. (Otherwise known as Saint Nicholas, this is a traditional Dutch feast on 5 December during which gifts and sweets are exchanged. Not to be confused with Santa Claus or Father Christmas.) I wonder if *Sinterklaas* visits people at sea. He might even bring me some wind! I've had no wind for two days and I've had enough of these strange cross-seas. Sigh. There's nothing I can do about it. I have to respect the ways of the sea and the weather; they rule out here and are mightier than *Guppy* and me.

I go to bed early, and while I'm asleep the wind picks up. I fly on deck and hoist the code zero. It opens up and stays that way. Yippee! I switch off the Yanmar that has been running for the past two days and listen to the silence and my courageous *Guppy*. She's making speed at last. My neck is still aching, and I wonder what strange posture I must have slept in with all that rolling.

DAY 5: *6 December*

The wind continues to blow. *Olé, olé, olé!* And this time in just the right direction. *Guppy* is sailing at some 5.5 knots on the code zero, mainsail and genoa, and, after four days at sea, I see my first yacht. I pick up my binoculars. Wow: four spreaders. It's a big ship. Why on earth are they sailing without sails? It's approaching fast and definitely not on the wind. I call the ship on the VHF and they tell me there isn't enough wind. *Guppy* is doing 4.5 knots with far less sail capacity, so a ship like that could be doing 5 to 6 knots in the same wind. Oh well, to each his own logic. It's a beautiful day; a little cloudy, but I don't mind that right now. The sea is still pretty turbulent. The swell comes from ahead, and the waves and wind from astern. The L-shaped chocolate letter I started eating to celebrate *Sinterklaas* has melted in the heat, so I gather the bits in a mug and let them melt to drink later.

A spell of teasing winds warns me of a possible squall. I know that the weather can change in minutes. Suddenly it starts to blow much harder and I spot a heavy downpour ahead. I run and quickly lower the code zero. Just as I've stowed the sail through the fore hatch, it starts to pour and there are enormous gusts of wind. I also take down the mainsail, and I'm left with just the jib and mizzen. *Guppy* sails on merrily. I'm fully enjoying the rain and strong wind on the foredeck. This is my first really heavy squall and it's quite an experience. The rain suddenly halts, but the wind continues and Guppy speeds through the waves at 7 knots. It's cloudy and I'm wet and soon feel cold. I take shelter behind the sprayhood until the hefty storm subsides. It continues to blow for a while. In the evening the wind drops a bit, but *Guppy* continues to sail at a steady 5.5 knots. After preparing a tasty macaroni cheese dish for myself, I relax on deck and enjoy the sunset that manages to be different every day. Today the unusual clouds make it even more awesome. At about 19.30, it's dark and I'm looking at a pitch black sea and sky. No stars tonight ...

DAY 6: *7 December*

Crash, bang! I'm thrown from one side of my bunk to the other. There's a strong beam wind and the waves are coming from all directions. *Guppy* is being tossed around, but is going like the clappers — up to 9 knots at times. There are no dry spots to sit, so I remain under the sprayhood near the cabin entrance. Oh crap! Not a day to sit inside and read, really ... *Burp!* It's OK, I'm managing to keep everything inside, but they could tone down these waves for me. I've just calculated that if *Guppy* keeps up these speeds, I could be on Saint Martin as early as 17 December. It would be so awesome to reach Saint Martin exactly a year after my attempted escape from the Netherlands to this island. I'm really looking forward to seeing everyone I know there again, and to explore the island properly this time. I wonder if that boat I wanted to buy at the time, the *Duende*, is still for sale.

It's wintertime in the Netherlands, where it's cold and dark, while I've got the sun shining right above me and it's really hot. It's wonderful to be alone at sea like this, hundreds of miles away from rocks, shallows and busy shipping routes. It does, however, make me super-happy when I receive a text message from Dad and I'm able to send one back.

I haven't exactly done a lot today, but the day seems to have flown past; and talking of flying, if *Guppy* continues this way she'll soon take off. The speed doesn't drop below 7.5 knots. I'm surrounded by dark clouds, but there's no rain yet. Wow, the average speed has now reached 8.5 knots. I think I'm going to reef, but when I get up on deck I change my mind. I'm so enjoying the feeling of *Guppy* speeding over the blue ocean so bravely. She gives me a wink with her foamy, white moustache, and I give her free rein for a while. This is such a blast! It's getting too dark to write. Let's hope the clouds move on so I can see the stars tonight.

DAY 7: *8 December*

When I poke my head through the hatch in the morning and wake up after a couple of seconds, I notice something that troubles me. *Guppy* is sailing calmly, but we're surrounded by pitch-black clouds. A lot of wind is on its way. I prepare a quick breakfast while I can, and my crackers stay on my plate for a change instead of flying across the cabin. I'm having my breakfast in the cockpit when a flying fish lands on my shoes and smears them with its sticky scales. There are another two on deck and one on the swimming platform. Air pirates! Can't they watch where they're flying?

The wind has picked up a lot and I see one curtain of rain after the other. Amazingly, none of them close over *Guppy*. I could've done with a freshwater shower. The weather remains variable all day and I have my hands full changing the sails.

As night falls, I have some frankfurters for dinner and experience a fleeting moment of loneliness. Strange ... I suddenly miss land, trees and people. It's not that I'm bored, and *Guppy* is putting in a great performance, but I really wouldn't mind going for a walk or a run or having a good conversation with someone. Fortunately, the feeling doesn't last long and I'm cheered by the fact that I could be on Saint Martin within 10 days at this speed.

DAY 8: *9 December*

The strong wind continues overnight, and when I wake up in the morning *Guppy* is going very fast. In the afternoon, I decide to reduce sail and reef the mainsail. Not a bad decision, as the skies get darker and darker and the wind velocity increases. Suddenly there's a mega-squall with a blast of wind. I try to roll in the genoa, but the furling-line guide block breaks in two. Shit! Now the furling line has to run straight off the winch, which damages the edge of the cockpit. The wind and waves come from all sides and I need to man the rudder. *Guppy* is still sailing with the mizzen, reefed mainsail and storm jib, which is way too much sail. The wind is now at least 9 on the Beaufort scale and I'm trying to keep *Guppy* hard up to the wind with her nose into the waves. The white horses are flying horizontally across the sea as *Guppy* is hit by wave after wave. When there's a lull after a while and both rain and wind drop a little, I take my chance to drop the mainsail. Just in time before the next squall hits us. *Guppy* can now run downwind and I finally have the situation under control. I'm freezing and let the windvane take over the steering while I shelter inside from the pouring rain and crashing waves. Shit, that wasn't exactly fun! Certainly not a good experience to be out in 45 knots of wind in the middle of the Atlantic Ocean with way too much sail up. If *Guppy* had been under full sail in those conditions, she would have surfed and risked capsizing.

From behind the Plexiglas door I watch the turbulent weather and high seas that are tossing *Guppy* around like a rubber duck. That's exactly how I feel, too, I observe, and wedge myself into a bunk to try to read while the wind whistles through the rigging and the sea thunders by. I love the sound of whistling rigging and breaking waves; it takes me back to my childhood dreams of storms and high seas. As an eight-year-old I loved to sail my Mirror over the tidal estuary in stormy weather and rain; sometimes using only the jib when it was really rough. But right now, I wouldn't really mind if the wind dropped a little.

DAY 9: *10 December*

The wind hasn't dropped much, but now that it's on a broad reach I'm going well on the mizzen and storm jib. It's not really comfortable and seawater continues to cascade over *Guppy*, but it's a little less cloudy than yesterday and the sun is warming up a little. Great, I love the heat! Sitting at the cabin entrance under the sprayhood I see the second yacht on this crossing. It gives me a good feeling to know that I'm not the only one who's knocking about out here. I'm a little sluggish today and not doing anything much. I look at *Gup* chasing through the water and that's enough for me. In the meantime, it's 13.30 Cape Verdean time, but that probably doesn't apply to my present location.

For some reason, the other yacht is going much faster than *Gup*, and this with less sail. It's a much bigger yacht, so that figures, but it bothers me … Shall I add the genoa? *Guppy*'s speed is now dropping below 6.5 knots sometimes, and that's not good enough. It could be better. With the genoa up, she's going much faster, but not in danger of broaching. Great! Below deck, I write up my blog at the chart table and then send it through to Dad via the satellite phone. The wind seems to have dropped a bit, and *Guppy* is again going a little too slowly for my liking, so I decide to hoist the mainsail with a reef in it. The wind has dropped to about 25 knots on a broad reach. It should work, so I go on deck.

Guppy teeters on top of a wave and only just avoids surfing. It gives me a great view over … well, endless water. The mega-yacht has disappeared from the horizon. It's spectacular out here and *Guppy* is almost flying. The windpilot is doing a great job steering *Guppy* just as well as I could. I spend a while up on the foredeck until an enormous wave hits me and hauls me back to reality. My tummy is rumbling and I need to make something to eat. After having eaten my creation, I lie on the couch to digest the meal and read a good book. *Burp!* I may have eaten too well and too much. The sun sets again, making way for the night.

DAY 10: *11 December*

I've managed to sleep a lot better, despite the radar alarm going off from time to time to give warning of a big wave or a squall nearby. The wind is still around 25 knots. I eat a cracker with some jam in the ray of sunshine that finds its way inside the cabin. Yum! I've managed to find a brilliant spot to put my plate so that it doesn't fly off. I just set it down on my cardanic stove and that works. In future, I'll sit on the kitchen counter and eat off the stove.

After breakfast, I take the reef out of the mainsail. *Guppy* is now sailing with the mainsail, mizzen and half-furled genoa. It's ridiculously hot today. I stand on the foredeck for a while and enjoy the wind blowing through my hair and the fizzy bow wave. It's simply wonderful to think how everything has changed since my departure. I've been tested severely several times on this voyage. I've learnt so much and have changed my views about quite a lot of things in the world. Below deck, I continue to read *Dove* by Robin Lee Graham. It's a biography, and there's a lot that I can relate to. In 1965, the author is the first 16-year-old to sail around the world in his yacht *Dove*. On his voyage, he falls in love, marries and only gets back home five years later.

Halfway through, I decide to do something different and work on getting the hatches covered with insect gauze. I haven't had much trouble with insects so far, and certainly not at sea, but they almost ate me alive on Saint Martin the last time I was there and I want to get this done before I arrive.

After a meal of mashed potatoes and beans (the meat is finished, alas), I put on Metallica. I'm loving it and get totally hyped-up and happy. Before I realise it, I'm giggling. I tell myself that this is really silly, and then shut up when I realise I'm talking and listening to myself …

DAY 11: *12 December*

I wake up very early when I hear an enormous bang and rising wind. I look outside to see that the mainsheet is hanging in the water, having torn off the trackway. I see that the shackle holding the sheet block has broken off. Damn! Now the boom is chafing against the shrouds and has already caused some damage. I haul the boom in to avoid any further damage, find a new shackle in my box of spare parts, and the problem is soon solved.

It's daybreak and I stay in the cockpit to enjoy the sunrise. *Gup* is sailing fast, but it's comfortable. I now realise that what I experienced yesterday wasn't a long squall but a full-blown storm. A passing cargo ship informed me that the wind velocity had reached between 40 and 45 knots and that makes it a storm. The wind is now about 30 knots and *Guppy* is doing well with reefed mainsail, mizzen and storm jib. A little too much sail, but we're really going fast. It's wonderful to see *Guppy* sailing like this, and I love it. *Guppy* and I can weather everything and every storm. Yes, we can!

Timewise, I'm four hours behind the Netherlands. When I text Dad a 'good morning', the answer comes quickly: 'thank you, but it's already afternoon'. Hmm … This is going to take some getting used to.

I can't find flying fish on deck this morning. They probably were there but got washed off in the storm. I play some music and try to make some breakfast in the swinging cabin. It's cornflakes this time as the bread is finished.

There are only a few clouds, which means that it's probably going to be a hot day. The wind has dropped and it's a perfect day for a freshwater shower. It feels so good to wash all that salt off my body and out of my hair. I've had my fair share of saltwater over the past few days. If there's anything I would change, I'd have freshwater in the sea. It would make life on board a lot simpler. Everything else would stay the same, of course.

I look at my log: 4, 3, 2 knots … Damn, the wind speed is dropping fast, and so is *Guppy*'s progress. I've now experienced every kind of wind from nil through to 45 knots. Why can't I just have a nice, moderate wind for once? The sails are beginning to flap. I really can't stand to watch how *Guppy*'s lovely sails are damaged when they hit the rigging. Please God, Jesus, Santa Claus, Neptune, or whoever, give me some wind! My prayers go unheard and it remains calm. I sit in the cockpit for a while before deciding to try the light code zero. An unexpected squall hits *Guppy* before I see it coming, and it makes the tear in the sail even bigger. After the squall, the wind disappears altogether. I drop all the sails and switch on the Yanmar. I choose not to use the spinnaker because of the threat of another squall. Oh well, I'll just have to accept it. Instead I go inside, warm up some ravioli and play my guitar; I haven't done that for a while. In the evening I'm at the chart table pouring over my geography book and reading all about trade winds. According to this book it's a 'constant wind from one direction' which was used by seafarers in days gone by to 'sail the oceans'. Well, they are certainly NOT constant now that I'm sailing here. Trade winds, where are you?

Grr … Rain, heavy swell and no wind … This is crap! I finally manage to sleep at about 02.00 when the wind eventually decides to behave itself. *Guppy* can now clock up some miles again.

DAY 12: *13 December*

She's still going well by morning and I decide to put some bread in the oven to celebrate. I spread butter and chocolate paste over it … Delicious!

I think I'm about to lose it; the wind is dropping slowly again and the sails have started flapping. It hurts with every slap, and I cringe. I look at the mainsail and see a small tear just above the foot of the sail where it has worn. Oh, *no*!

'Just look at what you've done to *Guppy*'s sails!' I shout across the sea. 'You've already ruined my code zero. Do you now want to destroy the mainsail too?'

When I've finished ranting, a light breeze springs up and I wonder how long it will last.

I didn't sleep much last night and go to lie down on the couch. I look at all the photographs pinned up on the partition: the Optimist, the Mirror, the Contender, the first *Guppy,* a Hurley 700; all yachts I used to sail the rivers in the Netherlands, the Ijsselmeer, the Wadden Islands and the North Sea, together with Spot. My life flashes by as I look at these photographs and I see myself as an eight-year-old on the Mirror. It's amazing how little I knew about sailing then. I wonder where the Mirror is now. I miss her. She gave me my first taste of freedom. The Mirror allowed me to escape when I wanted to. How little I was then! And the Hurley 700, my first *Guppy.* The photograph was taken during a competition in Culemborg when I was ahead of Dad and his friend, Mark. It was one of the last races I took part in. I wanted to broaden my horizon. At that moment, between the two river banks, I wanted to move towards greater freedom; to explore beyond the horizon ... And now I have found the answer: even more horizon. I take another look and remember that with each photograph I wanted more — more water, more freedom. What's that expression again? Oh yes: the grass is always greener on the other side. Now I have what I wanted then. So why aren't I satisfied? Because there's no wind, the sails are flapping and I'm getting nowhere at a speed of 2 knots? Because I'm having a little setback? All at once, I'm really content with what I have: freedom, peace, space and *Guppy.*

After having studied some geography, it starts to grow dark again. Know what I really feel like tonight? Pancakes, pizza and a movie. Well, the pancakes and pizza are wishful thinking, but I do have a movie. Once I've settled myself on the couch, I switch on my laptop and select

Trainspotting from the list of movies I have brought with me. When it's ended, I take a look at the radar screen. It's empty and *Guppy* is so quiet that it takes me a while to register that I'm actually floating somewhere in the middle of the Atlantic Ocean. Cool! It's calm enough to make pancakes and then sit in the cockpit to enjoy the stars and the moon that is casting a soft glow over the sea.

DAY 13: *14 December*

Wind! There's wind again! *Guppy* is sailing at about 6 knots and the swell isn't bad. It's cloudy and I'm feeling a little sluggish. I plan to learn the last three paragraphs of my geography lesson and then do a test. I start with German, but don't get further than two pages and don't feel like switching on the laptop to do the test.

Somehow the day flies past and I've done almost nothing. The wind is constant and *Guppy* is sailing without any help from me. Lying in the cockpit, my thoughts wander off and I think of what still lies ahead of me. I'm looking forward to it all. First Saint Martin, and then a few nice islands; then on to Bonaire in the Caribbean by February. Gran, Granddad, Dad and Kim plan to meet me there. It's all going so quickly, and I can't believe I left the Netherlands five and a half months ago. It all seems so normal. I can hardly remember what it was like to cycle to school through the snow and cold and be shouted at by a stressed-out teacher. Obliged to go to school and to sit there learning nothing … No, I really don't miss it.

Today's activities:

07.00: got up
08.00: flying fish control (threw back three)
09.00: bread rolls in the oven; enjoy breakfast
10.00: navigation, find out where I am on this planet
11.00: an hour of school, German this time
12.00: more schoolwork, geography and biology
13.00: eat something
14.00: read

90

15.00: enjoy looking out over the waves
16.00: write my blog and send it off
17.00: play guitar
18.00: eat spaghetti
19.00: read
20.00: listen to music
21.00: gaze at the stars
22.00: lie in bed and update my diary
23.00: try to sleep

The rest of the night I get up every two hours to have a look. The radar keeps watch. That's just about how it went today. The only thing that really changes is the weather, the meals and the number of flying fish and other sea creatures that I spot. Usually, I'm much busier changing sails and adjusting the course.

I wake up late at night. Damn, *Guppy* is sailing too high at 320 degrees. That's on course for New York! And she has been sailing too far north all night. This is crazy! I switch on the deck lights and go to work on the sails. The boomed-out genoa has to be set on the opposite side to take Guppy on a more southerly course. Now that I'm wide awake, I stay on deck in the cabin entrance to study the course as it gets lighter. I now see that there's a large worn patch on the genoa sheet. I'd seen a worn spot there earlier, but how has it managed to grow to this size so quickly? I soon see that it's the spinnaker pole that's probably done the damage. If I've learnt one lesson on this voyage, it's how quickly things can wear out. The code zero only flapped against the diamond rigging a few times and the result was a torn sail. The mainsheet broke loose and the mainsail chafed against the rigging; the result: a worn patch on the boom and a hole in the sail. And there are some other worn patches on the sail. There's no doubt in my mind now, and I decide to do something to prevent further wear and tear. The only solution I have is to apply some Rescue Tape. Armed with tape, I walk to the foredeck and wrap it around the sheet. The job is done in 15 minutes. Now let's hope it works, because *Guppy* and I still have some way to go.

DAY 14: *15 December*

The ocean crossing is actually going very rapidly. I can't believe I'll be walking on land in less than a week. Come to think of it, it's a pity there are only five days left. This is really a fast crossing, even though *Guppy* is now sailing close to the wind at about 4.5 knots and the weather forecast predicts that the wind is going to drop. Pity! But at least there's still some wind and I'll have to accept what comes. If it's gone, it's gone. Tomorrow the wind should pick up again, so we'll just have to bob about a bit until then. A cargo ship passes me. It can't have had its radar on because the Echomax doesn't respond. I'm eating some spaghetti and watching the ship. We're not on a collision course, so I carry on enjoying my meal.

DAY 15: *16 December*

I didn't feel that great yesterday and today my nausea and dizziness aren't any better. Time for a paracetamol. It doesn't help much, and I stay on the couch and grab a book. It's a dictionary of sailing terms, written by real sailors. On the cover: *Sailing (sailed, have sailed and had sailed)*. 'The fine art of getting wet and becoming ill while slowly going nowhere at great expense' is one of the definitions. It's very funny to read, especially as there's a lot of truth in it. The definition of 'galley': 'nowadays called the "kitchen block". Consists of a finger bowl in which to do your dishes, two tea-lights to prepare your meals with and two thousand nooks and crannies, compartments and shelves to pack your stuff into only to have it shoot out as soon as the boat is a little lop-sided.' Brilliant! I finish the book in one go and feel a little better. On deck, I eat a can of pineapple pieces. There are a lot of dark rain clouds around me, but none above me.

I have only just gone inside when I feel *Guppy* heel. Wind?! Yes, the sails are filling out and here comes the wind! I unfurl the genoa immediately, but the sheet jams behind the kicker. In my enthusiasm I run to the bow, but am suddenly pulled back into the cockpit with force. My lifeline got stuck somewhere and, because I ran so fast, I was catapulted back. Hmm, it makes me think of a similar incident many years ago. I was 10 years old. After a 24-hour race at Medemblik, on the Ijsselmeer in the Netherlands, I ran off the boat without realising that I was still fastened to the lifeline. It jerked me back with such force that I landed in the water between the boat and the shore. Everyone laughed, and I suppose it must have looked funny. Today, having recovered, I walk back to the foredeck, loosen the jammed sheet and unfurl the genoa. Yes, *Guppy* is sailing again.

DAY 16: *17 December*

I wake up in the middle of the night to the sound of a sail flapping. After a while it stops, but I go on deck to take a look. It's really dark. Damn, *Guppy* is once again sailing too high! I look at the windvane. It doesn't look right and isn't working. I take off the chain that connects it to the rudder and switch on the electric autopilot. It will be light in an hour's time and I will then take a look at the problem. Actually, it can only mean one thing, and that's that the rudder gudgeon blade that guides the windvane's steering mechanism is gone, either broken or bitten off. I have a vision of a rudder blade with a huge bite in it … Lifelike fantasies of sea monsters surface and I stride away declaring war against them.

At first light, I take a look at the rudder. The whole of the rudder gudgeon blade has broken off close to the stern post pintle. It's torn off. No tooth marks, alas … It's only 260 miles to Saint Martin and I probably have enough power to get there on the autopilot, but I don't want to depend on the autopilot and luckily I do have a spare rudder gudgeon blade in stock. There's work to be done. Standing on the swimming platform, which is jumping up and down and is regularly underwater, I know that this is going to be quite a job. I tie the tools I need to a bit of twine and then unscrew the large hexagon socket screw that still holds the top bit of the rudder. Suddenly I see a couple of fins protruding from the water. Hey, dolphins! They keep me company while I do the repairs. An hour and a lot of swearing later, *Gup* has a new rudder gudgeon blade and we're able to continue sailing using the windvane.

I've hardly finished my breakfast when a huge, black rain cloud comes over. I hope it's not accompanied by a lot of wind … It turns out to contain more water than wind, and I use the opportunity to wash my hair and scrub out the cockpit. It's followed by a lot more rain and I just let it flow over *Guppy* while I shelter below deck.

When the sun eventually comes through, I see a yacht behind me. It's clearly bigger than *Guppy* and is holding a course that's going to take it very close to *Guppy*. Why does it have to get so near in this rough sea when the ocean is so huge? I change my course and they pass me at a distance of about 100 metres. They call me on the VHF and I answer their questions:

> **Them:** Where are you going?
> **Me:** Saint Martin. And you?
> They mention a destination that I've never heard of before.
> **Them:** Are you alone?
> **Me:** Yes.
> **Them:** How old are you?
> **Me:** Fifteen.
> **Them:** Wow, damn! You're probably the youngest person to have crossed the Atlantic solo!
> **Me:** Uh, yes, I think so.
> **Them:** Cool — you go, girl!.
> **Me:** Thanks!

We continue to talk for a while, and then I decide to warm up some frankfurters as I'm famished. The next shower is coming towards *Guppy* and it's getting darker. I still have 195 miles to go before we reach Saint Martin. *Guppy* is now sailing a constant 7.5 to 8 knots. Will we be able to make it before dark tomorrow? One hundred and ninety-five miles in 24 hours is really absurd, but theoretically possible at this speed. Otherwise … Well, I'll just arrive in the dark. One thing is sure, and that's the fact that this is the last night I'll have the space and be far enough from land to be able to sleep a bit without having to be watchful. At least, I hope so. *Guppy* is giving quite a performance and is almost flying. We're sailing with mizzen, mainsail and genoa in a beautiful 25-knot beam wind. It's amazing to watch. On the low side of the cabin, I'd probably be able to see fish swimming past the portholes … Heeled over like this, the side of the cabin is now the floor, but it's so cool!

DAY 17: *18 December*

Only 70 miles to go. Oh damn, I'm beginning to get hyper! There's an island just 17 miles from here. I think I'm going to make it before dark; otherwise, it isn't really a problem as there's a full moon. It's strange being this close to shore and knowing that I'll be walking on dry land tomorrow. It's a strange thought to think that I'm the youngest person ever to have made this crossing solo and without any assistance. But the weirdest thought is that I'll be seeing Saint Martin again today.

It's lovely weather today; still blowing some 20 knots and *Guppy* is sailing at 7.5 knots. It's noon and I've 55 miles to go. The wind is dropping a little and comes from astern. I boom the genoa out again.

Oh no, it looks as if the whole of Saint Martin is waiting for me to arrive. Dad let me know via a text message, and tells me a helicopter will be filming my arrival. A little later, I hear engine sounds in the air. I shoot below deck to throw off the rags I've worn on the crossing and put on a decent pair of shorts and a T-shirt. The helicopter circles over *Guppy* for a while and then takes off in a westerly direction.

It's 17.00 and 17 miles to go. I'm arriving on time, but, alas, not in daylight. *Guppy* passes a number of small rocky islands and a slightly larger one. Saint Martin now lies 12 miles ahead of me. It's crazy to think that I fled to this island by plane exactly a year and a day ago. When I was forced back to the Netherlands under police escort three days later, I never dared to dream that I would ever sail here. And now it's actually happening … How super-cool!

It's slowly getting darker, just 10 miles to go. Wow, all those island lights — awesome! I suddenly hear the VHF crackling: '*Guppy*, *Guppy*, *Guppy*, this is …'

They are asking for my position. I first think it's the cameraman I heard from for the first time a few days ago. He wants to make a documentary about me. There's a boat approaching filled with Dutch people who live on the island and want to congratulate me. A little later it's the cameraman in a speedboat. The bay comes into sight. I start the Volvo engine and lower the sails. Petra Gilders, manager of the Saint Martin Yacht Club, has organised a mooring for me. When I eventually get to this location after 17 days of ocean crossing, the first thing I do is phone Dad to let him know that I've arrived and that he can now sleep peacefully. It's past midnight in the Netherlands. I close *Guppy* up and step onto land to go to the Saint Martin Yacht Club — the exact spot where I was taken away by the police last year.

Saint Martin

I recognise the island immediately. They guess I'm hungry, and they're right. I'm served chicken satay with French fries. Fries — now that's something I haven't eaten in a long time!

Everyone is congratulating me on my first solo ocean crossing. It feels strange to be surrounded by so many people, and what's also weird is that the land seems to be moving. I still need to swap my sea legs for my land legs, as I continue to feel everything moving up and down and need to sit down quickly. When I've finished eating, I accompany Petra and her husband to a Christmas party; it's the same Christmas party I attended the previous year.

I recognise everything: the road, the bridge, the airport … Wait a minute, the landing strip is longer and so is the road around it. Last year I could walk there, and now it's much too far to walk. We pass the harbour where the *Duende* lay, the Dufour Arpège that I wanted to buy on my last visit. Then we enter a residential area that I still remember, and it seems as if I was here only yesterday. This is really strange. At the Christmas party, I meet three people I know from the previous year. They are very happy to see me again, but it's really late and most have had a good bit to drink. It's weird to be here, and in a way it feels as though I was never gone. When I've caught up with everyone, I go back to *Guppy*. What a pleasure to be able to sleep the whole night through!

I wake up to a soft tapping sound. It's raining and it takes me a while to realise where I am. Why is it so calm on *Guppy*? Are we becalmed again? Huh? Do I hear an airplane? Slowly I realise that I'm not sailing anymore but lying at anchor. I get up and walk outside. It was dark when I arrived, and the first few seconds are a total surprise. I notice yachts anchored all around me. I see green mountains, a white beach and palm trees. I give myself a few minutes to absorb it all, have something to eat, wash up and tidy up. At 10.30 Petra and cameraman Peter Wingender are picking me up in a dinghy. Peter wants to film me the whole day. We first go to Immigration and Customs, and, as always, this takes a lot of time.

The bridge will open at 17.30 to let *Guppy* through, so Henk, Marja, Dominique and Ton, the Dutch people who had come to welcome me in their speedboat the previous night, take me to an idyllic beach. We first cruise around the whole bay and then out under the French bridge. At the beach we tie the boat to a mooring and swim to the shore. Here we have a meal and a chat before we swim back to the boat and motor back. An airplane comes in low over our heads and lands just as we pass the airport. They drop me off at *Guppy*, and I have three quarters of an hour to wait for the bridge to open and let me through. I've only just got on board when I'm called and told to cast off and follow them. What, already? I follow the speedboat that's now carrying all the children from the yacht club. Before I know it, there's a police boat behind me and a whole armada of boats following me. What's this all about? … The children in the speedboat are now unfolding a big banner with *Welcome to Saint Martin, Laura.* The bridge is already open and the fleet of boats and dinghies cruises along with me. At the bridge, people are waving, and at the yacht club there's an even bigger crowd. They're all welcoming me and taking lots of photos. Then there's an explosion of noise as all the mega-yachts blow their horns. Is it really all for me? I'm stunned. What a welcome! I tie *Guppy* up to the jetty in front of the yacht club. The jetty is full of people. Wow, everyone is being so kind!

It's very busy at the yacht club and I join a table of girls. One of them is 12-year-old Bodine, the daughter of Henk and Marja. While we are eating a hamburger, people stop to congratulate and welcome me every five seconds. It still hasn't really sunk in. Was it really me who sailed across the Atlantic Ocean on her own?

Then there's a woman who steps up to me and says: 'I'm from the boat across there, and the owner would like to invite you to come and have a drink.'

'OK, but, um, there are only mega-yachts on that side …'

I finish my hamburger, and half an hour later she's back again.

'Why not bring someone along with you?' she asks.

I look at Bodine, who asks her mum if it's OK. She in turn asks Bas Stamm, a boy of 16 who is also wandering around the yacht club, if he'd like to come along.

We are fetched by a tender that is bigger than *Guppy*, and the crew bring us to the yacht which is really enormous. I've never been on such a big yacht. It has a 2-metre flat screen that just drops out of the ceiling, and everything is so unbelievably luxurious.

After a few hours, I'm back on *Guppy* and I'm trying to digest all the impressions of the past day. I'm happy, but, strangely enough, not entirely. I haven't heard from my mum in weeks and even now she hasn't called or made any contact.

I immediately make friends with Bas. He was born on Saint Martin and has lived here all his life. Together with Bas, I take *Guppy* to Simpson Bay Marina the following day and then visit Philipsburg. We go for a swim, eat an ice cream and then take the bus back to Simpson Bay when we get bored. Catching a bus here is very different to catching one in the Netherlands. There are no bus stops. You just stand at the roadside and wave down the first minibus you see with the destination you want displayed on the windscreen.

Bas and I are together a lot. We sail, watch movies and have a lot of fun. When I'm not with Bas, I'm on the internet, trying to reach my mum, answering tons of emails, doing my schoolwork, updating my website and trying not to say 'no' too often to people who want something from me. One evening I stay awake until half past one in the morning for an interview with the VARA, the Dutch national public broadcaster. It's late because of the time difference with the Netherlands. By two o'clock, they still haven't phoned. Idiots! They call me the next day to say they had logged the interview incorrectly in their programme schedule. They ask if they can do the interview at the same time this evening. No, I tell them, I don't think so. Tonight I have 'sleep' logged in my schedule at that time. I'm afraid my opinion of the media isn't improving. Sometimes it's all a bit too much. Too many friendly people who unintentionally demand attention and can't stop talking. Preparing *Guppy*, my schoolwork, the media, parents and friends all demand my attention. Do I always have to be cheerful and put on a smile? Both at sea and on land, I have these 'it's all a little too much' moments. At sea I sometimes curse the waves and the wind and swear at every drop that finds its way into the cabin. It's a great tension-reliever, but when I'm on land and I refuse a journalist an interview because I've had enough, it usually results in bad publicity which only makes me feel worse.

The attitude of the cameraman who's doing a documentary on me doesn't improve matters either. I see him peering at me through his lens almost every morning when I wake up and look through my porthole. Why is he always there so early, and why does he need to see me get out of bed every day? For the umpteenth time I tell him that it's not appreciated, but he just doesn't listen. And so it continues for the whole week. I've also discovered that he can't film that well. His images are very shaky and he never uses a tripod. I just can't get through to him, and don't think this is going to work ... But, fortunately, there are also many friendly people and happy moments.

The replica of the eighteenth-century merchant vessel the *Stad Amsterdam* is lying at anchor offshore. What a beauty! I'm fetched by one of the crew and given a tour of the ship. They are busy taking supplies on board, and I give them a hand. It's a lot more than I ever need on *Guppy*. With 70 crew members, it's 70 times as much!

At 11.00 they take me back to *Guppy*. I'm going to pack my bags, because Henk and Marja, Bodine's parents, are coming to pick me up. We drive to Oyster Pond where Bodine and I are being picked up by Dominique and Bobo, the ship's dog, and then taken to *True Blue*, a 57-foot ketch. I'm going to spend my Christmas holiday on this boat with Ton, Dominique and their two dogs. Henk and Marja will come along in their speedboat, *Oyster*, and Bas and his father, Mike, in their 9-metre yacht, *'t Swaentje*.

We sail to Grand Case, on the French side of the island, in the three boats. Unfortunately there isn't much wind. Halfway, *Oyster* comes alongside and Henk tells us he's going to fill up with fuel. Bodine and I jump on board for the trip. After refuelling, we cruise to Grand Case where *True Blue* is already anchored in full Christmas regalia. The entire boat is covered in streamers, lights and Christmas hats. Once we are on board, I try to get onto the internet. There's a sort of super WiFi antenna on board *True Blue* that gives you access, even when you're lying at anchor. In this way I manage to wish Dad a Merry Christmas and update my blog. We spend the night off Grand Case, and sail on to Tintamarre, an island belonging to Saint Martin, the next morning. Here we have breakfast and unwrap our Christmas gifts. Father Christmas has brought me a pretty necklace and a T-shirt.

Later that morning, *True Blue* sails to St Barth, while Bodine and I kneeboard behind *Oyster*. It's a great Christmas, with warm weather, lots of kneeboarding, swimming and good company. At the same time, it's weird to be so far away from the Netherlands at Christmas where my family has watched my 12-year-old sister's televised performance in the *Magic Circus Show* in Geneva. Hopefully someone has recorded it for me to view later.

The next day, most people want to go to town to do some shopping. Bas, Bodine and I don't feel like joining them and choose to go kneeboarding behind the dinghy. This doesn't really work as the motor isn't strong enough to pull us, but snorkelling is also an option. I see a number of boys jumping off a 10-metre high cliff and want to try this myself. Five minutes later I'm standing on top of the cliff; Bodine and Bas are quick to follow. Jumping is much easier than climbing to the top, and after a few jumps, we're done with it.

During dinner, Mike says he needs to get back home. He asks me if Bas and I will sail 't Swaentje back for him. The next day we get her ready, leave the mooring and sail back to Saint Martin. On the way, Henk comes alongside to give us a cold beer. Nice!

As we approach Saint Martin, the situation gets interesting. Bas doesn't have a clue where to find the harbour where 't Swaentje is moored and we don't have a chart. We phone Mike, who tells us to go in the direction of Philipsburg. We need to sail past all the cruise ships, and of course the wind drops and we can't get the old outboard motor started.

Mike is waiting for us when we moor. He tells me I need to go to the yacht club because there's a surprise in store for me there. It's a big

Christmas gift. When I unwrap it, I see that I'm the owner of a brand-new laptop. The gift is from Tony, the yacht broker I met the previous year. Wow, what an amazing Christmas gift — I'm speechless!

New Year!

I think I need to start with some schoolwork today. When I've finished, I call Bas. He has to go to *'t Swaentje* to replace a line, and as I've had enough of my homework I decide to take the bus to Philipsburg to help him. There's a strong wind and we need to paddle to the yacht mooring on a raft. It takes a while paddling against the wind and waves to get there, but we manage to replace the worn mooring line and then have time to wander through Philipsburg. It's very touristy with all the people from the cruise ships, but once you're off the main roads you immediately enter the poorer suburbs.

I wonder what the year 2011 will bring. The last day of the old year doesn't get off to a good start, however. I haven't been feeling well all day and it's only getting worse. Leaning against a palm tree and sitting on the warm, white sand, I feel really dizzy. After having almost emptied the contents of my stomach over Bas, I begin to recover a little. That's as far as I'm concerned; poor Bas is not impressed. He's had to jump out of the way and is now asking me if I'm alright and to ensure there's no repeat performance. I'm feeling as right as rain by that evening; it must have been something I ate.

At midnight we watch the fireworks from the boulevard and wish each other a happy New Year. No fireworks are allowed on the Dutch half of the island, so I've brought along one of *Guppy*'s flares. After the fireworks display from the French side of the island, which takes about 20 minutes, we find a quiet spot to light the flare. Not strictly legal, of course, but what good are New Year's Eve celebrations without fireworks? It's the first time that I've lit a real emergency flare as it's forbidden in the Netherlands, even as an exercise. The flare hangs in the sky for a long time, and when it has landed in the ocean we walk back to *Guppy* where it's really quiet. Everyone has gone to bed and we decide to go to sleep.

Stad Amsterdam

My computer still can't receive any WiFi signal and I decide to take my new laptop to the shop where it was bought. They try everything to fix it, but without success and decide it needs to be sent off for repairs. When I leave the shop without my laptop, I receive a call from Arthur from the *Stad Amsterdam*. Would I like to join them for the next 10 days? What a question — of course! There are three conditions, though: that I bring my passport, that I have a note from my dad giving his permission, and that I bring along my schoolwork. I've been on board twice, and yesterday, when I heard that one of the crew was injured and had to be flown home, I grabbed my chance and asked if I could go along for the trip as a replacement.

I immediately phone Dad and ask him to write the note with his consent and fax it through. I then get *Guppy* ready for 10 days of silence and loneliness. The dinghy is stowed on the foredeck, the hammock is put away and, most importantly, the dishes are done and refuse removed. I arrange with Arthur to meet him at the bridge at three o'clock, but I pack my bag and am ready at two o'clock. I decide to be on my way, and call in on Petra at the yacht club to ask her to keep an eye on *Guppy*.

At three o'clock sharp, I'm fetched as arranged, along with two other crew members. I'm allocated a cabin and we sort out crew gear. I'm on 'red watch'; that's from midnight to four in the morning and again in the afternoon.

After dinner, there's a crew introduction (in which I need to take part — very weird). The one moment I'm travelling around the world on my own, and the next I'm introducing myself to the passengers along with 30 crew members on the 76-metre *Stad Amsterdam*. What an awesome experience.

As my first watch is at midnight, my roommate, Fleur, and I go to sleep at 20.00. I don't even notice when they raise the anchor an hour later and the sails are set. When I clamber on deck at midnight, it's pitch dark. It's the first time that I've sailed on a square-rigged ship.

A number of sails have been hoisted and I feel as though I'm in a dream. Slowly the heavy ship cleaves its way through the waves as the sails fill up. During the night, we adjust and trim the sails a bit and add an extra one. Otherwise, it's quite quiet. I get an explanation about the lines, sheets and rigging. There really are loads of lines to learn about. Some 800 of them; that's quite a bit more than I have on *Guppy*! At 04.00 I go back to my bunk, and when I wake up the next day we're already at Saint Kitts. It's really peaceful here, and I'm so comfortable in my narrow bunk with air conditioning. Everyone has a cold due to the air conditioning. It's so good to sleep in the gentle swell when you don't have to worry about navigating, ships, rocks and other dangers.

Once the guests have explored the island, the anchor is raised and by late that afternoon Dominica has come into sight. Fleur and I are furling the sails in the tops of the masts and tying them up. There's a name for it, but I've managed to forget it. Oh yes, it's 'stowing', I think.

Everything on board has a name that I've never heard of, but I'm learning fast: it's *afzoeten* instead of *ontzouten*, stowing, unfurling and many other sailing terms. I'm no longer getting lost, either, which was the case on the first day. While we are sailing, Arthur suddenly appears with an old on-board camera. The documentary cameraman had told me off for not taking a film camera with me, and now Arthur wants to make up for it. Argh — more cameras to contend with. I love making films and photographs so long as I don't feature in them. I just want to enjoy everything around me and not have to concentrate on the cameras. On *Gup* I know everything, but here everything is new for me and I want to enjoy the experience as much as possible — without a camera in front of my nose. Arthur only occasionally wields the camera and I can live with that.

It's 08.00 and I'm woken up by one of the crew. I gobble down my breakfast because I want to see Dominica by daylight. The island looks very tropical; it's tall and very green. Last night's rain is evaporating and drips off the palm leaves. As soon as the guests are taken to the island at 09.00, we sail towards the northern side of the island where we will pick them up this evening.

It's already 9 January and, after completing my schoolwork, I write an email to my family who are now celebrating Dad's birthday. There's a good wind, but, as is often the case, it's a headwind. It's only an hour's sail and the captain wants us to sail for that hour. I'm not the captain, but as soon as the sails are hoisted we can begin the task of taking them down again …

In the past few days we have sailed via Saint Kitts, Dominica, Îles de Saintes and Guadeloupe to arrive at Montserrat. We have a day off today. No 'red watch' for a change, and nothing to stop us from exploring the island. Fleur and I can't make up our minds whether to do some form of water sport or to see the island. After looking at the water sport facilities — a leaky boat, a fender/cushion and a homemade contraption of some 2 metres that's supposed to resemble a catamaran — we decide to tour the island.

This is the only spot on the island where they have any boats, the taxi driver tells us, and we go along with him to see a bit of the island. Either the driver is really dull or it's just a boring island, because he doesn't have anything interesting to tell us about it. Just 'This is a park and this is a house', and so forth.

After showing us a stream that's 15 centimetres wide and declaring that the water is 'holy', we leave him behind and carry on walking. Far better this way. After 10 minutes we're lost, but it's very pretty. When we reach another road after a long walk, we come across our taxi driver again. We wonder if this is pure coincidence.

We buy something to eat and drink at the local supermarket and, after much pleading from us, our taxi driver takes us to the 'No Entry' area. The island's capital was entirely destroyed during a volcanic eruption about 15 years ago, and because the volcano is still active it's forbidden territory. But not for us!

It's really impressive: a town totally deserted and buried under a metre-thick blanket of lava ash. In the abandoned homes there are photographs on the walls, Christmas decorations and calendars dating back to 1996. It wouldn't be difficult to imagine a few zombies walking around here. A true ghost town! We make our way back before it gets dark.

We are woken up early the next morning, enjoy an excellent breakfast, unfurl the sails, weigh anchor and sail in the direction of Tintamarre, the island that lies in front of Saint Martin. My trip on the *Stad Amsterdam* is coming to an end. When we're lying at anchor again, the guests visit the island while we swim. As soon as the guests are back, everyone has to be in their crew gear. There's a barbecue tonight and everything has to be set up for it. It's my last evening on board and I'm going to miss this. Of course I want to see *Guppy*, but this trip has been terrific. Hard work, but fun; and it makes a pleasant change to have so many people around me.

Early in the morning, we weigh anchor and sail past Philipsburg, where there are seven cruise ships, and back to Simpson Bay. I say farewell to everyone and get on the first tender back to *Guppy*. I then walk to the yacht club to meet Jillian Schlesinger, an American girl who is making a documentary about my voyage. I met her in the Netherlands last year and we get on well.

Mum and I have patched things up and I've received a long letter from her. The poor communication between us led to one big misunderstanding. She sent me a number of messages and I sent many, too, but somehow she hasn't received them because she's not all that good with computers. Anyway, to keep a long story short ... she still loves me and misses me and I love and miss her, too.

There's a new yacht lying next to mine, and the children on board are about my age. I don't recognise the flag, though, and look it up in the atlas. It appears to be Brazilian. I start talking to them, but soon notice that their English isn't that good. They're learning to play the guitar and we take turns to play a song and try to converse a little on board their yacht. It's difficult. They rattle on about all sorts of things, but I don't understand a word of it. I nod and say 'yes' and 'no' a few times, to look like I understand a bit, but they just carry on talking. It doesn't really matter because I like their company and they seem to like mine. I'm even able to teach them a thing or two on the guitar, which immediately makes me feel better about my own playing skills.

Early the next morning, I walk to the yacht club. I'm leaving tomorrow and have decided to buy an SSB radio here. Most sailors have them on board and are able to hold lengthy conversations with other sailors on long voyages and establish friendly radio networks in this way. After having phoned around and done some thinking, I finally select one. It's delivered the same afternoon; a brand-new SSB, antenna tuner and email modem that turns out to be much bigger than I expected. I don't have much time to set everything up, as Bas and Jillian are waiting on the jetty. I'm leaving today and they want to spend as much time as possible with me. I'm filling the oil on the Yanmar and am fumbling with it a bit. It resembles a circus act, and has me hanging over the main engine with my head turned slightly to the left and pressed hard against the scuttle of the engine space. That way, I can just about see the opening with one eye. Then, if I can get my hand in the right position, I can fill it with one hand. I have made a funnel from a plastic Coke bottle, because a standard funnel can't reach it. I only just manage to get it right, but not without some spillage this time …

Once the engine oil has been topped up, I can replace the steps in front of the engine space and get on with the next chore: fill up with diesel. The nozzle of the hose is too big for *Guppy*, so some diesel also lands in the cockpit. Once I've cleaned this mess up, too, I cast off and leave the jetty to go to the bridge where some busybody wants to tell me how I must manoeuvre to get my boat dead slow in the right position. I don't want to stop, I want to leave! Once outside, I tie *Guppy* up on a mooring and somebody offers to clean the underside of Guppy's hull. I accept. While Bas is making French toast inside, I'm sitting in the cockpit and looking at Saint Martin. It was so different here this year. Last year I could only dream of this, although it hasn't all been fun and I've had quite a lot of demands made on me and my time by nagging people, including the media. I'm really happy I can sail off again.

When we've finished the French toast and Guppy's hull is clean, I leave Simpson Bay. With Bas and Jillian standing there waving, I sail off in the direction of Îles des Saintes.

Saint Martin–Îles des Saintes: 154 nautical miles

DAY 1: *20 January*

Towards evening we pass Saba. A Coast Guard plane flies over a couple of times. With Saint Kitts just visible on the horizon, I enjoy a beautiful sunset. I'm so glad to be back at sea and the peace is just wonderful. No people, no demands; just the waves, wind, *Guppy* and me. Awesome! When we arrive at Îles des Saintes, I'm going to spend a couple of days just sitting around on *Guppy* doing absolutely nothing.

DAY 2: *21 January*

After a long night of struggling with periods of calm to leeward of the islands, I'm below deck enjoying some breakfast when *Guppy* suddenly grinds to a halt with a jerk. I'm thrown forward, then jump up and run outside. Almost immediately I see the cause of our sudden stop. There are about 50 metres of buoys, fishing nets and other rubbish floating behind *Guppy*. I climb onto the afterdeck, and from the swimming platform see that the flotsam has wound itself around the rudder. Fortunately nothing has twisted around the propeller, but there's a bright yellow buoy stuck to the rudder. I try to loosen one of the ropes with the boat hook, but the boat hook breaks and I have to let it drop if I don't want to land in the water myself. Argh! I then tie a broom and paddle together to try to clear the tangled mess. *Guppy* is now sailing at 1 knot, and that means I'll get to Îles des Saintes in the dark. It's very hard steering *Guppy* like this, and she's drifting further and further from Guadeloupe. I switch on the engine while in forward, in the hope of gaining some speed. It helps, but not a lot. I eventually have an idea. In the aft cabin, I find a long piece of rope that I can throw over a buoy that's being towed by *Guppy*. After many failed attempts and much swearing, I finally succeed and manage to draw the buoy alongside. I cut most of it free; just a small buoy and a piece of rope remain, but they don't really hold *Guppy* back much. I keep the engine running, and at around 16.00 we arrive at Îles de Saintes. I let the anchor out slowly, taking care not to drift astern. As soon as this is done, I dive into the sea with a knife.

Îles des Saintes

The neighbours give me a strange look when I surface a little later with a big piece of unravelled green rope and a number of buoys that I've managed to get myself tangled in. Once I've thrown the lot into the cockpit, I put the engine into reverse to see if the anchor is holding. All is well.

Only then do I have time to look around. Next to me is a Dutch catamaran, and a woman is swimming across to me from the yacht. They've heard from Ton and Dominique that I was on my way here, and she wanted to know if I'd like to come over for a meal in half an hour's time. I don't really feel like cooking myself and new contacts are always welcome, so I accept. A little later, I'm on board *Koolau*, but I don't stay long as I'm dead tired and worried about falling asleep on their boat.

Îles des Saintes looks lovely. It's a little island made up of a group of islands and has one touristy village. The anchorage is pretty full. After my busy time on Saint Martin, I take it easy on Îles des Saintes. I enjoy another two meals on *Koolau*, where we also enjoy a fun Rummikub evening. I go for a long hike on the island, read a lot during the day and watch movies in the evening. I don't meet many people and don't go ashore much. All I need is some rest; no people and no pressure for a while. After four days, I'm feeling a lot better and decide to continue on my way.

Îles des Saintes–Dominica: 20 nautical miles

DAY 1: *26 January*

The weather has improved today. I write a quick blog for my website and set course for Dominica, but as soon as I round the heads of Îles des Saintes I regret my decision. The waves are rolling over the deck and *Guppy* is jumping around like a kangaroo. This is no fun as there are lots of fishing buoys out here that I really don't want to get into. This is why the sprayhood is down and I'm drenched by the first wave that pounds over the deck. I'm normally able to switch on the autopilot from the cockpit, but it doesn't respond. I've experienced this before, but this is really a bad moment for it to happen again. Soaking wet, I run into the cabin and switch the steering from there to 'auto'. By the time I get back on deck, the waves have swung *Guppy* from the right course. Argh! I really hope the sea is less rough when we get to deeper waters, but that's not the case. The wind increases and one shower follows the next. With just the genoa up, *Guppy* has heeled over so much that water pours into the cockpit at regular intervals.

I hadn't anticipated such a rough crossing, so I hadn't secured the dinghy to the foredeck all that well, and now it's almost washing overboard. I crawl forward, but keep on getting water in my face, which means I can't see a thing. Hmm … I spot my diving goggles in the cockpit and decide to put them on so that I can see what I'm doing. This works a treat!

There is so much rain that I only see the tall green mountains of Dominica when I'm half a mile from the island. I really hope that it's a little drier and calmer when I try to anchor *Guppy*. Sure enough, the weather gods smile on me and it's fairly calm behind the island, and it gets dry, too. The first time I drop anchor, some local thinks that I'm too close to his mooring, so I have to take the anchor in again and try a little further down. I let out the anchor chain too quickly and the chain lands on top of the anchor, which means that the anchor doesn't hold. I heave up the anchor and try yet again. Third time lucky. Just then the next cloudburst hits *Guppy* …

Dominica

There are two other Dutch yachts next to me. When it has stopped raining, I see someone on board and paddle towards them. They're just about to go for a walk and I decide to join them so that I can see a bit of the island, as I haven't been further than the Customs office. It's a nice walk and we get back just before dark. There's a party at Big Papa's, the local bar, so we join in and enjoy the atmosphere and music. There's only reggae music, of course, and the constant smell of weed, or marijuana. It's the most normal thing in the world to smoke it here, and when you walk through the streets at least half the people you see are either stoned or drunk, but not aggressive.

Together with the crew on *Cornelis* and *Stamper*, the two Dutch yachts next to *Guppy*, I decide to see some more of the island. We get up early and look for the bus that takes you to the Indian reservation, but can't find it. A taxi costs 150 East Caribbean dollars (that's about €38), and we think it's too expensive. While we're trying to find a solution, a kind man approaches us and says we can take the bus to Marigot and then change buses. The taxi driver is furious with the man for spoiling his potential fare, and we board the very full bus to Marigot while the two of them are still arguing.

The route is beautiful. The island is very green and is apparently the last Caribbean island with an unspoilt tropical rainforest. Unfortunately, the bus passes all of this at full speed and we have to crane our necks to see the view. In Marigot, we hitchhike to the village that, according to the driver of the truck that picks us up, is the Indian village. We walk through it but don't really get the idea that Indians live here, and so we take a bus back. We stop in another village and — *voilà* — there it is at the foot of a mountain. It's not very exciting, just a few girls who are weaving baskets, a waterfall and … well, that's it! I pick a coconut to take with me and we go on to the capital, Roseau.

Back on *Guppy*, I take the dinghy and paddle to *Stad Amsterdam* that, by happy coincidence, has just arrived. I recognise Leo on the bridge, who sees me first. It's good to meet up with everyone, but there's been a big change of crew and many of them don't know me. Enough of them still do, though, and they ask me to join them for a meal.

Nearly every day the locals come to the yachts lying at anchor to ask if we're interested in tours on the island or trips down the Indian River for $30. Diane from the *Cornelis* and I have decided to do our own river trip in my dinghy. The locals, of course, say that this is prohibited, so we start out at five in the morning before it gets light. There's no one about and the faint light makes it even more mysterious. Wow, it really is stunning! We continue up the river, which is surrounded by mangrove swamps and palm trees, and we pass the spot where *Pirates of the Caribbean II* was filmed. The river is getting shallower, but the dinghy is light and we manage to carry it across the waterfalls and rapids that are becoming ever more common. We then decide to leave the dinghy behind and continue on foot. There are a lot of mosquitos, and some parts of the river are suddenly very deep, which means I go under a couple of times, but I don't mind — this is freshwater. I'd love to take some with me, fill the dinghy up with it or take a hose to *Guppy* from here, but that, of course, isn't possible.

When we get hungry, I try to open a coconut. It takes some doing, and to our dismay it's sour. We try another; this one is good. We each have half and it makes up for the breakfast we missed. Satisfied, we walk back to the dinghy. It's all downstream from here, and we have fun paddling fast and even rafting in some places. An awesome experience.

Running wild, we come to the mouth of the river where there are now a number of people. They aren't particularly happy to see us, and one man gives us a whole sermon about it not being allowed … I tell him that's too bad as we've just completed our trip. There's nothing much he can do about it as it's not his river. He grumbles and swears a bit, but leaves us alone.

When we eventually get back to *Guppy*, I feel I've had quite a day and sit and read in the cockpit. At 14.00 we all go snorkelling, and that evening I visit *Stamper* to make everyone some banana pancakes.

The next morning I wake up when I hear someone call my name loudly. Outside there's a boat carrying scuba tanks and a number of people who ask me if I want to go diving. Sure! I grab my diving gear and jump on board. It's beautiful underwater. I see two turtles and we dive through an underground cave. Back on *Guppy*, I tidy up and get some schoolwork done. That night, I make some popcorn and watch a movie. And so ends another beautiful day on this tropical island.

I actually want to sail on to Bonaire tomorrow, so I start getting things sorted for the voyage. After half an hour everything is neat inside, but now all the mess is lying outside. The whole cockpit is full. Half a fishnet, a huge shell, flippers, various wetsuits, grapefruit and lots more that doesn't belong here. En route from Îles des Saintes, the shell had dropped on my toes, so I put it in a box and secure it. I also pack the rest where it belongs. I paddle to my German neighbours and ask them if they can take me ashore with their fast dinghy because it'll take me forever to get there in mine. They're happy to help me and I clear outward at Customs. On the way back, I recognise one of the yachts: it's *Tante Rietje*. I ask if we can run past them, but unfortunately they aren't home. What a pity!

When I'm on deck a little later, I see that the *Tante Rietje* crew are on board and paddle across to greet them. They recognise me immediately and I'm invited to join them. The skipper tells me that his wife couldn't take the heat and has gone back to the Netherlands. Now he's sailing with an Italian whose relationship has broken up. They're busy making dinner and ask me if I'm hungry. The cook being Italian, it's spaghetti, of course. After catching up with all the news, I paddle back to *Guppy* and chat to Dad on Skype, but the WiFi signal is weak and falls away from time to time. As soon as it starts getting dark, I lie on the couch to watch a movie, *The Kids Are Alright*.

Dominica–Bonaire: 450 nautical miles

DAY 1: *2 February*

The alarm goes off at six in the morning. I stretch in my bunk and then start on the best morning exercise there is: heaving up the anchor. This is because my trusty 34-year-old *Guppy* only has a manual windlass. With some effort and a bit of sweat, I manage to get the 25-metre-long, 10-millimetre-thick, heavy anchor chain back on deck.

All is calm in the bay; one or two people are coming up on deck, and a yacht leaves just in front of me. As soon as *Guppy* is out of the bay, I hoist the sails and prepare something to eat. There's little wind and the last Dominican shower falls over me. To prevent *Guppy* rolling too much, I start the Yanmar. A little later there's a breeze and I can switch it off. As soon as I've checked the sails and seen to it that *Guppy* is on course, I start to feel bored. What's this? Have I spent too much time on land? Fortunately it doesn't last long. I eat a grapefruit, enjoy watching Dominica grow smaller on the horizon and make some macaroni. I'm never bored in the evening and enjoy my dinner watching the sunset. It looks like I may have company. A brown sea bird circles around

Guppy three times, flies straight into the mainsail and then perches on top of the mizzen. That's where it stays. I'm just beginning to enjoy its company when I hear *splat*, and see that there's a pool of thick bird shit that's landed 5 centimetres from me. Guess I'll take care of it in the morning …

The night is calm and I don't need to do anything. No changes of course or trimming sails. Great!

DAY 2: *3 February*

At 07.00 I'm woken up by a call from the Dutch newspaper the *AD* (*Algemene Dagblad*). Half asleep, I tell them about my experience with my shitty bird. The stupid bird left an hour ago having shat over the entire boat. My reward for the ride. Nice!

After a breakfast of cornflakes this morning, I clean the cockpit. I'm not planning to sit in this muck for the next two days. It sticks like glue and I've given the culprit a good warning not to come back. I'll take care of the mizzen, bimini and foredeck when I get to Bonaire.

There isn't a cloud in the sky and it promises to be a warm day. There's a nice breeze for a broad reach, and *Guppy* is sailing at around 6 knots. I'm getting into my rhythm again. A flying fish lands in the cockpit today. I throw it back into the sea and spend the rest of the day trimming the sails, checking my course, navigating, cooking and sending off a blog about shitty sea birds …

At night, a cruise ship passes *Guppy* in the opposite direction. I'm having ravioli tonight and, just when I take a bite, a big wave sends both me and the saucepan flying, spreading the contents from the galley to the chart table, with me landing on my back. How can a simple meal cause all this mess? After taking a photo of the ravioli battlefield, I set out to clean it up.

DAY 3: *4 February*

I'm going a little too fast this morning and decide to drop the mizzen. Not that it helps, because even at 6.5 knots I'll be arriving in Bonaire in the dark now. I fiddle with the sails until I get *Guppy*'s speed down to a nice 5.5 knots.

The sun is climbing and it's beginning to be very hot. In the aft cabin I check to see that the fenders and mooring lines aren't buried under too much mess. It's not too bad and I have them to hand. It's happened that I've come into a harbour after a long crossing and been unable to find or reach the lines and fenders that I urgently needed. That was a lesson to me. The wind drops gradually. I send Dad a text message that it'll probably stay this way until morning, and reset the mizzen. It's only half past four, but I'm really hungry and make myself a meal.

DAY 4: *5 February*

I'm not getting much sleep tonight. I'm nearing land and would prefer to keep watch, but we're still 40 miles off so I try to sleep. At 06.00 the first light comes into sight. I don't see any land, only a light; the lighthouse on the south point looks as though it's standing in the water.

When I round the south point at dawn at a distance of 3 miles, I see a strip of land. *Guppy* is sailing solely on the genoa. At 08.00, it's light and I still have 5 miles to go. At 09.00, I'm lying in front of a narrow harbour entrance and call the harbour master, Gerard van Erp, on the VHF. The harbour entrance is very shallow and he pilots me across it in his RIB. I thought I would be able to navigate with my plotter, but when I look at it I see that *Guppy* is going over land!

Bonaire

The harbour at the Plaza Resort is very full and *Guppy* is tied up alongside another yacht. That's good as it gives me more privacy. Gerard appears to live on a big boat in the harbour, and I go and eat a croissant with cheese with him and meet his family; his wife, Anneke, and children Laura (13) and Marijn (15). He then shows me around the hotel complex that includes the harbour. I see iguanas everywhere, some of them as big as dachshunds.

After a bit of rest, I set to work scrubbing the bird shit off the deck, and that evening I go to eat pizza with Gerard and his family. I haven't had pizza in a while, so I really enjoy it. I get back fairly early and try to get some sleep, but the mosquitos make it almost impossible. I flap my arms around to swat them and tell them to try someone else's blood, but nothing helps. In the end, I attach the nylon wind catcher to the front hatch and then lie right under it on top of some sails, spare parts, emergency rations and some other stuff. It's not very comfortable, but the mosquitos stay away from the wind that blows over me and I manage to fall asleep fairly quickly.

I wake up to the sound of someone calling my name out loud. When I eventually stick my head through the hatch, I can't see anyone. An hour later there's someone on the jetty again. Argh, the continuous calling of my name is beginning to get on my nerves! I finish my schoolwork and check my email. There's an invitation to go to the HISWA water sport fair (the annual boat fair in Amsterdam) that runs from the first to the sixth of March. I don't really feel like being in the limelight again, but on the other hand it may be a good opportunity for some clarity on the subject of my voyage and to have my own say about it all. I then make a start on installing my new SSB radio set. It turns out to be more work than I thought, despite the fact that the preparation has already been done. The antenna and most of the cables were installed in the Netherlands. It looks like I'm going to have to ask Gerard if he knows anyone who is familiar with these things. The instructions for the wiring between the enormous transmitter, SSB radio and modem aren't very clear, and joining up the wrong wires could mean the end of my SSB. Gerard tells me he knows someone who can help. I contact Hans, Gerard's expert, who assures me he'll be able to fix it in a couple of days' time.

In the meantime, the chaos on *Guppy* is driving me nuts and I make a serious plan called 'Tidy and Organise'. First I clean out the galley and do all the dishes. Then I start on the fore cabin, salon and the aft cabin. At the end of the day *Guppy* smells fresh and I'm exhausted, but order has been restored on board and that feels wonderful.

I'm still thinking about the proposal from the HISWA boat fair, and after an exchange of emails we have sorted things out. I'm off to the Netherlands in a couple of weeks.

I heard today that the Chief of Staff at the maritime NATO headquarters in England, Hank Ort, has warned yachts not to sail through the Gulf of Aden. He said no one could count on protection against pirates, and mentioned me in particular. He was speaking in response to a request for support by 30 yachts that wanted to sail through this area in convoy. I'm sorry that NATO no longer offers protection for small boats and only helps big ships. I don't think it would be too much trouble just to be on standby should a convoy of yachts call for help. It's a pity, even bizarre, that my name becomes associated with anything nautical. Why, I wonder? What I'm doing may be unusual at my age, something I'm becoming aware of myself, but why there's so much media attention on me is something I've never understood. The fact that a bird shitting all over *Guppy* makes the news on the internet the next day is too crazy for words. And so is the fact that I'm mentioned in a report about piracy in the Gulf of Aden when there are hundreds of other sailors out there … I happened to speak to some New Zealanders who sailed through the Red Sea just yesterday and they said nothing about pirates. I'm not saying that they don't exist, but it's not that you have a 100 per cent chance of being attacked when you sail through this region. And yes, potentially, there's danger everywhere.

I've spent the whole morning doing schoolwork, answering my emails, writing up my blog and other duties. I'm a little stuck where chemistry is concerned. Gerard attempts to help me, but even he can't quite figure it out … But he can help me get rid of all the media mosquitos that plague me daily. He organises a media conference at which journalists get the opportunity to ask all their questions in one go and then leave me alone — and it works!

When I get back to *Guppy*, a boy and a girl who are sailing with their parents on a Canadian yacht approach me looking for people their own age. They look friendly and I decide to go with them to their catamaran. This way, I meet Joey and Olivia. We watch a surfing movie, talk a lot and visit the neighbours, who are New Zealanders and have just made popcorn which we wolf down…

I've promised to be back in time to join Gerard, Anneke, Marijn and Laura for a barbecue on the beach. We're sitting near a local band that's playing on steel drums, which makes it impossible to hold a conversation, but they're not bad. During the barbecue, I get to meet Caecilia and Jan Godschalx, a Dutch couple who come over to enjoy the sun every year. I visit the Washington Slagbaai Park with them the next day. They've hired a car, and the four of us, including Gerard, set off. I learn that some trees are unable to grow vertically because of the wind, so they are sometimes only 2 metres high but 30 metres in length as they grow over the ground. I also learn that flamingos here are pink because they eat shrimp, and that iguanas have a taste for biscuits and creep onto you as soon as you put a piece in your lap. All very informative. That evening I watch a violent movie on *Rhythm* with Joey and Olivia. I don't really like it, but I enjoy the company.

I have a bicycle on loan and it's wonderful to go for a ride. In the Netherlands, I had to cycle 12 kilometres to school and back again. I haven't even cycled more than 5 kilometres this year and that's got to change!

My gran and granddad arrive today and I'm waiting for their plane from the beach. I'll see them land from here. The plane flies over at 18.00, and Gerard and I walk to the airport. They're happy to see me again, and, after eating a pizza together, we take them to their apartment. The next day Gran, Granddad, Gerard and I do a cycle tour of the island. Gerard has been involved with nature conservation on the island for a long time and knows everything about the nature and geology of the island. He takes us over a couple of hills to a big lake in a nature reserve. There are usually hundreds of flamingos in this area, but this morning we see only two ... It starts to rain on the last leg of our journey. The bicycles are hastily packed into the car and they all dive inside; anyone would think they were made of sugar that melts in the rain ... I tell them that's it's not that bad and carry on cycling as we are now going downhill. It rains harder and harder, and within two minutes I'm soaked, but it's so hot that it's actually quite pleasant. We end up in a restaurant with traditional food in Ricon where 'big mammas' conjure up delicious rice dishes with goat and fish.

The next day, I take a wonderful kayak trip through the mangrove swamps; the nursery of the ocean. It's a special place in which I find parrotfish, flamingos and a barracuda that has apparently lost its way. We drive back to the harbour via a narrow sand road and I'm sitting in the back of the vehicle when I see an enormous sand truck bearing down on us in a cloud of dust; it's too late to do anything and the truck crashes into us. I bump my head, but don't have any other injuries except a painful headache. Suzanne and Gerard, sitting in the front, also seem to be OK. The truck driver shouts that neither his brakes nor his hooter work and then starts swearing in Papiamento. After waiting for an hour in the boiling sun, we are finally fetched by Anneke and Marijn, who take me to the first-aid post for a check-up, just in case. After waiting a very long time, we find out that there's no doctor present. Eventually we seek out a general practitioner who speaks only Spanish and Papiamento. Fortunately, Anneke and Marijn speak both these languages. Anyway, it's now three hours since the accident and I'm finally standing at reception with some pills for the swelling and headache. I'm told to take some rest and to come back if I feel nauseous or if the headache persists. I'm feeling much better already; I'll just lie down and take a break … The worst part was the shock, but my head is still on my shoulders and I'm not squinting or seeing double.

It's only just dawning on me that we could all have died. I wasn't wearing a seat belt in the back of the car when the accident occurred. It's thanks to Gerard, who put his foot down on the accelerator instead of braking, that the impact was less serious than it could have been, otherwise we would all have been killed! You should have seen the car; both back wheels were standing out at different angles. Poor Gerard … Until yesterday he had been the proud owner of the only electric car on the island. His car is now a total wreck.

I'm standing at the airport today to welcome Dad and my sister, Kim. I spot them immediately and wave madly. They eventually see that it's me and wave back. It takes a while before they make their way through the crowd and it's wonderful to see them again. They'll be staying with me on board *Guppy* for a week. The next morning, Dad and Kim are awake very early. It's the time difference of five hours between the two countries, of course. I have to get used to the chatter in the early morning and can forget about waking up gradually while they are here. The day starts with rain; lots and lots of rain ... The hatches are open and the wind catcher has been catching water rather than wind, so everything is wet inside. I try to push it outside and close the hatch, but this only results in an extra pool of water. Dad starts seeing to a couple of chores on *Guppy*, and Kim and I try to make a kneeboard out of a bodyboard and a piece of wood. My dinghy with its 6-horsepower Mercury motor soon has us planing behind the boat. Kim is having a great time on Bonaire and enjoying the heat. After the kneeboarding, she invents another game; it's swinging around *Guppy* from a rope attached to the top of the mast ... My sister, the circus artist!

Within a day, the cockpit is full of rubbish and it's a mess inside. It takes some getting used to having three people on board, including a sister who creates havoc. It's also a bit unreal to have them both here with me. It's as though I'm watching a movie that's in fast-forward mode. That night we make pancakes and watch a movie. I take a break and enjoy Dad and Kim's company. We regularly visit Gran and Granddad, who are staying 2 kilometres up the road in their apartment, and we take a trip to the former slave quarters in their rental car. The days fly past. We swim and snorkel, but I have a bad headache every time I dive underwater. We also go sailing on Gerard's big yacht. Everybody loves it, except my little sister, who is seasick; she's too much of a landlubber. But she's keen to go sailing on the inflatable catamaran that we borrow every day. The Minicat is amazing and we scoot across the sea from Bonaire to the island just off the coast called Little Bonaire almost every day.

Unfortunately, it's still the rainy season on Bonaire and it continues to rain really hard. Our canoe trip to the mangrove swamp is consequently cancelled and so is our plan for a barbecue. Despite this, we have a good time on *Guppy*.

Tomorrow Kim has to go home on her own as she needs to get back to school. After she leaves, I still have a few days with my dad to check and repair a few things on *Guppy*. And then I leave for the Netherlands. How strange it will be to be there for a week! I'm looking forward to the HISWA boat fair but not to the cold. I'm told that temperatures are around freezing point and that there's snow from time to time. Brrr ...

Dad and I wait at the airport until Kim's plane departs. The flight is delayed and we spend three hours staring at the landing strip until she's able to board. Afterwards, she told us that she had the misfortune to sit next to a teacher she knew from school who had spent her holiday on Bonaire. Poor Kim! When Dad and I get back to *Guppy*, I notice that Kim has forgotten her coat. I quickly email Mum to take an extra coat to the airport when she fetches Kim at Schiphol. Hopefully, she'll receive the email in time.

A few days later, I'm standing at the airport for my own flight. When we've taken off and I look through the window, I find myself thinking of the person who was my heroine at the age of 10, Tania Aebi. She sailed solo around the world from 1985 to 1987 and saw and learnt so much about the world. I know I'm also going to learn a lot on this voyage, about myself, too, and that it will change me in a positive way. This adventure that I want to have with myself is so exciting.

It's dark and below me I see the lights of England. In an hour's time, after a flight of eight hours, I'll be back in the Netherlands. To think that it took me half a year to get to Bonaire from there! When I get to Schiphol Airport, my feet are freezing even though I've taken care to wear warm shoes. I manage to get my torn genoa, which I've brought with me to get repaired, through Customs. I then try to get my mobile phone to work and phone my friend Suzanne. She lives close to Amsterdam and it makes sense for me to stay with her. It'll also be much nicer than the hotel room offered to me by the HISWA boat show organisers. My mum lives miles off in Friesland, in the north of the Netherlands, and the rest of my family is still on Bonaire. My body receives a second shock when I go outdoors and feel how cold it really is. Oh, my God!

From Amsterdam we drive to Lelystad to drop my sail off for repairs. Everything feels strange yet familiar. The clouds, the cold, the trains, cars, motorways and high-rise buildings.

That evening, Suzanne cooks pancakes for me … As though I haven't had any in ages. Her five-year-old daughter, Sofie, is very happy to see me. I'm sharing a room with her and I am immediately her new best friend. Every time she gets a chance, she's either on top of me or next to me, talking 10 to the dozen. She's so sweet, I just have to laugh.

That night I go to sleep early, thanks to my jetlag. In the meantime, my phone rings non-stop and my mail box fills with interview requests from television, radio, newspaper and magazines. From *Jensen* to *De Wereld Draait Door* (both highly-rated TV shows in the Netherlands), they all want me as their studio guest. But I don't even know who Matthijs van Nieuwkerk (a popular Dutch TV show host) is! That evening I follow Suzanne's advice and take a look at his programme, but can't really see myself sitting in his show. What do they expect me to do there and why feature me in a television programme? I decide to give interviews only at the HISWA boat fair. Besides that I only want to make one public appearance and that's a lecture I've promised to give for the Ijmuiden Sailing Association.

At the back of the boat fair they've constructed a pool in which some boats are floating. Together with a primary school pupil from Amsterdam, I step into a boat that's been baptised *Guppy*. Olympic sailing champion Marcelien de Koning interviews me on the water while I sail to the middle of the pool and cut a ribbon to release a number of balloons. It's the official opening of the HISWA children's pavilion.

I have a busy schedule at the boat fair. In the mornings I give a presentation at the sailing auditorium, and in the afternoon I give sailing lessons to children in the pool. I sign the book that my gran has published about me, and today I give interviews in between my other commitments. My jaw is soon sore from talking and laughing.

I have no problem giving the presentations and I'm glad to notice that people's opinions about me have changed. The sailing auditorium is packed for my presentations, and people are no longer critical about me; just interested in my story. I finish giving my sailing lessons and then have time to stroll through the boat fair myself. Many of my friends have come to the event to see me. They've changed, and so have I probably. We talk about things in general and I soon notice how I've fallen behind on all the news since my departure on 4 August last year.

My lecture to the yachties at the Ijmuiden Yacht Club is special and teaches me a lot. In my preparation the evening before, I worked until the early hours of the morning to make a nice PowerPoint presentation with lots of photographs of my voyage so far. I didn't have a clue how to use PowerPoint when I started out, but I certainly do now. I think that the presentation with photographs and a few notes on paper will suffice, but when I see the crowd waiting for me in the auditorium, I get quite nervous. I rattle off my presentation far too quickly and, after 20 minutes, notice that I'm through more than half of my material. Suzanne is sitting in the front row and makes frantic gestures for me to slow down. I decide to read them an excerpt from the book I'm writing; the bit about the storm on the Atlantic Ocean. After the interval, people are invited to ask me questions and there's a virtual flood of them! All in all it's a good experience to stand before an audience of genuine sailing enthusiasts and give them a talk. I get the impression that people are more positively disposed towards my voyage than they were when I started out. That's something I need to get used to.

The next day, my best friend, Aileen, comes to visit and spends the night. We have a great time going to McDonald's and then seeing a movie.

My dad, gran and granddad have also landed at Schiphol Airport. They were still on Bonaire when I suddenly decided to accept the invitation for the boat fair and they had already booked their flight. My dad, mum and Kim come to the boat fair the following day. There's a little tension at the beginning, because various state organisations had tried to set my parents against each other in the attempt to stop me from undertaking my voyage, and this had led to some misunderstandings. At the end of the afternoon, something special happens. We decide to go out for a meal together and it turns out to be very enjoyable. My parents are nice to each other and tell us stories about their own voyage around the world when I was born in New Zealand. It's so good to be together like this. It's the first time in years that the four of us have done something together.

Dad, Mum, Kim, I and Spot, of course, have a photograph taken. This photo will be framed and go back with me to Bonaire where it will have a place of honour on *Guppy*. I don't possess a recent photograph of the whole family and don't know if I'll ever have one again. I grew up with my dad and seldom saw my mum over the years. I love them both, but gave up the hope of ever seeing the family reunited a long time ago.

Once the boat fair is over, I spend a few days with Mum and then some with Dad. I also visit the hospital, where they discover that I fractured my skull in the car accident. Fortunately, a scan shows that it's healing nicely and I don't need to worry about it. Then my time in the Netherlands comes to an end and I'm really looking forward to getting back to *Guppy*. I notice that I don't miss my home country at all, even though it's good to see my family and friends again.

After a 10-hour flight to Bonaire and with a big smile on my face, I stumble over the bridge to the marina and back onto *Guppy*. I'm dragging a repaired sail, my backpack and a lot of spare parts for my mate, *Guppy*. I never thought a week in the Netherlands would be so tiring! It was really cool being back, but exhausting. My visit to the Netherlands had been one long chain of events that had me flying, running and jogging. I managed to do an enormous amount but there were also things I ran out of time for. Luckily, I'm back on my faithful *Guppy* and have a few days to recover before I start sailing again.

After a bad night with a lot of mosquitos, I get up. I'm going to sail today, but before I do so there is a lot that needs to be done. I start by removing the sail covers and the wind catcher, after which I check the rigging and the engines. Then it's time to check the weather on the internet and chat to Dad via Skype. At about half past eight, Gerard takes me to get *Guppy*'s outward clearance at Customs and Immigration. The immigration official is not yet at his post, so together with Anneke we decide to have breakfast at City, a restaurant on the boulevard. During the breakfast, a Customs officer comes to tell us that the immigration official has arrived. After clearing outward, I get back to enjoy my breakfast of bacon, egg, fruit and bread. It's yummy!

I go back to *Guppy*, cast off the mooring lines at 10 o'clock and make for the San Blas Islands. I've decided to give Curaçao and Aruba a miss. The Aruban prime minister's advisor has invited me a few times to please attend a special party to be given in my honour on the island. He's even offered to pay for my presence, but I don't want to be the focus of any more attention and don't need a party. Right now, I just need space, water, waves and *Guppy*.

Bonaire–San Blas Islands: 670 nautical miles

DAY 1: *14 March*

It's blowing hard and, after a month on land, it's great to be out at sea again. After rounding Little Bonaire with just the mainsail, I set the genoa and *Guppy* gets up to 7 knots with ease. Awesome! I've been doused by my first wave. Halfway to Curaçao that afternoon I'm really tired, but I'm on the windward side of the island and too close to land to afford nodding off. I'm just counting the waves when I suddenly see a huge cargo ship bearing down on me at full speed. I'm looking into the sun and can't see on which side to pass her. I call her on the VHF … no answer … Then she suddenly emits a big cloud of fumes and alters course to avoid me. Thanks for keeping an eye out! I hate cargo ships, but this one has certainly woken me up. On the SSB radio, I listen to some of the chatter as I sit and watch the sunset from the cockpit. I've finally passed Curaçao, and as soon as night falls I manage to steal a couple of hours' sleep.

DAY 2: *15 March*

I've had a bad night and wasn't able to drop off once, but I must say that the full moon was amazing. A little light is always better than a black night. Sometimes it's so dark at sea that I can't see *Guppy*'s bow. I'm still not feeling a hundred per cent and have a headache. That accident on Bonaire has had more impact on my health than I expected.

I'm trying to call Hans, who helped me to install the SSB, on the radio, but get no reply. I'm warming up the leftover pizza from Monday and eat it in the cockpit while gazing out over the vast expanse of blue. What an awesome sight! I'm so glad I persevered and overcame all those setbacks in the Netherlands. Usually, my first full day at sea is great and everything is good, but my mood swings in the afternoon and I'm asking myself why I didn't stay at home. This is what I experienced yesterday, too. Towards evening the sunset compensates for everything and I know that it's all been worth it.

My gaze falls on the chart with the time zones. In the Red Sea, there will be a three-hour time difference with Europe. I'm hoping that it will be safe by the time I get there and that there will be fewer pirates. *Guppy* isn't exactly a trophy, but I'm worried that they may regard me as a hostage that could be worth some money. My voyage is enjoying world coverage and pirates also have access to the internet ...

DAY 3: *16 March*

I've managed to cover 175 of the 675 miles and expect to arrive at the San Blas islands in three to four days — my last stop before the Panama Canal. I've been studying all the books and information from other sailors on this canal. It's a very busy shipping route and you can't just sail through it. First my boat needs to be measured and inspected, and then I'll have to find four extra crew for the line-handling in the locks. The Panama Canal is always busy and they want to avoid accidents at all costs, so pilotage is compulsory. In the locks a yacht rises by 9 metres each time, and you need to remain in the centre of the lock. This is done with the help of four lines that are heaved across by the canal linesmen. These lines need to be kept taut at all times by the crew.

Organising all of that costs time, and only afterwards are you given a date to pass through the canal, and this can take a couple of weeks. That's why I'm glad I can keep going now. I'm sailing about 50 miles off the coast of Colombia and pirates are reputed to be active here, too. Although I've mainly seen water around me for the past couple of days, I've regularly passed cargo ships. Two of them sailed straight for me and one didn't respond to my call on the VHF. Fortunately, that was during the day and I could see them coming from a good distance. I'm also lucky that it's almost full moon, so that I have good visibility at night, too. It also helps with spotting squalls, although the radar is better at picking them up than I am. Until now it's been perfect weather and both *Guppy* and I are enjoying this. A wonderful following wind is helping to blow *Guppy* onward at a speed of 7 knots. I notice that I can amuse myself for hours just looking at the sea and waves — they never cease to fascinate me!

DAY 4: *17 March*

I counted a record number of flying fish on board this morning. There were six in the cockpit and five on deck, even though I managed to save two of them the previous night. As soon as I threw one back, the next one came on board! I suppose it's logical, as predator fish hunt them at full moon and they have to fly to evade them. Bad luck that this lot landed on *Guppy*.

I managed to sleep last night despite encounters with a couple of short squalls. It's still overcast outside but most of the threatening cloud masses pass by. The sun is tanning my face and I'm able to sit in the cockpit without getting a wave over me most of the time. This is the life!

There's now 340 miles to go. We have wind from astern and *Guppy* is sailing at about 7 knots, bringing us to San Blas with speed. Besides the flying fish keeping me busy and a couple of passing ships, it's a boring day. There's little to do in terms of sailing. I change tack with the genoa a couple of times and play with the course. I don't feel like reading or writing; I don't really feel like anything. After a few unsuccessful attempts at trying to call Bonaire on the SSB, I give that up, too.

Otherwise, I'm agonising about being able to reach the San Blas Islands by daylight in two days' time. If I don't make it by daylight, it will mean that I have to wait offshore on Saturday night. The islands are surrounded by dangerous reefs and I'll need to find the entrance to the lee side, and I'm not going to risk doing this in the dark. We've another 317 miles to go and it's now 15.20. *Guppy* is fast, but is she fast enough? I hope so. I text Dad my position via the satellite phone from time to time because the tracker on *Guppy* has been unreliable since Bonaire.

I'm sitting in the cockpit gazing out in front of me. A wave washes over me and I look for a spot that stays dry. There's a white bird with a long tail flying around the boat. Is it a cockatoo? It's beautiful, but I really hope it's not going to land and shit all over the boat. Fortunately, it rejects *Guppy* as a landing site and flies on.

It's blowing harder and harder, which is something I was prepared for. The area between Barranquilla and Cartagena can be very windy. Just before sunset, I put a reef in the mainsail. Night falls fast.

DAY 5: *18 March*

We sail through the night with a wind of 35 knots and ever-rougher seas. Everything, but everything, is salty: my bed, the floor, the cockpit and the cushion I sit on to observe my surroundings. Everything I'm wearing is also soaked in salt. The wind has gradually dropped to 30 knots but the waves remain high, which means that one moment *Guppy* is in a trough surrounded by water, and the next is on the crests of waves; on a sort of rollercoaster surfing on the swell at enormous speed. A lot of wind is OK, but the high waves are dangerous. The windvane steering system is only just coping, and *Guppy* is being thrown on her side from time to time. It's really my fault because I've got a little too much sail up in my attempt to reach the San Blas Islands before dark.

This afternoon, three cargo vessels decide to pass me at the same time. One from ahead, one from astern and one on the beam. Luckily they keep their distance. It's overcast and it remains that way for the rest of the day. I leave the reef in the mainsail as we're still doing speeds of above 6 knots. We've covered quite a distance during the night, so I'm fairly sure that *Guppy* will succeed in getting us to the San Blas Islands by daylight tomorrow.

The heavy clouds and waves that continue to wash over *Guppy* make it a sombre day. I'm feeling a lot better today and am reading *Tijdelijk Adres: Andes,* a book by Dutch author Agnita Twigt about her backpacker trip through South America as a young woman.

How long this day is! The overcast weather makes it seem much later than it actually is. I think of the Netherlands where it's probably just as sombre and grey. The nightfall takes forever, too, as if it will never get dark. Dad is already fast asleep so I can't text him now. I'm trying to kill time by reading magazines, eating, walking around and staring at the clock. It's seven o'clock and still not dark. I think I need to set my clock for the next time zone because it's almost always light at 06.00 and dark at 18.00 when you're in the tropics.

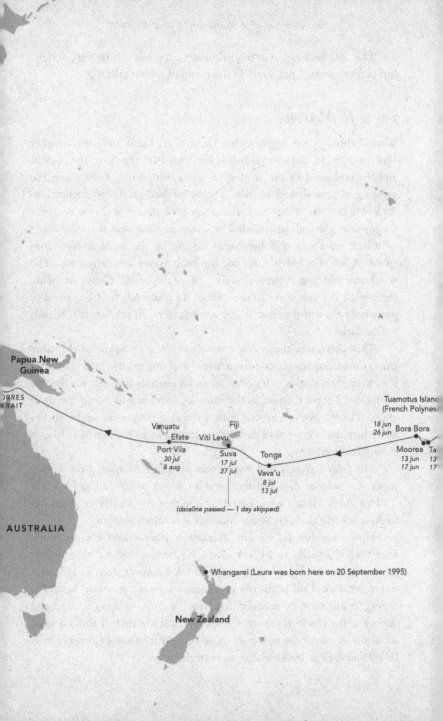

Papua New
Guinea

TORRES
STRAIT

Tuamotus Island
(French Polynesi

Vanuatu   Fiji
Efate   Viti Levu   18 jun   Bora Bora
Port Vila   Suva   Tonga   26 jun
30 jul   17 jul   Moorea   Ta
8 aug   27 jul   Vava'u   13 jun   13
8 jul   17 jun   17
13 jul

(dateline passed — 1 day skipped)

AUSTRALIA

● Whangarei (Laura was born here on 20 September 1995)

New Zealand

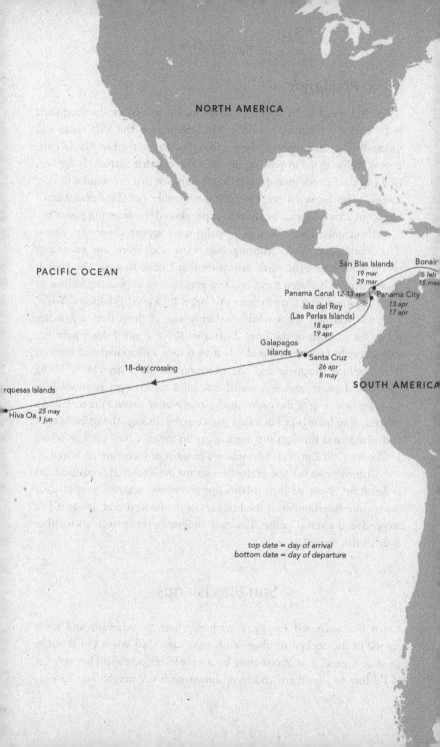

NORTH AMERICA

PACIFIC OCEAN

Bonair
5 feb
15 mar

San Blas Islands
19 mar
29 mar

Panama Canal 12-13 apr

Panama City
13 apr
17 apr

Isla del Rey
(Las Perlas Islands)
18 apr
19 apr

Galapagos
Islands

Santa Cruz
26 apr
8 may

18-day crossing

rquesas Islands

Hiva Oa   25 may
1 jun

SOUTH AMERICA

top date = day of arrival
bottom date = day of departure

DAY 6: *19 March*

The wind speed has dropped to 20 knots, the sun is not showing itself today and it's drizzling non-stop. I'm listening on the SSB radio and suddenly hear that someone else is also on his way to the San Blas Islands. I soon realise that I'm picking up the radio net that surrounds the San Blas Islands. I check in and ask if there's a chance that the wind will ever subside. The answer is no. They ask me whether I'm alone and when I expect to arrive. I speak to all sorts of people and the morning passes by.

All at once I see the tops of palm trees appear above the waves. The islands are slowly coming into view and there are enormous waves crashing on the reefs. Knowing that I need to enter the lagoon somewhere in between these breakers gives me an unpleasant feeling.

I see something flash in front of *Guppy*. It's a pod of dolphins. Wow! I haven't seen any for a while. Suddenly one of them does a 3-metre jump just in front of the bow. Awesome! What a pity I don't have my camera ready, but then I'd probably have missed a jump like that anyway. The dolphins disappear and the enormous breakers get closer. Using the VHF, I ask if anyone is available to pilot me in. I get an immediate response from one of the yachts that's already safely beyond the reef, and a quarter of an hour later I'm following a dinghy through the maze of reefs and islands and through the narrow gap in the reef into the bay of the Hollandes Cays Kun Yala Isles where a number of yachts are anchored.

This overcast version of the film set for the *Bounty* chocolate advert is beautiful, with its little islands, pearly white beaches, crystal-clear waters and the thunder of the breakers in the background. It's as if I've stepped into a travel guide. The only difference is the overcast weather over all this beauty.

San Blas Islands

Once I've anchored *Guppy*, I wash my hair (wonderful!) and settle myself in the cockpit to observe my new view. Just when I'm about to prepare a meal, I'm approached by a couple of yachties. They ask me if I'd like to join them and have dinner with my neighbour. Sure ...

that will be great … and a quarter of an hour later I'm enjoying the company around a table on a Danish yacht.

At night, it starts to rain and doesn't stop. It's still pouring when I wake up. Listening on the VHF, I hear some chatter about a party the next day. While I'm reading (blush) Donald Duck, some yachties invite me for dinner. They fetch me at five o'clock and we eat on board the *Icarian*, together with Brian and Marilyn, an elderly Canadian couple who've been sailing in the Caribbean for seven years. The food is delicious and my English is sorely tested, even though it has been improving fast since the beginning of the trip. We chat about all sorts of things that evening, but especially about sailing, travelling and our experiences. I don't get back late as I want time to enjoy the full moon. It's such an awesome scene — the clouds, the dark, mysterious palm islands, the yachts and … *Guppy* and me.

In my thoughts, I once again see myself at the age of eight, dreaming of the high seas and the uninhabited islands that I was going to discover in my travels on my boat. Then it was a dream and now I am here. It's amazing! Even as an eight-year-old I was already looking for adventure. Wandering through cornfields and having sword fights with sticks. I laugh when I consider my simple nature at that age. Even then I was sailing as much as possible, summer and winter, come rain or shine; I was at one with the water. Wearing plenty of clothes, a dry suit and a life-jacket, I was at my happiest when dark clouds passed overhead and waves swept over my little boat. Then I would dream about the big oceans and unknown parts of the world. Nowadays, I'm a little less cheerful when a wave soaks me, but I'm still thrilled at discovering new countries and meeting new people.

The day starts with rain, but fortunately the sun finally shines through. I'm sitting at the chart table trying to solve some maths problems when the Canadian couple from *Icarian* come to ask me if I'd like to go snorkelling. I grab my gear and jump into their dinghy. The snorkelling is fantastic and we see turtles, stingrays and starfish. Tonight there's a party for all the yachts at anchor on one of the little islands. I speak to many different people and they all have a lot of questions. The Kuna Indians who live here are also present. They live in small huts and make beautiful embroidered *molas*. Three families live on this island. They keep an eye on any pollution and on the coconuts, of course. Coconuts are a means of payment over here. A rich family owns many coconut palms and the coconut is used to barter for anything they need. It's also prohibited to collect any coconuts on the islands. A funny coconut economy!

I open my eyes and see ... maths problems. Sigh. They keep me busy, but I manage to solve them and can now amuse myself. There are now two Dutch yachts anchored near me. They're both called *Pjotter*! The owners of the bigger *Pjotter* were the former owners of the smaller *Pjotter*. Without planning it that way, they both happened to be sailing around the Caribbean at the same time and have met up unexpectedly. The crew of the smaller *Pjotter* have come to visit with their two children, Emma and Maxim, who soon discover my stuffed animals, including my Donald Duck. He's immediately renamed Donald Dekker and I let them have him. Just as they are leaving, Mike and Deana Ruel come by. They're all people who I met at last night's party. Mike and Deana come from California, coincidentally from the same town as the Sunderlands. Zac Sunderland held the record for a while for the youngest sailor to have circumnavigated the world. His sister, Abby, wanted to break that record last year. She needed to sail non-stop to do this because of her age, but landed in a heavy storm while crossing the Southern Indian Ocean where her mast was swept overboard and she had to abandon the attempt.

We decide to go snorkelling together, but first have something to eat on *R Sea Kat*. I spot a turtle with three pilot fish at a depth of 10 metres. The water is so clear and the colours are stunning. Looking down on the water, light blue indicates a sandbank, brown a reef and deep blue the ocean depths. That night we all have dinner on board *R Sea Kat* with Mike and Deana. The day has flown past and I've made a number of good new friends.

In the morning, I decide to finish preparing the ratlines to the first spreaders. I complete this chore just before it gets really hot. Now I can get up the mast with ease and I enjoy the view from the first spreader. After we've looked at each other's photographs on *R Sea Kat*, we go snorkelling. It's so beautiful underwater here that it never fails to impress me. The tide is coming in and we decide to let ourselves drift while hanging on to the dinghy. It's as if we are flying over this underwater world. A small black-tip shark passes us and I'm surprised that I'm not scared. On the contrary, the shark is the one that catches fright and, unfortunately, disappears quickly.

This morning, I see that *Rhythm* has anchored here, too, and it's great to see her crew. We've been invited for a barbecue by the charter yacht next to us this evening. During the barbecue, and on other occasions, I've been able to gather quite a lot of useful information about Panama. I'm very curious to know how long it will take me to get permission to go through the Panama Canal. During my parents' world voyage, they had to wait for three weeks before they were allowed to pass through with their yacht.

One evening, I enjoy some pancakes on board smaller *Pjotter*. Yum! With seven adults and two kids running around it's really busy on the 10-metre *Pjotter*, and it takes some getting used to, but luckily the kids calm down when they start watching the movie *Happy Feet*.

The next day a new yacht arrives, full of backpackers. Looking at the dome antennae up their mast, it seems they have internet. I introduce myself to the crew and am invited on board. Great, I'm allowed to use their internet! In a way it's wonderful to live without internet. It does, however, have a magnetic attraction, and once again I'm reading my emails. Fortunately, the connection doesn't last long and I'm able to enjoy the real world rather than the virtual one.

That evening we have a farewell dinner on *R Sea Kat*. Our ways part tomorrow as the *Pjotters* are going back to the Netherlands via Iceland, but I will probably see Mike and Deana in Panama later on. I wave goodbye to *Windwalker*, *R Sea Kat* and the *Pjotters*, and now there are only three boats left. A feeling of loneliness comes over me and I don't quite know what to do with myself. For the past few days I've had people around me all the time and every second has been filled. Now I have to amuse myself, but that doesn't really worry me. I'll soon be heading for Panama myself and can start getting *Guppy* ready for the voyage. I can also visit the other yachts, do my schoolwork or read. Getting some schoolwork done seems a good option, and when I've finished that I climb up into the mast and sit on a spreader for an hour to record all the recent happenings in my diary. The view from the lower spreaders is stunning. It's quiet and I can sit here for hours just daydreaming; and that's exactly what I do. From my position high in the mast, I see a stingray and then a turtle swim past.

I take a walk around Tiadup. The island is not very big and it takes me less than half an hour, but at least I've had some exercise.

Towards evening, Brian and Marilyn from *Icarian* come by.

'Do you feel like having dinner with us?'

'Sure, that would be great!'

I jump into my dinghy and minutes later I'm chatting away. When I get back to *Guppy*, I once again climb up to my new perch in the mast to think back on yet another wonderful day on this voyage of mine.

I've decided to continue my voyage tomorrow afternoon and am busy stowing all the loose stuff away; flippers, towels, wind catcher, bottles, clothes, books, laptop, tins, the dishes, sail covers and charts. There's plenty to do. It's amazing how one person can create so much mess in just one week …

San Blas Islands–Panama: 80 nautical miles

DAY 1: *29 March*

Just before sunset, I steer *Guppy* through the reefs and into the choppy sea. Late in the afternoon, I have the sun on my back which is ideal for spotting the reefs, and sailing through the night will bring me to Panama by daylight. The waves are something to contend with in the shallower parts, but once out at sea *Guppy* is doing an average of 6 knots under full sail on a moonless night in the direction of Panama. It's pitch dark and hard to distinguish the sea from the sky, and it feels like I'm floating through the universe. Although I would have been able to see the stars if that were the case.

Slowly the shipping traffic picks up. I spend the whole night in the cockpit tucked into my red sleeping bag. I'm sorry to have said goodbye to everyone I met in the San Blas Islands, but that's the way it goes: travelling and parting go hand in hand, and I'm finally getting used to it. I can now enjoy the first day at sea without missing everyone and everything. Besides, the Panama Canal and the Pacific are waiting for me. And so we sail through the black night with an increasing number of lights moving past, and the radar fills with approaching dots.

DAY 2: *30 March*

It gets light slowly and I should be seeing the coast now, but there's a thick black cloud blocking my view. I can't make out if it's a high or low coastline we are approaching. With the heavy cargo traffic, I've hardly been able to shut my eyes, but I'm used to this kind of traffic from my crossings between the Netherlands and England. At about nine o'clock, I pick out more and more detail and see the piers of Colón harbour. With all the cargo ships, cranes and traffic, it feels as though I'm approaching the busy harbour of Rotterdam. The only difference is that there are mountains and palm trees here and, fortunately, it's considerably warmer.

I'm in contact with Mike and Deana on *R Sea Kat* via the VHF, and they have organised a spot for me at the marina. Once inside the breakwaters, it's beautifully calm. There are a number of people waiting for me in the harbour and I get a spot right in front of the restaurant … Oh no! Well, you can't look a gift horse in the mouth.

Colón

Almost immediately there are lots of people around me all wanting something from me. I clear in and then start to organise everything for my passage through the Panama Canal. *Guppy* gets measured and inspected and I need to fill in a pile of forms and answer the same queries each time. Hopefully, I'll get a place on the waiting list for the Panama Canal soon. There are dozens of yachts in the harbour and another 15 are lying at anchor; and they all get to go before me.

On my way back from clearing in, there's a cameraman standing in my way again. Argh! I say that I'm tired and that they should come back tomorrow, but they continue to take photographs and carry on filming. I then say something unfriendly to shake them off, but it doesn't make any difference. They keep on asking questions and I repeatedly tell them to go away. When they eventually make a move to depart, there's one final question: 'By the way, what's your name?'

Seething with anger, I storm back to *Guppy*. It's amazing how rude people can be; they haven't even taken the trouble to find out who they are interviewing. After taking a shower and writing my blog, my anger subsides and I walk to the yacht where I've been invited to have dinner. After a delicious *bamischottel* (Indonesian noodle dish) and having not slept for 39 hours, I quickly fall into a deep sleep … zzz …

At half past eight José, who works at the harbour, should have been taking me, Mike and Deana to Colón. At half past nine he still hasn't arrived and he only pitches up at half past 10. Panamanians! The radiator needs to be filled with water every 10 minutes, but we eventually get to Colón. Colón is a decaying, overcrowded town where everyone does his or her own thing. There's little law and order, and the residents, often armed, shoot at each other as they walk or drive around. Everyone has warned me not to go there on my own.

The Immigration Offices are on the second floor of a derelict building. Once there, they tell me that I don't need a visa for some reason but that Mike and Deanna do. We can't work out why this is so, as José was convinced I'd need one.

It's hot and humid, without a breath of wind. When we get back to *Guppy*, we first cool off in the pool that belongs to the harbour. There we learn that we can borrow bikes from someone, and a little later we're on our way to Fort Lorenzo. Mike has heard about this place and we're curious to see it. We cycle for about 10 kilometres, uphill and downhill, and then straight through some jungle over a good tarred road on our folding bikes without seeing anyone; just the odd monkey. We hear thousands of jungle noises all around us, of which I can identify only a few. This is fun!

The fort is a ruin, but its location is beautiful. We are rewarded with an awesome view over the sea and of a winding river running through a jungle. Just before sunset we make our way back. Slowly the jungle comes alive. Monkeys and all sorts of other animals alert the jungle of their presence with their loud cries. I'm busy looking at a couple of monkeys overhead when I have to brake sharply to avoid running over a snake. It raises its head and hisses at me. I get the fright of my life, but it seems as shocked as I am and disappears into the grass.

Mike, Deana and I have put our names on the list of yachties for the free bus trip to Colón that goes twice a day. We walk to the bus at 07.45 and it's already jam-packed with people. Officially, only one person per boat is permitted on the bus and a number of people are unceremoniously thrown off. Now Deana and I have managed to get on the bus, without Mike, but he manages to get on somehow. The trip is bumpy and we have to wait a long time for the locks to close and the bridge to open. On the return journey, the bus is overloaded with big bags and boxes of groceries. I'm relieved to be back on *Guppy*.

One of the nicest things about sailing around the world is that you meet the most amazing people on your voyage. Mike and Deana, whom I met on the San Blas Islands, are an example. Mike was a heart surgeon when he was diagnosed with cancer of the throat. He survived against all odds and this made them decide to change the course of their lives. They sold their home and most of their possessions and bought *R Sea Kat*, a 42-foot catamaran, to sail around the world in. They have invited each of their three adult children to sail a section of the voyage with them, as they want their children to share these special memories.

I've become good friends with them; not only because they're genuinely nice people and always ready to help me, but because they're very special. They met each other during their studies when both of them had part-time jobs as trapeze artists in a circus. According to Mike, Deana was the only woman who could perform a two and half forward-somersault from a swinging trapeze. Mike himself also has some amazing stunts to his name; such as setting himself alight and then diving into a tiny pool from a great height. They are in their sixties but you'd never think it. I hope to be just like them when I grow old.

Mike and Deana are passing through the Panama Canal at the same time as I am. *Promise*, another 42-foot catamaran with Joy and Gordon on board, is leaving today and we're going with them as line-handlers so that we know what we can expect. The old tyres that will serve as fenders in the canal are loaded onto my deck today. I'm on the list for 9 and 10 April, which means *Guppy* and I will be in the Pacific Ocean in a few days' time.

I'm able to take a quick dive in the pool before *Promise* gives me a sign that she's allowed to leave. We are on the first shift and on our way to the first three locks, the Gatun Locks, with two other yachts. Before we can leave, the two other yachts have to raft up alongside *Promise*. It's chaotic moving between huge, loudly hooting cargo ships, with much swearing and shouting going on. Hmm, I notice these people haven't done much manoeuvering before ... I'm a line-handler on *Promise* and I'm observing the chaos next to us while waiting for a line from the other yachts. Finally, they succeed in tying the three yachts together. We're in front of a cargo ship that, despite sounding various warning signals, almost landed on us, and we're now moving into the lock. Heaving lines are thrown across to us from the top of the lock by canal linesmen. We attach our ropes to them and the canal linesmen haul them up with the heaving lines. We are the middle boat so we don't have much to do, and I use the opportunity to study the whole procedure. Everything goes well until the last lock, where we see an ambulance approaching ... Something has gone wrong with handling the lines on one of the yachts behind us and someone has lost a couple of fingers.

It takes a day and a half, and we drive back from Panama City to Colón on the second night together with all the other line-handlers. Tonight, a party is being given in my honour at the club. In exchange the local media are able to do a few interviews. It's much better to do it this way. They show respect and are far better prepared, so I don't have to field stupid questions.

It's dark and calm outside and it's raining. Jillian arrived today and we are having a good time. We get the last provisions in Colón and then take a swim in the pouring rain. That evening we want to make hamburgers, but when I open the packet I see a dirty white mess. The packet shows me that these should be chicken burgers, but what is this mash? I throw it in a pan and cook it. It's not that bad once it's covered in bread, cheese and a lot of ketchup.

It's *Guppy*'s turn to go through the canal tomorrow and I'm busy with the preparations. I cover the solar panels with cushions because the weighted lines or 'monkey fists' don't always land where they should. I lash the tyre fenders to *Guppy*'s sides, fill the water tank and do the dishes. I then mess up my tidy galley by baking cookies with Jillian. Tomorrow there'll be six people on board *Guppy* and I need to be able to offer them something to eat.

Colón–Panama Canal, Panama: 43 nautical miles

DAY 1: *10 April*

I'm busy with the final preparations until noon, and at 13.00 we untie our lines and *Guppy* makes for the Flats where I bring her alongside the anchored *R Sea Kat*. While we are waiting, I decide to do something useful and dive overboard with a putty-knife to scrape the barnacles off the propellers, as this makes a big difference in speed.

The pilot, Francisco, looks at me in amazement when I tell him that I'm *Guppy*'s captain, and shakes my hand. He gives me a thoughtful look and then continues to explain how I have to take *Guppy* through the busy shipping traffic to reach the first locks in the canal.

Just before we get to the first three locks that will lift *Guppy* 27 metres to the level of the Gatun Lake, I greet an Australian sailor whose yacht is going to be tied to *Guppy* when we slowly move together into the first lock.

'Did you see the crocodile on the bank?' the Australian asks me. 'It just slithered back into the water.'

'No. What a pity!'

Now I really must pay attention. Not to the crocodiles, but to the weighted heaving lines that they'll be throwing across from the sides of the lock. The line-handlers on either side of the yachts need to tie these ropes and keep them taut while the water level rises. It all goes well and isn't as complicated as some nervous yachties have told me it would be. It's just a little bigger than the hundreds of locks I've passed through in the Netherlands. Once past the locks we enter Gatun Lake, which is surrounded by tropical rainforest. Here I have to moor *Guppy* to a big doughnut-shaped mooring for the night. A little later, the Australians and Mike and Deana, who come through the locks a couple of hours later, tie up next to *Guppy*. I cook pancakes for the whole crew and play my guitar. We exchange beers and swap notes with our neighbours about our experiences.

Guppy is overcrowded, and Jillian and I decide to sleep under the stars on the suspended net on Mike and Deana's catamaran. All the comfortable places on *Guppy* have been taken by the crew. At five in the morning, we're woken up by the calls of howler monkeys from the jungle bordering the lake. It's fascinating. One monkey starts howling and it sets off a wave of howls that reverberate through the jungle.

An hour later, a new pilot boards. He urges me to hurry so that I can reach the Miraflores Locks by midday. Mike and Deana are sailing close by. We cross the Gatun Lake playing loud music. It's hot and very tempting to have a water fight. We end up sailing close enough to be able to throw buckets of water at each other!

Before we know it, we've reached the final locks and our journey through the Panama Canal is almost done. The descent through the last locks goes smoothly, but now the sun makes way for a downpour. My entire crew flees below deck so that I have to motor to the anchorage and drop the anchor on my own. Sailing with a crew is complicated, as you have to take each one of them into account and need to explain everything all the time. It's a huge mess on *Guppy* and everyone is tripping over each other, but it's been fun, too. Tonight we're all looking forward to a barbecue that's being given by a Dutch project developer for us and the crew of some of the other yachts anchored off the coast of Panama City. It appears that he and his family live in a beautiful house in a rich suburb of the city. Towards the end of the party, one of the host's friends gives me money to pay for the journey through the canal. Totally surprised, I thank him for his generosity. I say goodbye to my line-handlers and am kindly taken back to *Guppy* by car.

Panama

In the evening, Jillian and I go to the Shakira concert. Not that we're such fans of hers, but we've been listening to the sound-check from a distance all day and the teenagers on *Rhythm* have asked us to come along. It's good fun, even though we can't hear each other speak for all the noise, and we eventually motor back to *Guppy* in the dinghy at two in the morning. Now to catch a few hours of sleep before Jillian flies back to New York tomorrow morning.

I plan to sail to Las Perlas the day after tomorrow. The Minicat, my small inflatable catamaran, needs to be stowed and I need to buy a new cushion for the cockpit. The old one has sadly fallen apart, and it's not much fun sitting on salt-encrusted wood for days on end. After folding away the Minicat, I accompany Deana to the shopping mall. It's not easy to find a suitable cushion, but we succeed in the end. I spend the rest of the day tidying up. The six crew members have made a mess of *Guppy* and it takes some time getting her shipshape again.

Once I've completed all my chores, I visit *Salamander*, a boat on the other side of the pier. One of the crew, Hilary, turns 19 today. It's a great party, but at one in the morning I decide to go back to *Guppy*. I'm on my way back when I bump my injured toe really badly at the dinghy dock. I'm tired and dive into my bunk, bleeding toe and all.

Panama–Las Perlas: 50 nautical miles

DAY 1: *16 April*

At 07.00, I'm on the bow doing my morning exercise, raising the 30-metre anchor chain that has kept *Guppy* in her place for the past few days. *R Sea Kat* is right behind me and together we leave this big city, the dirty anchorage and the blanket of heat and smog that hangs over it. It's cloudy and it remains that way. We don't get to see the sun, but we do see plenty of marine life. After an hour's sailing, I spot a whale. I call Mike on the VHF and shout: 'I saw a whale!'

A few hours later a ray jumps in front of the bow, then a shark passes by, and a little later some dolphins jump high out of the water. Each time I alert Mike, who's sailing a few miles behind me, but besides some sedate dolphins, they don't see much. After a tricky entry into Las Perlas, we anchor in front of these islands.

Las Perlas

It's not really pretty here, and there are rocks jutting out of the water as the water ebbs. The difference between low and high tide is enormous compared with the Caribbean end of the Panama Canal. I show Mike the photographs I took of the animals I spotted. He and Deana had been asking themselves 'What kind of crack is this girl smoking?', but now they believe me. Ha, ha! I make popcorn, something that I've almost perfected and doesn't come out black anymore. But I still manage to put in too much corn, with the result that the lid flies off the pot and popcorn shoots through the entire boat. Mike has taken care of my injured toe and it's less painful. It might be sensible to wear shoes from now on.

I wake up with a shock. Loud, cheerful music is coming through *Guppy*'s hull. I bounce out of bed and hit the low ceiling over my bunk. It sounds like Mike and Deana are awake … It's a beautiful day and I quickly jump into some clothes. The sun is shining, there's a little wind and, after enjoying some of Deana's delicious banana bread, we set sail for Bahia Sel Telmar some 20 miles further on. I navigate *Guppy* through the many sharp rocks under full sail. The charts are incomplete and I need to stay focused. After an hour, the wind drops and the speed falls to a miserable 1.8 knots. There's a little teasing breeze from time to time, but too much current to make any headway. Damn! I continue to knock my toe and it hurts like hell, but not enough for me to put on shoes. The sails are flapping around and my toe is throbbing. It has taken the whole day to cover 20 miles and we still have a few hours to go … In the meantime, *R Sea Kat* has had radio contact with *Rhythm*, who we've been trying to reach for some time. They are near Isla Contadora and may be coming this way tomorrow or the day after.

We finally get to the bay of Isla del Rey, one of the Las Perlas Islands, at about five o'clock. It has a well-protected anchorage in front of an estuary with high cliffs, and it's very green. I tie up alongside *R Sea Kat*, which spares me the sweaty task of heaving up the anchor again tomorrow. *R Sea Kat* has an electric anchor winch that raises the anchor in a few minutes. I was planning to give *Guppy*'s hull a good scrub, but change my mind when I feel the cold current and see all the jellyfish floating about.

We've used the engines quite a bit the past few days and decide to top up our tanks at a fishing village called La Esmerelda further down the bay. We take a chance and carry the jerry cans with us in the dinghy. Mike speaks a little Spanish and is able to explain what we're looking for. We follow two locals through the narrow, fishy-smelling streets. Children follow us at a distance, and curious eyes peer at us from everywhere. We're taken to a shed with two rusty diesel tanks. We drag the full jerry cans to the beach in a cloud of flies. Mission accomplished. Now that was an interesting way of refuelling.

I'm not feeling all that fit today; I don't know why. I try to remain cheerful and I'm fairly successful. It's high tide and we explore the river where we're anchored in the dinghy. The surroundings are beautiful, but the water is brackish with more mud than water. It soon becomes too shallow and we decide to go back to our boats. Dinner is a lively event, but I go to bed early.

Las Perlas–Galápagos: 900 nautical miles

DAY 1: *19 April*

At 09.00 we let our lines go and *R Sea Kat* and *Guppy* are ready to race in the direction of the Galápagos Islands. There's little wind and it will probably stay that way in the coming days. With the code zero, mainsail and mizzen up, *Guppy* is running at about 4 knots. The forecast for the next eight days doesn't look any better, and I don't really feel like making the crossing without wind. *R Sea Kat* thinks the same, but there's nothing we can do about it. Even the dolphins and jumping rays can't cheer me up. Ah well, it's all part of the deal. We try to make radio contact with *Rhythm* and by the end of the day we manage to get hold of them. They are 50 miles behind us and are running at only 2.5 knots. The wind eventually falls away entirely and it's our lot to float around in the ocean.

I was just getting into my rhythm again, and I'm disappointed about this calm. Towards sunset, a pod of dolphins swims by to cheer me up. They dive under *Guppy* and swim close to the bow. They're playing with the boat and jump right out of the water. I sit and watch this game for more than an hour. This is the longest dolphins have been alongside *Guppy* and given such a performance.

The wind has now skedaddled entirely, and I take down the code zero while the most beautiful sunset banishes my bad mood. It's like a painting, with a riot of red, yellow, purple, orange and pink tints all trying to outdo each other.

DAY 2: *20 April*

An unexpected fresh wind springs up in the middle of the night and *Guppy* manages to gather speed to 7 knots so that we cover 140 miles in 24 hours. I sail past Punta Mala where there's a great deal of cargo traffic, which doesn't allow for any sleep.

In the morning, the wind dies completely. I start the engine and try hoisting the code zero. Last night I had dropped this sail and secured it to the deck. Just as I'm loosening it this morning, a last blast of wind comes up, and before I know what's happening the whole code zero is blown overboard. Fortunately, I still have it tied to a sheet and now try to get the sail back on deck with all my might, which isn't easy. The water has made the sail very heavy, and the momentum of the boat and the rising wind don't make it any easier. It means I have to stop the boat and use the winch to haul the sail back on board. Half an hour later, it's done and I return to the cockpit. The code zero is up again and I'm thinking: Great move, Laura. Good start to the day!

It's going to be a very hot day with little wind and I try to stay cool by throwing buckets of water over myself. Towards the afternoon, I see two sharks swim by, but no dolphins today.

The sun sets and it finally cools down to more human temperatures. I'm re-reading Tania Aebi's book *Maiden Voyage* for the umpteenth time. I can't tell you how often I've read this book, but it continues to thrill me. When my stomach begins to grumble, I heat up some of yesterday's leftover macaroni and enjoy the sunset. With a bit of luck we should see the Galápagos Islands in eight days' time. When we get to Santa Cruz, I want to pay a visit to the Sea Shepherd Conservation

Society, which I support. Sea Shepherd helps all forms of marine life. On Galápagos there are protected tortoises that are 150 years old. That's exactly 10 times my age … I can't wait!

DAY 3: 21 April

In contrast to yesterday, there's totally no wind tonight and *Guppy* slowly glides across the moonlit sea. Thanks to the calm, I'm able to have a good night's sleep. Towards morning there's a gentle breeze and the speed moves up to 3 knots. Just then I feel an enormous bump! During the day I sometimes see whole trees floating by and that's the first thing I think of. Shocked into action, I hang over the bow to see if *Guppy* has any damage. So far as I can see there is no visible damage. Fortunately, we were only going at a speed of 3 knots. Slowly but surely the breeze freshens and *Guppy* is in her element again. Luckily, there's some welcome cloud coverage and I no longer have the feeling that I'm being cooked alive.

I amuse myself by reading, adjusting the course and looking out over the ever-undulating blue ocean. At noon, I manage to contact *Rhythm* via the SSB. For some reason or other they can hear *R Sea Kat*, but not me. Well, at least I know that they're about 40 miles behind me and should be within VHF radio contact within two days.

Later, the wind dies again and I'm treated to some rain. It starts as a drizzle but soon comes pouring down. After five minutes, there's 10 centimetres of rain in the bucket that I used to throw water over myself yesterday. I make myself some popcorn and carry on reading *Maiden Voyage*.

After an hour it grows lighter and I'm on the other side of the rain front. Then the sun comes out. The wind has shifted and there's now a headwind. With full sail, *Guppy* is running at 4 knots but not entirely in the right direction.

The sun is setting again and I'm sitting on deck looking out at the infinite blue mass all around *Guppy*. The sea remains a mystery. It has a huge attraction for me, but that appeal is tinged with fear. You have to understand its infinite moods and make the best of the circumstances. The sea can change from being calm and gentle to a monster that will devour you from one moment to the next! However, the odds of being hurt in a car accident are far greater, as I came to realise on Bonaire.

As the sun slowly sinks on the horizon, I'm staring ahead and thinking of home where everyone is fast asleep. I think of all the places I've been and the places yet to come. I'm curious about the Galápagos and look forward to crossing the Equator. I'll be in the Southern Hemisphere again; the hemisphere in which I was born, learnt to walk and spent my first years at sea.

DAY 4: *22 April*

After bobbing around the whole night, there's some wind now. Thanks to another calm night, I've again been able to sleep well. There's always someone on watch on *R Sea Kat*, floating a few miles behind me. Although my radar always detects anything first, I'm also able to respond to a shout on the VHF. I switch the radar alarm to a 300-degree angle so that it doesn't pick up *R Sea Kat* and give a false alarm. That gives me some rest and I have one of the best nights ever at sea.

Early in the morning I hear a loud hoot. Alarmed, I sprint on deck to see *R Sea Kat* at a distance of 20 metres from me and receive a cheerful 'good morning'. Half asleep and sitting in the cabin entrance, I decide to have something to eat. After a little discussion with myself, my choice falls on a peanut butter sandwich. I've just finished reading *Maiden Voyage* again and select a new book.

At 08.00, *R Sea Kat* and I try to reach *Rhythm* on the SSB. Just like yesterday, they can't hear me on this frequency. They're still 40 miles behind us and we don't think they'll be able to catch up with us anymore. I chat to the crew of another ship, the *Connect 4,* for a while, and listen to some of the other conversations on the net. In the meantime, the wind comes and goes and we alternate between motoring and sailing on the wind. Mike tells me over the radio how far we've come and how far we still have to go. I've stopped making any calculations and notice that it no longer interests me that much. Up until the San Blas Islands, I'd calculate the distances four times a day during a crossing. I just don't do it anymore; just like the contact with family and friends in far-off places is also beginning to fade. I do get emails and text messages from time to time, but I really only communicate with Dad, and increasingly with my mum who's slowly beginning to understand my dream a little better. There's more empathy from her side, although she does let me know in her texts that she worries about me.

I realise how lucky I am to have the parents I have. They may not be average parents, and they are too different to be able to live together, but they do have one thing in common: they both love me and show it. My mum a little later in my life than my dad, but then she didn't see me grow up and we had little contact. I have the support of both of them when it comes to realising my dream. Without them, and especially without Dad's support, I would never have been able to do this voyage.

DAY 5: *23 April*

The sun and Mike shouting over the VHF wake me up and shake me out of my dream world and back to reality. I go up on deck and take in my little world: yep, I'm at sea, *R Sea Kat* is behind me and there's wind. Wait a minute — did I say 'wind'? At last! I switch off the engine and make myself a peanut butter sandwich, for a change. The sun rises and the wind fills *Guppy*'s sails.

Mike calls me on the VHF: 'Hey, there's a big rain cloud hovering close by. Have you noticed?'

Still a bit sleepy I answer: 'Uh, no.'

'It's carrying a lot of rain,' Mike warns.

'Uh, yep.'

'It's going to miss me, but I think you're going to be hit,' he adds.

'Oh, yes?'

Only then do I look up.

'Oh, shit!'

A threatening black cloud is moving towards *Guppy*. I study the dark sky and figure that it probably carries more rain than wind, but one thing is sure: it's coming straight our way. I put up the sprayhood, throw the books and cushions inside and grab the shampoo. Here comes the rain … hard rain, a downpour. I wash my hair and fill eight two-litre bottles and a bucket with freshwater. Before the rain came I'd been burnt by the sun, and now it's cooled down beautifully. I wait until the shower is over in the comfort of the cabin. It slowly clears and I see *R Sea Kat* reappear on the horizon. There's some wind and we are moving again. The rain has invigorated me and cheered me up. I put on some music and start to make some food. When I go on deck again with a saucepan that I set to dry, I'm swinging to the sound of the music when I spot some dolphins. Now I'm really happy and move to the bow to watch them for a while. In the meantime, the spaghetti has boiled over and my galley is once again a mess …

I bring my spaghetti à la Laura up on deck and watch the dolphins. It looks like I'm getting a private performance with all the special stunts they're doing for me. After about half an hour, the show is over and they disappear into the dark. I'm sailing into the night with a big smile on my face and listening to loud music. I would certainly welcome more days like today!

DAY 6: *24 April*

It's 02.00 in the middle of the night and I'm cooking pancakes. I woke up craving pancakes and just couldn't sleep. Anyway, it's far too hot to cook once the sun is up. I eat two and crawl back into my bunk with a satisfied feeling. I'll have the rest of the pancakes for breakfast. A good beam wind continues to fill *Guppy*'s sails. I'm expecting to cross the Equator sometime between tomorrow night and the day after tomorrow. It's good seafaring practice to make an offer to Neptune on this occasion. All sorts of suggestions came in via the SSB; a catch of fish, rum, bananas, a pair of goggles … Nothing seems to be too weird to appease Neptune, the god of the sea.

DAY 7: *25 April*

Another 50 miles and I'll leave the Northern Hemisphere behind me. This part of the ocean is a place of either calms or heavy storms, but I've had more than 24 hours of good wind. The excitement mounts as I expect to cross the Equator at about 22.00 — that's if I can find it in the dark! From the Equator, the distance to the Galápagos is about 80 miles and I hope to be there before dark tomorrow.

Late in the afternoon, *R Sea Kat* (who's now sailing a few miles ahead of me) and I see another yacht, *Double Diamond*, that we'd met earlier in Panama. The three of us set off for the Equator together. My voyage has been really enjoyable so far. I've had more wind than I expected and no rough seas, but there's a very long 3-metre swell and *Guppy* is bobbing over it like a rubber duck.

DAY 8: *26 April*

I've killed two birds with one stone: I've managed to find the Equator *and* the Galápagos Islands! It's dark at the Equator, but the moment I reach it the sky is lit by lightning and Neptune rises above the sea to admire *Guppy* ... I open my eyes, but there's just the darkness, no flashes of light and no Neptune. I step out of my dream to check my position. We're still 20 miles away from the magical latitude.

R Sea Kat, *Double Diamond* and *Guppy* pass the Equator with a blast of music at 21.00. Having heard that Neptune has a weakness for pancakes, I've made an offering of a special pancake with a drawing of *Guppy* on it. Crossing the Equator feels just like New Year's Eve. Yes, I've reached another milestone. After the celebrations, I decide to go to sleep. *Double Diamond* and *R Sea Kat* promise to look out for me. When I wake up an hour later, *Double Diamond* has disappeared from sight and I'm alone with *R Sea Kat*.

After a few more catnaps, we reach the island of Santa Cruz in the morning. There's a lot of wind and we race to our destination over the last few miles towards land. The anchorage is busy; not only with yachts, but big motor boats, too. The anchorage appears to be a bad one and the anchor doesn't hold. So I have to heave the 30 metres of chain back up on board. While I'm busy doing this, two men appear on board and tell me that I need help. Help? I flip and tell them to get off my boat immediately. *R Sea Kat*, who's watching everything from a distance, phones me to let me know that they are keeping an eye on them. The two men appear to be from Immigration. OK, well, now that they're here, they can raise the anchor if they really want to. After 3 metres, they decide it's too heavy and let all 60 metres of anchor chain rattle into the water ... I'm livid and let them heave the chain up themselves. I then sail *Guppy* to another spot to check if it's any better. Fortunately, the anchor is holding now. The men from Immigration leave with the instruction that I need to clear in at their office soon. A little later, I accompany Mike and Deana to do just that. Next we bump into Gordon and Joy from *Promise*. It's great to see them.

Galápagos

Although it's incredibly hot, the water temperature is really cold for the Equator. This is due to the cold Humboldt Current that sweeps up the length of South America.

Sea lions are lying all over the dinghy jetty, and the only way to get ashore is to step over them. They don't like that, and the first time I try to reach land I'm unable to pass them. They grunt and threaten me because they see me as an intruder in their territory, but I eventually succeed. At Customs, they tell me that they first need to see my fumigation form. When I ask them why it's called 'fumigation', they explain that in the past ships arriving would be smoked out and the crew weren't permitted on board for two days. They assure me that *Guppy* doesn't need to be fumigated in this way, and a little later I take a taxi to the village and ask for directions to the office where I can drop off this form. But it's not as easy as that … First an official needs to come on board to inspect *Guppy* for vermin and I'm warned that any fresh food that's found will be confiscated. Once on board, I have 10 minutes to eat my last apple. A kind of paste is smeared into all the nooks and crannies to kill any vermin that may still be present. I can now pick up the form that says that *Guppy* has been fumigated and is free of vermin and contagious diseases. The following morning I'm back at the Customs Office for my clearance stamp. You do, of course, need to pay for the stamp, the fumigation papers and the time spent on the island. You have a choice of 10 or 20 days. Ten days should do, and I also pay for my entry to the Galápagos National Park.

The animal world on the islands is very special; there are sea lions everywhere, enormous iguanas and giant tortoises that are world famous. There's a heavy swell in the bay and at night the wind drops, which causes *Guppy* to roll heavily. It's so bad that I'm thrown from one side of the bunk to the other. Just when I was hoping to have an uninterrupted night's rest! I honestly managed to sleep better out at sea. In the morning, I wake up covered in bruises. As always, it feels strange to break my wonderful rhythm at sea for the busy life on land.

I walk to the Charles Darwin Centre with Mike and Deana. We see many giant tortoises, including George who is more than a hundred years old and is the last of its kind. The name 'giant tortoise' is certainly no exaggeration, because George weighs 300 kilos. The Charles Darwin Centre has posted a reward of $10,000 for anyone who can find a female Pinta Tortoise, in an attempt to save this species.

When the sun is high in the sky, we decide to go surfing. But where? We hear that Tortuga Beach is a good spot, so Mike fetches his surfboard from the boat and we get there after a walk of about half an hour. It's my first attempt at surfing. Mike says I'm a natural when I manage to stay on the board the first time I try it. Probably a bit of beginner's luck and the fact that the waves aren't that high. But I'm keen to learn, and continue surfing until it gets dark. On our way back, I decide to practise this more often; it's a fantastic sport.

I'm woken up by Mike on the VHF. He tells me to have a look over the side of the boat ... There are dozens of small black-tip sharks swimming around *Guppy*. Stunning to see how they're looking for their prey with their gliding movements. This place really has the most amazing animal life. I walk across Santa Cruz together with Mike and Deana to a place where there are more giant tortoises. They must be the slowest animals on earth! Unfortunately, it's all very touristy and a bit disappointing. They really try to make money out of everything. The 'wild' tortoises are not even in their natural environment, and there are at least 40 people around them with cameras. We decide to leave.

In the afternoon, we meet people from Sea Shepherd who run all sorts of conservation projects here. They protect the tortoises and give presentations at schools. They teach children to leave the tortoises alone and to handle nature with respect. They patrol the coast in boats to prevent illegal fishing, and have a special programme to protect the different shark species in these waters.

Guppy is still rolling like mad at her anchorage, while I go on as many tours as possible and make new discoveries every day. I visit a crystal-clear lake that lies between some cliffs on the island together with Mike, Deana, Gordon and Joy. You can jump into it from a height of about 10 metres which, naturally, I can't resist for long. Great fun, but very painful if you make a bad landing.

I do the half-hour walk to the beach to surf nearly every day, and I'm picking it up fast. Diving around the Galápagos Islands is also very special. I join a group to dive at Gordon Rocks. While swimming through the Galápagos underwater world, we see mantas, many colourful fish, different sharks and even a group of hammerheads! We are hoping to see a whale shark that was spotted here yesterday, but this giant eludes us. All the sharks we've seen more than compensate for this, though. The water down here is very cold and, despite wearing a 7-millimetre-thick wetsuit, I'm almost frozen when I get back on board. Even with the outside temperature being 37 degrees, it takes me two hours to warm up again.

It's 3 May today — exactly a year since *Guppy* was lowered into the water and I sailed the first few metres. A year later, she's covered more than 8000 nautical miles and is lying off the Galápagos Islands. This has to be celebrated! I spend the whole day making her spic and span. Not only inside, but also the body and hull. Armed with goggles, snorkel and putty-knife, I spend hours under the boat to clear the hull of algae and crustaceans. It's hard work, but it's got to be done every month because they grow at such a rapid rate in these tropical waters.

The rest of the day I spend repairing small things that have broken along the way and checking that all the systems on board are in good running order. The diesel tank is full again and I have enough food. I just need to top up the water and then *Guppy* will be ready for the 3000-mile crossing to the Marquesas Islands. I'll stay here for a few more days, but certainly not for the wonderful anchorage. *Guppy* is still rolling terribly and life on board is not much fun in this bay.

In the morning, another island visitor of about my age and I plan to go on shore to go to the fruit market, do some washing and then visit Isla Isabella. It's an island 40 miles further up, which you can't visit in your own boat without a special permit. I don't have a permit, of course, so we are to be taken there by a local fisherman. It's apparently very beautiful, not that touristy and it has penguins … on the Equator? I have to see this, of course.

The fruit market is nothing special and is crawling with vermin. I buy some apples and pears and then fetch my dirty washing. My washing hasn't seen any soap since Panama and I've run out of clean clothes. I walk to the laundrette with a bulging bag of sheets and clothes. I manage to fill the only washing machine and do the remaining half by hand. Back on *Guppy* everything is soon dry, thanks to the heat.

I pack my bag and we go to the boat that's going to take us to Isla Isabella. It's about two hours' sailing over a choppy sea. We moor off the village of Isabella, which consists of a few sand roads, some houses and two small hostels. We bump into the *Rhythm* crew who are here on a three-day tour and this is their last island. They are staying for two nights just like us, and have booked a hotel.

'That's great. May we put our bags in your rooms?' we ask them.

'Sure, where is your hotel?' they ask.

'We're sleeping on the beach,' we say and point out the sleeping bags that are tied to our bags.

We hire surfboards and surf until the sun goes down.

Sleeping on the beach is less successful. What a lot of mosquitoes! After an hour we pick up our sleeping bags and run off screaming to look for a better spot. We end up sleeping at the end of a long jetty, but the tide rises during the night and we are woken by the splash of a wave in our faces. We go to the other side of the jetty and fall asleep to the soothing sound of waves. The first thing I see when I wake up and open one eye is a crab right in front of my nose. Argh! We are surrounded by an army of big red crabs! We wake up instantly, but once we've chased the crabs off our sleeping bags and gear, the world looks a little better and we can laugh about it.

We go surfing, catch a ride into the mountains and spend a lot of time in the harbour where there are dozens of sea lions and penguins swimming around. After two wonderful but tiring days, we go back to Puerto Ayora in another fishing boat.

I'm glad to be back and to see *Guppy* again. I borrow some jerry cans and, together with Mike, fetch water to fill up my tanks. We return the jerry cans and, while Mike removes the refuse, I take a shower on shore near the laundry. I feel reborn as I step back on *Guppy*. I'm so exhausted that I'm dizzy and can't take another step... I fall into a deep sleep within minutes while *Guppy* continues to dance the salsa in the swell.

I feel much better after I wake up and enjoy a breakfast of French toast and maple syrup. A boat comes alongside *Guppy*. It's the director of Sea Shepherd, Alex, who gives me two huge bunches of green bananas. I give him a tour of *Guppy*, and then he motors back to shore in his boat after wishing me a good voyage.

In the meantime, Mike is cleaning his hull and I jump in the water to help him. When we've finished this chore two hours later, I make banana pancakes on *R Sea Kat* for the last time. We're sad as our paths are going to part tomorrow. I'll continue going west, while they'll go north towards Alaska. Mike and Deana are probably the best sailing friends I've made and the most special.

As always, I'm longing to leave the day before my departure. *Guppy* and I are yearning for the Marquesas and we're ready to go. Hopefully the winds will be favourable this time. A few hours before a long ocean crossing like this, I'm always a bit nervous. Am I sure I haven't forgotten something? Do I have enough food, liquids, etc, on board? I'm always worried that I've forgotten something, but as soon as I've sailed off, everything usually feels fine and I sail to meet the ocean with a big smile. Oh yes, now I know what I forgot ... my blog! The photographs! I download the last of my photos onto my site and write a blog at the internet café. I give one of the banana bunches that I received from Alex to *R Sea Kat* and we raise our anchors together.

Galápagos–Hiva Oa: 3000 nautical miles

DAY 1: *8 May*

The high seas roll over *Guppy*'s bow; *R Sea Kat* hoots one last time and our ways part. The waves are crashing over the deck while I hoist the mainsail. My course is close to the wind and *Guppy* is sailing well heeled over. It's cloudy, and wave after wave lands in the cockpit, but *Guppy* is sailing at a good 7 knots. I wipe away a last tear as *R Sea Kat* and Santa Cruz disappear from sight. After two hours of good sailing the wind improves, but the speed drops to 2 knots. There must be an enormous tidal current to cause this. Slowly the last island, Isabella, disappears and I have only ocean around me.

At 06.00, I check the SSB radio. I hear *R Sea Kat* faintly, but unfortunately they can't hear me. I listen to some of the chatting on the SSB while eating the last piece of banana bread that Deana gave me the day before our departure. *Discovery* appears to be 30 miles away and *Rhythm* is leaving either today or tomorrow. I'm feeling well. *Guppy* is sailing at more than 6 knots and is a lot steadier in the water than she was at anchor in Academy Bay.

I've said hello and goodbye for the umpteenth time; hoisted the sails to go to the next set of unknown tropical islands, but for the first time it feels really good. The dip that I usually experience on the first day after my farewells doesn't come this time. Instead, I'm standing on the aft deck holding on to the rigging and enjoying the ocean, while worshipping the sun and letting a thousand thoughts run through my mind. I love daydreaming while I look out over the sea. How will this trip go? How many days will it take? How much wind will I have and how will I feel? What do the Marquesas look like? So many questions and so much to dream about. Before I know it, the sun is setting again. I cook spaghetti and wait for 18.00 to switch on the SSB and, hopefully, make contact with *R Sea Kat* or one of the other yachts.

DAY 2: *9 May*

I've just finished throwing some flying fish and squid off the deck when I come eye to eye with a bird. It's about 10 centimetres from my nose, perched on the sprayhood and swinging to the movement of the waves. When I turn around, I see that its mate has landed on the solar panel rack. I notice a loose cord and decide to fix it before I give them a sermon.

While the birds listen patiently to me, I tell them that they're welcome so long as they do their business off my boat and don't come inside to distract me. They look at me quizzically and I decide to drop the speech.

The birds stay where they are and I go and read a book in the cockpit. There's more wind today and it's cloudy. Wave after wave lands in the cockpit. I'm just sitting on the toilet and holding on when an enormous wave turns *Guppy* into a swimming pool. Despite the sprayhood, saltwater flows halfway through the cabin. I mop up as much as possible and then take a seat in the companionway. The cockpit is wet and so are my cushions, which, fortunately, weren't swept overboard. Grrr! Bloody wave!

The sun slowly sinks into the sea and the day makes way for the night. I've made macaroni cheese tonight, but it doesn't taste that good to me today and I have to force myself to eat some. The world around me is tinted orange, red, purple, inky blue and then, finally, black. I pick up my sleeping rhythm again while *Guppy* gallops on faithfully.

DAY 3: *10 May*

I'm reading a book in the cockpit while a heavy, long swell rolls under *Guppy*. That's until a wave breaks over *Guppy* and soaks both me and my book … I curse the wave and continue reading my soaked book. It's my third day at sea and it already feels so familiar. It was great being on Galápagos and Santa Cruz, but I'm certainly not missing the anchorage there. Back at sea, I'm slowly catching up on my sleep, but I do need to get up every hour to check that *Guppy* is going in the right direction and that nothing else has gone wrong. I've got used to that. Anyway, I now dive into my bunk at eight in the evening so that I get all the rest I need. In this way I wake at daybreak and am totally refreshed.

Another 2480 miles to go, which means that I have the first 500 behind me. Up until now, everything is going well and I'm feeling fine. The wind has been very kind to me, too. Life at sea is wonderfully simple. The days come and go in more or less the same way, every day. In the morning, I'm in contact with other ships via the SSB, and the rest of the day I'm either reading, checking the course, trimming the sails, getting rid of the flying fish and squid that come on deck, or eating bananas.

Unfortunately, there were two stowaways in my bunch of bananas; two huge cockroaches that immediately got a burial at sea from me. I show a little more mercy to another stowaway, a cute little lizard that is welcome to stay on board for a few more thousand miles.

DAY 4: *11 May*

At last I hear about *Rhythm*'s location via the SSB. They are 420 miles behind me. They left two days later with the notion that they might catch up with me, but *Guppy* is a lot faster than they think. With the much bigger *Rhythm* behind me, it's a challenge to get *Guppy* to sail even faster. There's a wonderful breeze and, according to the chart, the current is adding half a knot to our speed which rarely drops below 7.5 knots and usually sits at about 8 knots, while *Rhythm* is sailing at 7 knots.

I haven't passed any ships or seen a dolphin, but the number of stranded flying fish and squid on *Guppy* increases daily. When I get up in the morning, the deck sometimes looks like a marine cemetery! My feathered passengers, who sailed with me for two days, left today. They had enjoyed a good rest and were ready for the next stage of their journey to some unknown destination. Sea birds seem to be constantly in search of fish and skim over the waves for days, diving into the sea and then flying on over the tops of waves, dipping their wings, only to rise with the next wave. Well, now I'm alone again. My resident lizard has gone into hiding … I'm enjoying the lovely weather; a strong beam wind and a clear blue sky with the odd, lost puff of cloud. If it stays this way, I don't need to see any land on the horizon for a while.

After the busy life and bad nights at anchor off Santa Cruz, I'm now fully recovered and ready to get back into my schoolwork. For some reason or other, this day goes by faster than yesterday. I read, gaze at the water, cook, write my blog, trim the sails, and before I know it another day has gone. The sun sinks into the sea, the air cools down and the night moves in like a dark blanket. I switch on the radar, creep into my bed on the low side, and gently sway into dreamland.

DAY 5: *12 May*

The blanket of the night disappears over the horizon and a new day breaks. *Squeak, crackle, pop* … The daily hour for sailors on the SSB radio has begun, and I try to interpret some of the crackly English that comes from the black box in front of me. Sometimes the sound is clear; at other times, not that good. One boat is easier to follow than the next, and when you can't get hold of one particular boat, the conversation continues via one or two other boats. It's the only way of finding out the locations of the different yachts in the ocean. The coordinates that are passed on by various people on the SSB make it clear to me that I'm not the only one sailing in the Pacific.

When I hear a crackly 'Guppy, Guppy, do you copy?' I fly upright, bump my head on the low ceiling above my bunk and grab the microphone. They've heard from someone that I'm somewhere on this ocean. Unfortunately, I have no luck reaching *R Sea Kat* or *Rhythm*, but it's great to hear about other yachts that are, as yet, unknown to me. I think the SSB radio is a fantastic communication system.

In the meantime, *Guppy* is flying along at a speed of 8 knots. She really has ants in her pants, just like the wind. I check my position: another 2140 miles to go. Wow, we're really moving! I pick a couple of bananas from my big bunch at the back and try to avoid the waves. I'm eating myself silly on bananas as they are all ripe at the same time. My gaze wanders across the deck and I discover a record number of flying fish. There must be at least 20 of them. For some strange reason they are all in the middle and on the port side. It could be that there is less water washing over the windward side. I pick them up, one by one, and throw the slimy fish back in the water, along with some rotten bananas and mildewed bread. Well, that was my contribution to all those hungry sea creatures, and now I'm going to feed myself some scrambled eggs this morning.

The day is spent reading, gazing at the indomitable sea and fighting off another three cockroaches that have suddenly crawled out of the bunch of bananas. Suddenly it's evening. The wind is coming from the port quarter, the speed is dropping and the sails are beginning to droop a little. Damn! I prefer a good beam wind. When I check the distance covered in the past 24 hours, I see that we have covered 194 nautical miles. An absolute record for *Guppy*. You rock, *Guppy*! You can do it, I love you! I haven't only established a personal record, but have also beaten my dad's record on his world voyage with *Diario* by one mile.

DAY 6: *13 May*

Despite the fact that it's Friday the 13th today, it's going to be a lovely day, right? Well, not exactly ... The stainless-steel ring to which the windpilot steering-cable pulley is attached has broken off. I manage to attach the pulley to the taff rail with some twine and get it working again. I also notice that the batteries are running low. This can't be due to my use of electricity — or can it? It takes me half a day to discover that my big 12,000-watt converter is on. I only use this converter for power tools such as the drill. I'm not sure that this is the source of the problem, but hope so.

It's a beautiful morning, the night making way for a glorious blue sky. Later, when I'm reading a book in the cockpit, I'm suddenly bored ... I gaze over the sea and talk to the wind, but as soon as the sun sets and it cools down a bit, I cheer up. I've almost finished my huge bunch of bananas. I'll have to eat the nine remaining bananas tomorrow or throw them away. There's a following wind and the waves have stopped washing into the cockpit, so I'm able to enjoy reading on deck without my pages getting wet and sticking together. The speed remains at around 7.5 knots and I'll reach the halfway mark in 450 miles.

DAY 7: *14 May*

The sea is choppy, but *Guppy* just thunders on regardless. There's hardly a cloud in the sky today. Another beautiful day passes, just reading, drawing, filming, sitting, thinking and adjusting the course. The wind is now close to the beam and I'm playing around with the spinnaker boom. After eating, I decide to take down the spinnaker boom after all. This is how it goes: ease the sheet ... heave the sheet in ... tighten the other side ... wait for the right wave ... sprint to the foredeck. Hold on! Lift the spinnaker boom. *Bang!* Shit! The genoa is flapping over the bow while the boom swings from side to side. I heave in the spinnaker sheet and the boom swings towards me. *Ouch!* My index finger turns red. I manage to get the sheet loose and quickly snap the spinnaker boom to the mast. I sprint to the stern and let go of one sheet so that

one girl, one dream

I can rapidly heave in the other. The genoa is set again. After holding my finger under the saltwater tap, the injury appears not to be serious. Good, now I can deal with the night.

DAY 8: *15 May*

I've had a bad night thanks to the damn swell and squalls which have had *Guppy* on her side, sending everything that's loose flying through the cabin.

A little while ago, I noticed that the batteries are almost flat. The converter has been on and I probably left the electrical autopilot on too long, and, yes, maybe I should have turned the plotter off during the day. The batteries really are almost flat, but fortunately the radar is still working. Tomorrow I'll switch everything off except the SSB.

I'm trying to sleep, but don't succeed. Approaching squalls keep me awake and the cold drizzle is making me shiver. I'm standing in the companionway admiring the spooky glow of the moon when an unexpected mega-wave engulfs *Guppy*. I fall backwards and manage to crawl and get up in the middle of the cabin. A pain shoots through my foot. It's always my feet and toes that take the brunt of any fall. Mike didn't give me the nickname 'Yo, Toe' for nothing! I walk to the bunk, switch on the light and inspect the damage. My whole foot is covered in blood which drips off the ends of my toes. The floor is covered, too … Wonderful! I wipe most of the blood away with a facecloth and notice that there is a deep hole in my heel. I hop to the first-aid kit and back, leaving a trail of blood. I manage to bandage my foot up and then clean up the mess. It's too painful to put my heel down and I have to stand on one leg like a flamingo. Charming on a yacht with a 6-metre swell! But once I've recovered from the shock and pain, I manage to see the funny side of it. Sailing is so nicely unpredictable, and that's what's such fun about it. That you have to do it all on your own; whether it's reaching a new harbour thousands of miles away, or in this case sorting out a hole in your foot.

It's 04.00 and I'm trying to get some sleep, without success. The pain in my foot and worrying about the flat batteries keep me awake. Let's hope it's a sunny day tomorrow so that they can charge up a bit.

Since I was very little,
I could always be
found on the water

Lanzarote

The first big ocean
crossing:
the Atlantic

Arrival in Saint Martin

Equator
crossing

Galápagos

Reception on Hiva Oa

Bora Bora

Moorea

Messy arrived one night during
a squall, and stayed with
me for several days

Darwin

Departing from Port Elizabeth

An approaching squall

The day before the storm

Chaos after
the storm

Guppy is welcomed into Saint Martin

CAPE OF GOOD HOPE
THE MOST SOUTH-WESTERN POINT
OF THE AFRICAN CONTINENT

Christmas at sea

I hear from other sailors on the SSB that the ridiculously high swells we're experiencing have been caused by a storm in the south and that it will continue for at least the next two days.

DAY 9: *16 May*

I sleep until half past seven when I'm woken by the first rays of the sun. The sun is now rising two hours later than at the start of this stage of the voyage, and is setting almost two hours later.

Hopping on one foot like a regular circus act doesn't really work for long. Because the injury is in my heel, I can get around on the toes of my injured foot and continue to use my good foot. I soon have muscle pain in my toes, but I should get over that with a bit of exercise.

Last night, I passed the halfway waypoint. Unfortunately I can't carry out a little celebration dance, but I manage to enjoy the celebratory biscuits I baked for the occasion. The swell has got even higher and longer, which makes it more tolerable, but it does make me dizzy when *Guppy* teeters on the crest of a 7-metre wave. My batteries have been charged a little by the sun, which has finally shown itself. I discover that when I switch on the plotter the radar automatically switches to standby, and uses current in this way.

Towards evening, the wind suddenly swings round, which means that I'm now running downwind. Something tells me that those dark clouds may have something to do with rain and squalls, but I set my boomed-out genoa on the windward side anyway. When I'm back in the cockpit, the wind changes direction. Well, I take the spinnaker boom down again and we sail into the night with a beam wind. Nature rewards me for passing the halfway waypoint by sending me a full moon. Together with the sunset and the clouds, it makes a beautiful picture.

DAY 10: *17 May*

After my cracker-with-jam breakfast has flown through the entire galley, I decide to boom out the genoa. The wind has shifted and it looks as though the steady trade winds are back. During the day, the high swell flattens out slowly. Little by little my awareness of time is disappearing. If I didn't write up my diary, update the blog for my website every day and chat to other sailors on the SSB, I really wouldn't know what day of the week it is or how long I've been underway. Like the fact that I'll have been on my voyage for a year in three months' time. It feels as though I've never done anything else but sail, up one wave and down the next; sleep, read, think about the future and take care of *Guppy*.

I've been thinking about which route to take. Shall I go via South Africa or through the Red Sea? Both routes have their advantages and disadvantages. The biggest disadvantage of sailing around South Africa are the Roaring Forties winds that lie just below this route. You can experience a lot of south-westerly storms down there, with high waves up to 20 metres that are whipped up by the very strong Agulhas Current travelling in the opposite direction to the wind. These storms come upon you suddenly, and you need to wait for the rare moment between them before sailing further. The distance around South Africa is only 1000 nautical miles, but progress can be slow as you sail against the prevailing winds. If I choose to do the Africa route, it will mean rushing through the Pacific in three months. I love sailing and especially long crossings, but I also like visiting new countries and meeting people.

On the other hand, the Red Sea is not much better. There's the danger of pirates, and sailing in that part of the world is not much fun. If you're sailing during the good season, you're likely to have a strong headwind for the first 600 miles, which is not much better. But I still have time to make up my mind.

My foot is healing well. I probably won't have to stand on one leg like a flamingo when I reach land in eight to nine days' time, and until then the longest distance I'll have to walk is 12 metres. For now I enjoy the simplicity and ease of a long crossing: no islands, no shallows and reefs that can wreck you. There isn't much shipping traffic either, which means that I can rely on my radar and enjoy a good sleep. Seeing that we're still a long way from the Marquesas, due west is good enough for now; I can adjust the course as we get closer. It's really relaxed sailing. Better enjoy it while it lasts, because after the Marquesas there's a minefield of islands, reefs and atolls.

DAY 11: *18 May*

There are some wind directions that I really hate. One of them is a strong headwind; the other, a little wind from astern. This time it's the wind from astern that keeps me up all night! Because *Guppy* isn't being heeled to one side, as would be the case with a beam wind, she just rolls on the ever-present swell and her sails start to slap. This means having to change course constantly and adjusting the sails to stop the *clunk-slap-bang* chorus. This only succeeds when I change the course to the extent that *Guppy* gets a broad-reach breeze, which means I'm way off-course. In the meantime, I'm enjoying the full moon and the lovely trail of phosphorescence that *Guppy* leaves in the infinite swell. The sun has begun to rise, which tells me that I've been battling with the sails all night. The wind has increased a little; just enough to stop the *clunk-slap-bang*, I hope.

I eat my cornflakes in the morning sun and hope to catch a bit of sleep. Then — *bang!* — the mizzen's sheet-pulley block that sits on the rail is suddenly hanging in the water. My temporary repairs haven't held. I hadn't used a self-locking screw and now the screw is gone. Damn! I use some twine to fasten the pulley to the eye on the rail. Just as I'm finally sleeping, the *clunk-slap-bang* chorus is back. Grr ... Stupid wind, look what you are doing to *Guppy*; you break everything!

A little later, I hear another *bang* and just see a bent shackle fly overboard. Followed by the pulley blocks from the main falling on deck. Sigh ... I find a new shackle and tighten it as much as possible with a pair of pliers. I then adjust the course some more, and that seems to help. Only problem is, we're now sailing in totally the wrong direction. After a while the wind picks up, and I can now bring *Guppy* back to her proper course without the *clunk-slap-bang* of the sails. At last, time for some sleep.

DAY 12: *19 May*

During one of my night shifts, I notice a yellow glow on the horizon. It looks a lot like the gleam of light from an island, but there isn't an island anywhere near here and I can't figure out what it is. It's too big to be a ship and, if it isn't a ship, what on earth could it be? It doesn't feature on the radar, either. I continue to watch … The glow gets bigger and the light stronger. Suddenly, a yellow ball pops up on the horizon and grows larger and brighter. Just like magic and so beautiful. How can I have mistaken the rising moon for a ship?

There are a few showers in the early hours to annoy me, but they disappear quickly as the sun rises. It's definitely cloudier than yesterday, but it's going to be a lovely day. *Guppy* is reaching at 7 knots. I have been reading less these past few days and spending more time looking around me and walking around the deck. My injured foot feels a lot better, and I'm able to stand on it a little. The clock shows that we are 11 hours behind Europe. When the sun sets here on 19 May, people in Europe will be starting their day on 20 May. Another 920 miles to the Marquesas Islands. They're approaching fast.

DAY 13: *20 May*

Because of atmospheric conditions, the daily SSB radio hour is now at 05.00 local time. This upsets my morning routine … After a bit of a chat, I hear that *Rhythm* is still 280 miles behind me. I've also been chatting to *Discovery*, who now lies 80 miles ahead of me. In the meantime, I take a look to see how many more miles we still need to cover. Neat, just 800 miles to go! I have a good chance of seeing land in five days' time and that's a weird thought.

Thankfully, I've been spared flying fish for a few days now. A good thing, as it means I don't have to scrub the deck to get rid of their sticky scales. Nothing stressful has happened and I've been sleeping well, so I'm using my extra energy to walk up and down the deck like a flamingo and trimming the sails to the best of my ability. I can now use the spinnaker boom again, and I spend hours sitting on the boom next to the mast gazing at the spray of water as *Guppy*'s bow cuts through the ocean. What an endless sense of freedom this is.

Suddenly I'm hungry and need to cook, and that's a challenging task. As soon as I put something on the kitchen counter and turn to reach for the next ingredient, I can be sure that it takes off into the air with me as its target. Gravity sucks! With this in mind, I take extra care with the handling of the spaghetti sauce. It won't be the first time that this ends up dripping down the galley wall, but all goes well this time and the meal tastes even better than usual.

In the middle of the night, I'm woken by a pot that manages to free itself from the sink and fly through the cabin before landing on the floor with a lot of noise. I leave it where it is and go back to sleep. Having forgotten all about it by the next shift, I step right into it and lose my footing!

DAY 14: *21 May*

The time difference with Europe is now big. When my parents in Europe have their dinner, I'm waking up from my last catnap. The wind is of the 'little wind from astern' variety, so I'm battling with the sails again. It's pitch dark when I try chatting on the SSB, but this morning I can't seem to get a coherent word out of it. While I'm listening to the *snap, crackle, sssst* on the radio, I unravel the bandage around my foot. It looks like it's healing well, and it might be good to let it have some fresh air. Needless to say, I bump it a little later and the wound is open again.

'Well done, Laura,' I mumble to myself and wind the bandage back on.

My mood doesn't improve when my breakfast goes flying a little later. Well, at least it keeps me busy.

I try to take no notice of the way *Guppy* is rolling, nor of the dropping wind and speed, because it's a lovely morning anyway. *Guppy* has gained another 10 miles on *Rhythm*, who is now 300 miles behind me. My mood is improving, and how could it be otherwise? There are only 700 more miles to go, the sky is blue, the sun is warm and *Guppy* is running at 5.5 knots. I spend the greater part of the day reading in the cockpit. I wash my hair with saltwater and do the dishes. In between, I gaze at the sea and think about home and the future. My thoughts are a jumble, and 10 minutes later I can't remember what I was thinking about. Life on board is timeless and everything just happens. The day ends and the night falls; the sun and moon chase each other overhead and say, 'Look at us. We're much faster than you — we get around the world in 24 hours.'

DAY 15: *22 May*

While I'm still enjoying my warm bed, the SSB radio begins to chatter. I find out nothing about *Rhythm*'s position and decide to get up. It's a beautiful morning. Not a cloud in sight, and I'm surrounded by a spectrum of blues from dark to light.

After eating a cracker with jam, I decide to grab the sextant and take some sun sights to establish my position in the time-honoured manner. This is much easier on a big ship than on my rocking horse, but practice makes perfect.

Guppy has another 500 miles to go, and if the wind cooperates a little I should be throwing my anchor into the bay at Hiva Oa in three days' time. It suddenly seems so close. I'm still wondering whether to go on shore or not. My foot wants to stay at sea so that it can rest, but the closer I get, the more I'm hearing that I-want-to-go-on-shore voice. Instead of running everywhere, I could just walk carefully, of course.

This day seems to take an eternity. I play the guitar, sit on the spinnaker boom and climb up the rigging, but when I look at the clock it's only 12.00 noon. Time is going so slowly … Towards sunset, the clouds come in from the south, as they often do. They float by threateningly, but only shed their tears on the northern horizon. The swell is still 3 to 4 metres high but very long, and *Guppy* just glides over it. What a difference from the Atlantic Ocean and the Caribbean with its tall waves and the powerful trade winds!

DAY 16: *23 May*

Fortunately, I'm able to recapture my wonderful feeling of timelessness today. I read *Dove* and then start on *Spray* by Joshua Slocum. There are clouds again today; many, many clouds of all sorts and sizes. Really cool! And I sit and gaze at them for at least two hours. You get the dark, low ones that chase ominously overhead. You also have the huge, white ones that look like giants and tower above you as they float past faster; and above them the long wispy ones. And all this against a background of clear blue sky with the sun burnishing the sea into a blazing, golden disc. Awesome!

There is more wind and *Guppy* is sailing at the great pace of 7 knots. We still have 300 miles or two days' sailing to get to Hiva Oa. Incredible! I walk around the foredeck to check that all is in order and — *whoosh* — receive an impromptu shower as a wave breaks over *Guppy*. Thank you very much, now I'm wide awake and decidedly salty.

The wind has accelerated and the waves are now high enough to wash over the foredeck, but *Guppy* simply thunders on and I can continue to play my guitar in the cockpit. The guitar sounds so cool in combination with the hiss of the waves as *Guppy* cuts through the water that I forget all about the egg I'm frying for myself. All at once I smell something … Luckily, I catch it before it burns and most of it is edible.

DAY 17: *24 May*

At 05.00, I switch on the SSB. *Snap, crackle, pop* … can't understand a word. Well, no problem, let me catch some more sleep. Mother Nature thinks otherwise, and a little later I'm unceremoniously ejected from my bunk. *Guppy* has suddenly been thrown on her side, and, instead of it getting lighter, it's now pitch dark outside. Rain and wind are breaking over *Guppy*. I furl the genoa in as fast as possible and change to manual steering now that the waves are growing in size. *Guppy* is surfing, with the wind and waves coming from a broad reach. With just the mainsail and mizzen she is picking up speed to well over the 10 knots on occasions. This is going way too fast! After a while the rain stops, but the wind and high seas continue. I change the steering back to the windvane and decide to take down the mizzen before she broaches. *Guppy* is sailing better this way, but the wind gets stronger and I'm forced to put a second reef in the mainsail. I then unfurl the genoa — still attached to the boom — a little on the windward side to improve the balance. While I'm busy, I'm being pelted by one shower after the next.

The rest of the day remains dark and rainy. I hope the weather is better tomorrow. Hiva Oa is a tall island and I've been looking forward to seeing it from a distance. Reaching the Marquesas Islands is a milestone; something I hadn't dared to dream of a year, even three months, ago. They seemed so far-off and are so near now. I'm longing to see with my own eyes whether the Pacific Islands are as idyllic as everyone has told me they are.

DAY 18: *25 May*

The squalls kindly keep me busy all night, but, just like me, they are now tired and have retired after a couple of final stunts. It's slowly growing lighter and clearing up. The shadow on the horizon is growing larger and larger, and with just 16 miles to go to the anchorage I'm getting more impatient by the mile. When I finally sight land on the horizon in between downpours, I dance for joy. I've found it! But my happiness soon changes to sadness when I consider that the longest and probably the most beautiful crossing is coming to an end.

The shadow grows and takes shape slowly. I can't believe my eyes when I see a wall of rock rising out of the ocean at the place which has been water for the past 17 days. The water gets shallower, and because of this the swell gets higher, which has *Guppy* now surfing from the wavetops down into their troughs 4 metres below. The land is approaching fast and I'm getting really nervous. *Guppy* has never approached such a tall and craggy island before. Finally the bay is in sight. On the VHF I hear that *Papillon* has already spotted me. The swell subsides as I enter the bay of Hiva Oa.

I throw out bow and stern anchors in the muddy waters of the bay, and *Guppy* lies still at last. I then inflate the dinghy and first do a lap of honour around my home, my loyal friend, my everything. She's dirty and has accumulated a lot of marine growth during the crossing. I put the covers over the sails and talk to other sailors who come by in their dinghies. It's only 19.30, but I'm dead tired. I can't get used to the fact that I can go to sleep now without being constantly alert and having to keep going on deck to check that everything is still in order.

Hiva Oa

When I wake up in the morning, I work out that *Guppy* has covered 3000 miles in 17 days and 22 hours to get to the Marquesas. Wow, it's the longest and the best crossing I've ever made! The Atlantic Ocean crossing, from the Cape Verde Islands to Saint Martin, was 'only' 2200 miles and also took me 17 days. I don't quite understand how *Guppy* did it; especially when I hear from the other boats in this bay that a number of yachts that left a few days before me still haven't arrived.

In the morning I hitch a ride to Atuona to clear in. It's a small village on a hill. As always, the Customs officers ask me several times if I've honestly sailed over all on my own, and then they stamp my documents while shaking their heads in disbelief. After buying a delicious fresh French loaf in a local shop, I walk back to *Guppy*. It's quite a distance, but after 17 days of little exercise I really feel like walking. Unfortunately, the hole in my heel still hasn't healed properly and it becomes difficult and painful to walk.

When I finally get back to *Guppy*, the local mayor suddenly appears on the dock. I receive a beautiful flower lei from him and am invited for a meal. This I gather from a mix of French, some broken English and many gestures. The food is delicious and the people are extremely friendly. They say they're sorry they weren't able to organise a big feast when I arrived, but they had no idea I would be coming. I'm actually glad it's worked out this way: when I arrive somewhere, the first things I need are rest, a shower, food and sleep. I like to be treated like everyone else.

The weather isn't really smiling on me. It has rained solidly for the past three days. That's normal here and it gives the island a beautiful and very mysterious air. The huge green mountains are almost always shrouded in a band of mist, and the peaks with scurrying clouds. According to local legend, the islands were created to house the gods. The famous Belgian folk singer Jacques Brel is buried here, as is the French painter Paul Gauguin.

Although I've just arrived, I've the feeling that I've been here for a week. We drive along the winding roads on the island with Hilary from *Salamander* and a woman from Atuona that we've met. It's really stunning, very green and mountainous. As soon as we are in the clouds, we are surrounded by pine trees; the air is rarefied and the temperatures plummet. I find it hard to believe that I'm on an island in the middle of the Pacific in this landscape. The local woman shows us the centuries-old *tiki* — sculptures, usually of faces in stone and wood. We stop at places where nothing seems to have changed in the past 400 years.

New yachts arrive every day and I get to meet new people. Everyone is amazed that I did the crossing in less than 18 days. They ask if I've been towed by a whale, and I'm immediately given the nickname 'The Flying Dutchgirl'. Except for a yacht that's 10 metres longer than *Guppy*, no one seems to have a better crossing time up until now.

Unfortunately, my speed has not prevented loads of algae, snails and other crustaceans from growing on *Guppy*'s hull. This means that I'll have to spend half the day under *Guppy*, armed with goggles and a putty-knife. I've just got into the water when I hear my name being called.

There's a woman standing on the jetty who says they have a surprise for me and that I must follow her. It's the same woman with whom I toured the island. She begs me to come. The people on the island are so friendly that you can't refuse. We walk to a big field where there's a hut with a display of food. Outside, a beautiful traditional dance is being performed. The dancers have lovely costumes and are dancing to the beat of the drums and song. They had gone ahead and prepared the welcome they had wanted to give me when I'd arrived unannounced. Now that I've recovered from my voyage, I can really enjoy their hospitality. I receive another flower lei and two necklaces made of beans. The food is delicious, and at the end of the feast I'm given some more to take home. That night I share it with the other sailors. It's a late night but a great party.

I'm woken by the sun instead of rain for a change. It's suddenly stunning weather and very hot. I see the mountains peaks appear from under the clouds and the mist slowly lifts from the palm trees. But the good weather changes quickly and we're back to normal: rain and calm. Luckily, the rain is warm here and easy to live with. It's a good day to visit all the neighbouring boats and to exchange books and movies. Cruisers do this a lot when they meet up, so that we all have something new to read when we're at sea. It means that I'm reading purely English books now. I also make an attempt to bake bread. I haven't been very successful so far, but armed with a new recipe and the right ingredients, given to me by another sailor, I've just managed to produce a loaf of bread that is now standing in front of me on the table emitting a wonderful aroma.

The islanders are always very friendly and cheerful. You're promptly offered a ride when you walk along the roadside, and as soon as they see my bandaged foot they want to help me. The wound still hasn't healed, mainly because it's often wet from stepping in and out of the dinghy. It's easy to pick up an infection here, and I'm constantly offered well-meant advice. Recently, I was looking for an internet connection when a total stranger offered me his office. He gave me the office keys and left me to it. If I'd wanted to use his car, that would have been fine, too! You don't experience this kind of trust in the Netherlands.

I've passed on the flower leis I received at the unforgettable feast given in my honour to other sailors who have just arrived, as a kind of good-luck charm. I don't have much use for flowers at sea. My gran has given me plenty of flowers and plants in the past, but they never survive in my care. When I managed to kill even a cactus, I was given a plastic plant that could, at worst, only get dusty …

Tomorrow I'm heading for Tahiti. I just need to study the charts and figure out a route between all the atolls before raising the anchor. It's about 700 miles and I expect Guppy will need about six days for the passage. Dark clouds fly overhead and it's raining non-stop when I wake up at 07.00, but I'm definitely leaving today. I start by stowing the dinghy, the bimini and the sail covers, and then heave up the stern anchor. It brings a huge amount of mud on board, and both *Guppy* and I end up not only wet, but dirty, too. I eventually get the bow anchor out of the muddy muck at about nine o'clock. Then *Guppy* glides peacefully through the floating coconuts towards the open sea, while the sailors in the anchorage call out their best wishes for a pleasant and safe journey.

Hiva Oa–Tahiti: 700 nautical miles

DAY 1: *1 June*

I set the sails but there's no wind; just endless rain. I'm sitting on deck in a pool of water with a bucket collecting the runoff of heavenly freshwater from the boom. Slowly I drift past Hiva Oa. *Guppy* passes towering waterfalls cascading from the top of the island cliffs almost straight into the sea. The swell is not as bad as when I arrived, but some wind would be welcome. I see a yacht approaching in the opposite direction and hear '*Guppy*, *Guppy*, *Guppy*, this is …'

It's *Discovery*, who has recognised *Guppy* from a distance. There aren't too many red two-masters around. After this contact, *Discovery*, *Papillon*, *Promise* and *Juliana II*, who've all been following the conversation, call me. They're all anchored in the bay I'm passing and wish me a good journey. It will probably be the last time I see them, as I'm travelling much faster than most of the cruisers.

It's still raining and I've had enough of it. I'm cold, even though I'm wearing a raincoat. I put on a thick, dry jersey and dive under the covers to get warm while *Guppy* moves on. I read a book and keep an eye on what's happening outside and on the radar. I've often sailed this way in the Netherlands. Hmm … The rain, the cold and the dark clouds remind me of home. Not long from now and the cold, grey Dutch coast will show up before me! Night falls slowly as the last islands disappear in the rain.

DAY 2: *2 June*

At first light, I see that there's the promise of a lovely day. The last showers of the night disappear on the horizon, and the wind spurs *Guppy* on to sail at about 5 knots under a clear blue sky. There are dolphins swimming alongside *Guppy*, and one of them swims on its back near the bow and seems to smile up at me.

Jillian, who's come to see me in Tahiti, landed there today and texts me that it's an awesome place to surf. I was looking forward to getting there, but even more so now. I'll have to be patient as I'm using one of the slowest means of transport in the world and still have 600 miles to go, which, with a bit of luck, should take me five more days.

DAY 3: *3 June*

The teasing squalls are giving me a bad time and I'm constantly busy with the sails. Unlike yesterday, it's cloudy today. In between the squalls, with winds of more than 30 knots, there's a breeze of some 15 knots giving *Guppy* a speed of about 5 knots. I'm sleeping when I can now, because that's going to be difficult when I navigate between the atolls and reefs and have to do a lookout every 20 minutes to ensure that *Guppy* doesn't hit anything. The atolls and reefs are so low that even the radar doesn't always detect them. When I look at the chart, I see that *Guppy* has entered a new time zone and that there's now exactly 12 hours' difference with the Netherlands.

Half-absorbed in my book, I'm startled when I think I've sighted a small whale. On closer inspection it's a big dolphin, and it swims along with *Guppy* for a few minutes before continuing on its way. A pity *Guppy* and the dolphin didn't enjoy each other's company for a bit longer. I would have loved to have studied this sea creature more closely, as I've never seen such a big dolphin!

DAY 4: *4 June*

Flap, clang, flap — every time I've just got into my bunk, I'm woken up again. I'm having a night of wind from astern, wind from ahead or — no — it's a beam wind! But even in this weak and shifty wind, which has me adjusting the sails constantly, we've an average speed of 5 knots. Towards morning, the wind has disappeared and I've been coaxing *Guppy*'s small secondary engine to do its job. It doesn't give us much speed, but it does save fuel and helps to prevent *Guppy* from rolling so that I can get some sleep. I'm hoping to reach the first of the Tuamotu Islands by tomorrow evening. People have been warning me about this area; very pretty but tricky at the same time; and with very little opportunity for sleep …

While getting ready for some breakfast, I notice that my delicious French loaf has mould on it. I eat the good bits and throw away the rest. It's going to be muesli from now on. It's calm and hot and *Guppy* puffs along at 4 knots. I've spent the past hour looking at the point on the horizon where I expect to see land. It's my first atoll and I'm dying to see it, but however hard I peer, I see nothing but water. Normally, you can see an island from a distance of 30 miles if the weather is clear, but atolls are so low that you see them from only a few miles off and the first sign is usually just the top of a palm tree.

On my copied chart, I see a wreck marked on the north side, with the comment 'If you're gonna run aground, there are worse places than this.'

'I suppose that's one way of looking at it,' I tell *Guppy*, when I spy something sticking out on the horizon.

Within seconds I climb the ratlines up the mast and sight a low, ring-shaped coral reef island less than 3 miles away. I'm happy for a moment, but then feel rather hemmed in by all these reefs. With the knowledge that dozens of yachts are wrecked on them annually, I keep a sharp lookout. After a hefty squall with a lot of wind and rain that allows me to collect some freshwater, I can no longer see the island. The calm returns while night falls and the sea is tranquil. There are still 12 miles of open sea before the next atoll, so let me take a nap. The radar wakes me after only 15 minutes when it detects a fishing boat. So much for some rest!

DAY 5: *5 June*

When I wake up in the morning, there's an absolute flat calm; the ocean has changed into one enormous mirror and it's as hot as hell. I sail between two atolls and see them both. Just as I'm sailing through the last two atolls, there's a sudden strong gust of wind accompanied by very heavy rain. The waves soon build up and the wind shoots up to 30 knots within minutes. I need to put in the second reef and unfurl the small jib. Below, everything I had left out when the sea was calm now lies on the low side of the cabin. Damn, couldn't this have waited until I'd left all these dangerous-looking atolls behind me?

Two hours later I've passed the last atoll within sight and *Guppy* is happy to be in deep, open waters again. But the waves continue to grow in size, it's dark and very cloudy as the sea ceaselessly crashes over the deck. I hope Mother Nature is having fun!

The companionway has to remain shut or the cabin will turn into a swimming pool. I'm lying on the couch looking up at the hatches, which are awash with water, and listening to the violence of the waves. *Guppy* is putting up a good fight under difficult circumstances as I watch the last atoll disappear off the radar screen. It's comfy inside and I know that my faithful *Guppy* can take it.

In the middle of the night, I'm woken by wildly flapping sails. I rush on deck and see that the emergency repair job on the severed ring on one of the pulleys of the windvane steering system has broken again. I decide to sail on autopilot for the rest of the night and to sort the problem out tomorrow. Soaked to the bone, I lie in bed but battle to sleep. The waves are high and *Guppy* is constantly falling into the troughs at the bottom of the waves, flattening me against the side of my bunk. It's just like a rollercoaster that takes you up slowly and then is really fast going down. I study the chart in the dim light of the control buttons. It had looked as though I would get there in daylight, but now that *Guppy* is going so fast I'll probably get there by tomorrow evening in the dark. I confer with *Guppy* about navigating through the pass in the reef into Papeete's lagoon at night in this weather. *Guppy* isn't fond of reefs and prefers the open sea … Hmm, there are still 120 miles to go and circumstances may change. Time to catch up on some sleep! I have just found a good position against the bulkhead when — *bleep, bleep, bleep* — the ear-splitting radar alarm goes off. A big ship has just appeared in its detection zone. I keep a sharp eye on the sea giant's course until it's safely past me, and then try to catch up on some sleep again.

DAY 6: *6 June*

It's slowly getting lighter. Going on deck without getting wet has become impossible, as *Guppy* seems to be practising to be a submarine. The waves are still flying over the deck, but I've got used to that again. The transparent flap in front of the hatch is down and I'm looking at the radar screen from the low side of the couch. I'm spending most of the day below deck, sleeping, reading and playing with the cameras, but they, too, seem to be having trouble with the salty conditions and aren't working as they should.

In the afternoon, there's a cargo ship on a collision course that's not responding. Hmm … Not good, as I don't know whether they are aware of me. Luckily, I know it's there and manage to avoid it.

About 30 miles from Tahiti, I suddenly see lights on the horizon. Yes, land ahead! *Gup* and I have decided to enter the pass through the reef to Papeete by night. I'll anchor her somewhere in the harbour across the channel and look for a better anchorage tomorrow. There's a good one 5 miles further on, past a number of reefs, but it's not a good idea to do this bit in the dark.

As night falls, I'm at the chart table studying the approach details while listening to a Tahitian radio station. I don't understand much French, but that doesn't matter. This is Tahiti! Unbelievable! French Polynesia always seemed the most beautiful part of my voyage to me.

Around midnight, I'm approaching the pass that leads into Papeete through the reef. The leading lights correspond with what the charts show me, but as we enter the pass the thunder of breaking waves on the reefs is ever closer and nerve-racking … I keep a sharp eye on the leading lights, and after a while *Gup* and I pass into calmer waters. Yes, I'm really proud of myself and *Guppy*. We've succeeded in coming through the reefs that surround Tahiti at night in bad weather without damage. When I wake up the next day and look at the reefs we'd gone through during the night, I shudder.

The passage from Hiva Oa to Tahiti was one of the most hazardous so far. There are lots of reefs in this region and many ships perish here. You need to think ahead all the time; know exactly where you are and make sure you keep your distance from the reefs. The danger is that you can be hit by a heavy squall at any given moment, during which you aren't always able to steer the boat in the direction you wish to. The good thing about the reefs that circle Tahiti is that the waves break on them. Once you get inside the reefs, it's safe and calm.

Tahiti

Clearing in goes smoothly and I spot some sailors I know as I walk back. They tell me about the other yachts in the bay. I can now see the reefs clearly in the calm waters as I sail the last 5 miles to the anchorage.

I anchor *Guppy* in the crystal blue waters between Papeete and Punaauia. It's 10 metres deep and I can see the anchor clearly. The beautiful silhouette of Moorea is on the horizon, and I'm admiring this view when I hear my name being called. I see Jillian walking in the distance, but I don't feel like putting the dinghy together, so I dive straight into the clear, warm water while Jillian waits patiently on the beach.

'Typically Laura' is Jillian's first comment when I get to shore and wring most of the water out of my clothes. We walk to the marina to find out what a berth costs, but this is way over my budget. Not a problem, I'm fine just where I am. Jillian is staying in a hotel in Papeete and we're just trying to figure out what a bus ticket costs when a woman at the bus stop offers to help us. She counts out the coins and then donates the fare and refuses to take it back.

Papeete is very big and modern. Seeing so many people, motorways, traffic jams and a McDonald's takes some getting used to after two months. Besides the bustle, Tahiti is beautiful; very green with lots of tall mountains and very friendly people.

We catch a ride to the marina with three surfies who have just been surfing at Teehoopoo and enjoy a $10 ice cream. My most expensive ice cream ever! But one of the best, with chocolate, vanilla, coconut, whipped cream and cinnamon.

As I'd swum ashore, we wait at the dinghy dock for someone to give us a ride to *Guppy*. It takes forever and we decide to walk to a spot close to *Guppy* to swim across. As we're walking off, we pass a man with a surfboard on his way to the dinghy dock. Jillian and I turn and follow him to ask if he will give us a ride.

'Yes, of course. Aren't you the girl from *Guppy*? I think my friend Paul just gave you girls a ride.' Small world! We start to chat, and while Adrian takes us back to *Guppy* he tells us that there's a better anchoring spot on the opposite side of the bay. And so I heave up the anchor and take her over.

We swim to Adrian's boat and ask him where the internet reception is good. He offers to take us into town. We go to a big square with lots of stalls that sell cheap but good food. We then sit outside a café where Adrian waits for Paul. Paul is here with his yacht *Kipuku*, and is working to earn some money to be able to continue his voyage. He comes from Australia and has spent seven months on Tahiti. He's working on a mega-yacht here and isn't planning to leave French Polynesia just yet. Paul takes us to a park where they're practising Tahitian dance and drum performances for the festival planned for July. It's awesome, and I end up learning a few more French words. Paul gives us a ride back in a car that he traded for a fishing rod. I can't help wondering who got the better deal. A friend of his who borrowed the car managed to lose the keys, so now he starts the car by connecting two wires and using either an ice cream stick or a screwdriver to turn the ignition. It's a miracle it doesn't fall apart, but the engine keeps on running.

The next day Paul takes us to see a few stunning waterfalls off the beaten track in his wreck of a car. After travelling down a long, sandy road meant for four-wheel-drives, we come to a river. From here, we walk through rivers, over rocks and past pretty little waterfalls and finally get to a huge waterfall in a beautiful, green valley. Paul and I jump into the water and swim in the direction of the waterfall. Jillian is hesitant to join us as she swims under some trees that have fallen over in the water.

'Come on!' I shout.

We are swimming against the current and the wind generated by the cold water plunging over the edge. Paul has climbed onto the rocks and is ready to dive into the waterfall. I follow — what an awesome feeling this is! After a while, Jillian also takes the plunge. We get cold and swim back to enjoy the beautiful view of the waterfall and eat a coconut. When we get back to the car, Paul shows us the waterfalls on the tourist route, but swimming is not allowed here and they are no longer idyllic. We decide to go back, but first visit some surfing spots and a blowhole. This is an extraordinary geological phenomenon that results when sea caves tunnel inland and have a hole near the surface. This means that seawater can suddenly spout into the air. I'd never heard of it and was an easy victim for Paul when he told me to peer down the hole. The result: a rush of seawater in my face.

We fill up with petrol, eat at McDonald's, get some groceries and figure that we could use Paul's mooring. He is leaving for a while and it's a much better spot. But then Adrian appears to tell us that he'll be using it. He agrees to let *Guppy* tie up alongside and the problem is solved. When Paul leaves for Moorea on *Kipuku* the next morning, we rearrange the yachts.

Today, Jillian and I take up the offer of borrowing Paul's car. After connecting the wires and starting the car with a screwdriver, I tell

Jillian she can drive. But being American, Jillian has never driven a car with manual gear changes. I'm 15 and don't have a driver's licence, so she's going to give it a try. I slowly start to lose confidence in Jillian's driving ability and after 10 minutes and several narrow misses, she stops the car on the roadside and refuses to go any further. Dad has taught me to drive on deserted parking grounds and some quiet roads, and so Jillian reckons I should drive. I need to get used to it a bit, and practise at a big parking lot further on. I'm enjoying it, and after a while feel confident enough to drive through the traffic and onto the motorway.

We stop at an ice-cream parlour and find a mango. Then we swim at a pretty beach, before driving further and further inland until we find ourselves on the other side of the island. It's much greener and less busy here. It's all going well, until we need to climb a very steep hill ... Jillian observes that the cars in front of us are producing a lot of fumes, but while I'm looking at the smoky scene on the road I suddenly realise that it's not the other vehicles but our own car that is smoking! I turn the car and drive down to the fuel station I saw five minutes ago on the way up. Halfway there, the engine stalls and we freewheel the last mile to come to a stop at the sign with the fuel prices. People come to our aid, but how to open the bonnet? As expected, the handle for this purpose is missing. I eventually manage to open it with some pliers and we can now get to the engine. The water level appears to be too low, but when we try to fill it, it drips out of the radiator. We have to make frequent stops to top the water up for the rest of the day. This explains the jerry can of water in the car. Hmm ... That's something Paul forgot to tell us about!

It suddenly starts to pour with rain and it takes us a while to find out how the windscreen wipers work; something else that doesn't work as it should. On the way, we see some funny sights, such as a boy holding onto a rope tied to a bridge and surfing on the current of a river. We drive all the way around the island until we are back on the motorway to Papeete. We want to go to McDonald's in the city centre, and getting us there safely is the first real test of my driving ability.

Petrol and food are very expensive here. It all costs two to three times more than in the Netherlands, which is not strange when you consider that everything has to be brought to the island by either ship or plane.

We had forgotten all about the mango we'd plucked from a tree earlier that day, and when we get back to the marina we can't find it. That's until Jillian gets up and I start to laugh. She soon realises that my hilarity is directed at her bottom which is plastered with squashed mango. Still laughing, we walk down the jetty to the dinghy. I miss my footing and land in the water, much to everyone in the marina's amusement. Anyway, it's a great way to wash off the dust and heat after the long ride.

After a shower, we visit the owners of a 40-metre yacht who had invited us to dinner. I'd met them at a barbecue earlier. It's a lovely evening, with delicious food and good music. I then say farewell to Jillian who flies home to New York tonight.

After two really busy days, I decide to take it easy and focus on the things that need to be done. I fill up the 'wreck-on-wheels' with water and drive into Papeete for some groceries. There's no parking anywhere, and I drive around and around until I find a tiny space into which the car just fits. After picking up some supplies, I then drive to the Immigration Office to clear out, as I plan to leave the next morning. This is always quite a mission, mainly because they pose the most impossible questions: where you're going to, what time exactly you are leaving, and where you plan to go on to from there and after there … As if I know! *Guppy* follows the wind and I go with her. I depart when it suits me and not according to what's written on a piece of paper. Anyway, a little later all the documents carry big, fat stamps. I drive back through all the hustle and bustle and I am glad to see *Guppy*. The first thing I do: take a dive and decide to stay on *Guppy* tonight to watch one of the many movies I've exchanged with the other yachts.

Tahiti–Moorea: 18 nautical miles

DAY 1: *13 June*

Once I've topped up the diesel tanks, I raise the anchor and *Guppy* leaves Tahiti just before noon. The little wind there is comes from the direction we are heading for, but the waves aren't high and we make our way out through the pass between the reefs with ease. Once at sea,

I try tacking but *Guppy*'s speed is diminished by each wave. There's just too little wind and I start the engine to make some headway. Suddenly a breeze springs up and it's as if it's saying 'Hi, here I am!'

Whoosh — more wind. *Bang, clang, tinkle* and I'm flattened to one side with everything that's loose in the cabin. *Guppy* heels over heavily, but at least we're moving in the right direction at 7 knots, thanks to the sudden gusts off the tall mountains. *Whoosh!* Damn waves! They're building up fast. It's going to be a short, rough but enjoyable trip.

Towards 14:00 Moorea lies before us, and we're soon surfing into the pass with the sea breaking on the reefs to the left and right. Between the mountains in Opunohu Bay the water is beautifully calm, and I drop the anchor near the other yachts.

Moorea

Although it's only a few hours' sail from Tahiti, Moorea is a totally different world. The island is much smaller and not so busy.

There's a family with four children between the ages of 11 and 15 on the big motor boat that's anchored next to me. They've been making a round-the-world journey by plane with their parents for more than a year. When I tell them about my voyage, they want to sail around the world, too, but quickly change their minds when their parents tell them that you can't just walk away when you're on a boat together, and that you have to do all your own cooking, washing and groceries. The French captain of the motor boat is a fanatical sailor and has taken part in and won many competitions. He invites me to stay for dinner and starts to tell me all about his exploits. Such as the story about his crossing of the Atlantic Ocean in a Hobie Cat; a 5-metre open catamaran. It sounds like a stunt by a great daredevil, but not something I'd attempt; especially after he shows me some films of the action. Personally he thinks it's all terrific.

I treat myself to a real holiday on my first day in Moorea. I swim, read, eat and paddle around the whole bay in my dinghy. I don't really feel the need to go ashore. The view of the island from *Guppy* is awesome. The water is a lovely blue colour, very clear and you can see easily 15 metres deep. I experience a fear of heights when I swim and look down. In the beginning I'd sometimes been anxious when sailing *Guppy* over crystal-clear water where I could see the bottom. It made it difficult to judge the depth and space between the rocks and *Guppy*'s keel. Good thing the depth-sounder brings the definitive answer.

I wake up late the next day because I've spent half the night trying to download photographs onto my website; alas, without success. Half awake, I hear a dinghy tearing around the bend. It's Paul, whose yacht is further up the bay. He asks me if I'd like to join a few people and visit a place where the stingrays and black-tip sharks eat out of your hand. But of course!

We sail off on a neglected, homemade aluminium catamaran for about 3 miles to the swimming location. I'm not entirely at ease while standing in the water. I feed dead fish to the stingrays that are about one and a half metres long. They swim around calmly and bump up against you, even when you're not feeding them. But I stay away from the sharks. There's a sudden downpour with gusts of wind, and I shiver when I'm out of the water, but it's been a great experience and I wouldn't have missed it for anything. We motor back and decide to tie *Gup*, the catamaran and *Kipuku* together for a party on board tonight. We also invite the crews from the two mega-yachts that are in the bay to join us.

Guppy's mainsail needs to be repaired, as it has worn from all the flapping when sailing on the calm days. Paul used to be a sailmaker in Australia and wants to help. We take the sail to the mega-yacht that he works on. Here they have a good sailmaker's sewing machine on board and plenty of room. We work until it gets dark and starts to rain again. Oh well, we'll just continue tomorrow. Paul takes me on a tour of the enormous yacht. Wow, everything is huge and so luxurious! *Guppy*'s 17-metre mast only just reaches the first of the five spreaders on this yacht's mast.

The party on our boats has begun, but I still have to send a blog off via the satellite phone that cheerfully continues to give me an error warning. My thumb is numb from texting, and I try it one last time and finally get *text message sent* in the display. It's an awesome party and goes on until the early hours, but, fortunately for me, I don't have to get up early for work in the morning like some of the others.

I get to bed by 04.00, and it's later for some of the other party-goers, but I don't have a hangover like most. I join Paul on the mega-yacht on which he works, and help him with some chores. It's nice to meet the rest of the crew who weren't at the party the previous night. At five o'clock, Paul is finished for the day and we can continue mending the sails. The sewing machine isn't cooperating, and after two hours we take a break and then tackle the problem with renewed zeal. We spend a few more hours sewing *Guppy*'s mainsail in the bright lights of the mega-yacht. Just before midnight, the sail looks like new and we've sewn extra patches over all the worn areas, making it stronger than ever.

In the morning, I'm about to take my bike ashore for a tour of the island when a dinghy from one of the mega-yachts comes alongside to invite me over. They're a nice crew who sail around half the world and get paid for it. They usually have the whole mega-yacht to themselves, as the owner is seldom on board. At night, I try to upload some photographs for my site, but the internet is too slow.

I decide that I've had a good time here and want to move on tomorrow. Why am I so restless? Why do I constantly feel the urge to move on? What else lies beyond the horizon? When I'm at sea I want to be on shore, and when I'm on land the sea pulls me like a magnet … Which way shall I go now? Huahine?

Moorea–Bora Bora: 130 nautical miles

DAY 1: *17 June*

I toss off the lines, and *Guppy* sails towards a sea that's as smooth as a mirror. This means that the reefs aren't marked by the breakers. There's almost no wind, and Moorea disappears very slowly in the distance. But the good thing about this is that I can take my time. It's something different to be sailing out over a super-flat sea.

I'm very tired and am dozing off in the heat of the cockpit. At 17.00 I try to sleep, but don't really succeed. A few hours later, when it's dark and I've finally fallen asleep, I'm woken by the radar alarm and see a cargo ship in the distance. I'm shocked when I discover that the masthead light and the Echomax aren't switched on. Cursing myself for my carelessness, I follow the ship's echo on my radar until it has passed, and then go below again. Although the boat is quite steady, I just can't sleep. The wind has dropped and the radar alarm keeps on going off because there's quite a bit of traffic now, so I decide to sit on deck and enjoy the stars while *Guppy*, rolling gently, glides over the water on a purring engine. In the meantime, the first few islands are coming into sight, but *Gup* and I decide to sail on to Bora Bora.

DAY 2: *18 June*

As dawn breaks, the dark shapes take on some colour. I'm sailing between Huahine and Tahaa and have 30 miles to go. I hope to be there before dark. There's still no wind, but the tall mountains of Bora Bora are in sight. As is often the case with these coral islands, I have to sail halfway around the island before coming to the only opening in the reef by which you can enter. From the sea, I see a beautiful anchoring spot. There's another big yacht there, so I assume that it's deep enough. *Guppy* sails between the reefs into a lagoon that's as smooth as a mirror, and then it's another few miles to the anchorage I spotted. I'm halfway between the coral reef and the anchorage, and feeling very optimistic, when *Guppy* hits a mega brain coral. Although it's just a nudge, *Guppy* is not happy with me. On the second attempt, I run aground.

At this stage, I give up trying to get to my ideal spot as it's getting dark. I now have two options: anchor in very deep water or go to a mooring. The water is very deep, dropping away steeply near both the land and the coral reefs; a depth of more than 50 metres! Now that it's getting dark fast, I bring *Guppy* up to a mooring close to other boats. It's not ideal because I never entirely trust moorings. You never know how long it's been since the moorings were laid and what condition they're in. It also costs money, something I don't have a lot of. Well, *Guppy* will be OK for tonight, and we'll look for another spot tomorrow. Preferably one that *Guppy* can reach without being scoured by coral. Satisfied, I finish reading *The Girl with the Dragon Tattoo*, the delicious aroma of my homemade biscuits spreading through the cabin.

Bora Bora

Cornflakes again for breakfast. Hmm, high time I went to buy some bread. I inflate the dinghy, drop my folding bike into it, and ask my neighbours for directions. It's just 10.00 and already getting hot. I cycle fast because I can do with some exercise, passing through the village to another bay where I buy bread and eggs. I get back to *Guppy* at about 13.00.

After my little exploration, I decide that the moorings also being used by other yachts are probably the best option. There aren't any better spots, and to attempt anchoring where the other yacht is lying is too risky to try again. I'm still worried about our brush with the coral, and dive overboard to take a look at *Guppy*'s hull. All I can find is a small scratch in the paint on *Guppy*'s keel. She can definitely take a bump or two.

Meanwhile, I get to meet some of the people on the other yachts. One of them has a computer problem that I manage to solve, and as a reward they offer me the use of their internet. The moorings belong to the yacht club and I'm assured that they are checked regularly, so *Guppy* and I can relax and enjoy a good night's rest.

Yesterday's cycle has given me a taste for more, and I decide to cycle around the whole island as my morning exercise. It's easier than I thought it would be, as the road around the island is almost at sea level and there are few hills along the way. It takes me about three or four hours to cycle around Bora Bora's tall mountain and back to *Guppy*. I'd left fairly early and am back at 13.00.

At the yacht club, I meet the family that manages the club. The club was destroyed by a heavy hurricane the year before, and they're still busy rebuilding it. Although they speak only a little English and I speak only a few words of French, we manage to have a lot of fun. They offer to take me to parts of the island that can't be reached on a folding bike. From the top of the mountain there's an awesome view of *Guppy*. You can look down on Bora Bora and also have a view of all the surrounding islands — it's stunning.

When I get back, I move *Guppy* closer to the jetty. She's now moored between two of the yacht club moorings and feels entirely safe.

I think I'll cycle around the island again tomorrow, as a little more exercise won't do me any harm. Let's see if I can do it in two and a half hours this time.

As usual my plans change, and my second trip round the island is postponed when my neighbours, Tom and Janis on *Tomboy*, ask me to join them on a mountain hike. And so cycling makes way for hiking. What strikes me about the houses is that most have a graveyard in the garden where they bury their deceased family members, instead of making use of a communal cemetery. After a three-hour walk, I get back to *Guppy* and join up all the available hoses so that I can reach the tap on the jetty. Awesome! Now I can fill the jerry cans and bottles, do the washing and hose down *Guppy*.

I don't feel so well in the afternoon and decide to take it easy for the rest of the day, but that doesn't really help. Oh well, I should feel better tomorrow. I'll go to bed early tonight.

I'm feeling much better the next morning, but not super-fit. I can't, however, withstand the temptation of putting my Minicat together and taking it for a sail around the bay. There's a lot of wind, with some strong gusts off the mountains. I capsize several times and I'm catapulted overboard, but the few scratches I sustain are worth all the fun. The Minicat is fast; a bit too fast … and after a few rounds, my body reminds me that it would be better to take it a little easier. I go back to *Guppy* and read in the cockpit, with a beautiful view of the island. I don't always listen to myself, but I've started to learn from my mistakes.

With all the tropical fish that are swimming under us and the coral that surrounds us on Bora Bora, I have the feeling that *Guppy* is floating in a living aquarium. I fully understand why so many couples come here for their honeymoon. It's a stunning, tropical green island with pearly white beaches and wonderful diving spots.

In the morning, I continue to explore the island on my bicycle, but soon it's too hot to continue and I decide that snorkelling is a better option. The stingrays and black-tip sharks are fairly tame here, too, and they swim around me cheerfully. I then enjoy a Coke at the yacht club and check my email. When I get back to *Guppy*, my laptop slides out of my hands, but I manage to break the fall with my big toe. Good for the laptop, but not good for my toe, which is turning blue …

I was planning to move on, but the locals tell me that there'll be a big traditional festival on Friday and Saturday and that I shouldn't miss it. The yacht club owner, François, with whom I've become friends and who lets me moor my boat for free, tells me it's very special and that it's worth staying for. So I decide to stay for a few more days.

'Lauraaa, Lauraaa!'

I wake up to the sound of someone shouting my name, forget that I'm sleeping in my hammock, and fall to the floor. Still half asleep, I jump into my clothes and paddle to the jetty where François is standing. He asks me if I feel like going to some shark-feeding with them. No, thanks, I want to work on *Guppy* today and don't feel like going to a tourist attraction, but I won't say no to a nice breakfast. After breakfast, I'm allowed to use the internet for as long as I like, but I'm soon bored. The internet doesn't really suit my lifestyle and isn't really recreation for me. A neighbour who lives next to the yacht club comes by in her Land Rover and asks if I need to do any shopping. I jump at the offer and take my jerry cans along to fill up with diesel. Her English is not good and my French isn't any better, but we get along fine. Having run by all the shops, we get back to *Guppy* with heaps of stuff. I top up the diesel tank, clean up and then decide to go sailing in my Minicat again. There's a lot of wind, but I manage to capsize only once. I'm managing to sail the Minicat on one hull, which is not exactly what the inflatable Minicat was built for!

Without being aware of it, I've been amusing half the people at the anchorage and the yacht club with my sailing stunts for the past two hours. When I get back to shore and am busy rinsing the boat, they drop quite a few comments. Didn't I think there was a little too much wind for an ant like me to take her inflatable catamaran out today? But it was fantastic and I'd never gone that fast on the Minicat.

In the meantime, the dance festival has begun and the first performances will be given today. I walk to the village with Tom and Janis from *Tomboy*. I'm very surprised when the festival starts with three groups street-dancing to techno music. This is certainly not what I was expecting and I have to suppress a giggle. Tom and Janis are also taken aback. After the dancing, there's a long speech in Tahitian of which we don't understand a word, but it sounds good. After the speech, I accompany François to a friend of his who wants to give me some fruit for my voyage. They offer me bananas, grapefruit and pineapples that have just been picked.

I have dinner with Tom and Janis on *Tomboy* that evening, and we go back to the dance festival afterwards. For the first time it's really cool and there's a lot of wind, but now the traditional dances are being performed and they really are impressive. They resemble nothing I've ever seen before in terms of dancing. There are about 80 dancers who all follow the exact same movements in exotic costumes to the sound of the drums, making it look very spectacular and intense. I get back to *Guppy* very late and thoroughly cold, but it's been an unforgettable experience.

Kathy, François' wife, is taking part in the traditional canoe race the next morning and I very much want to watch it. At eight o'clock, I'm in François' speedboat with two of his children. It's great to watch one of these traditional canoe races. They're incredibly fast and the course extends the full length of the bay. Kathy's five teammates don't row as well as Kathy does, and they come in second to last, but no one seems to mind. They laugh a lot and, well, better luck next time, right?

Every day brings something new, but I decide that *Guppy* and I will be on our way tomorrow or we'll be here forever! This means that I must start the preparations: fold up and stow away my Minicat and bicycle, secure the loose bits and pieces in the lockers, and of course fill the water tank. The weather charts promise variable winds, but with a bit of luck *Guppy* and I will find a favourable breeze for Niue.

As soon as I'm ready, I go ashore to see whether I can persuade François to sail his Hobie Cat with me. I start taking off the covers and soon see that the boat hasn't been used for quite a while. Several pulleys and other bits are missing, but *Guppy* has a good stock of these, and, with much improvisation and the removal of a palm tree that blocks the way, we get the boat in the water.

We sail very fast, and within half an hour we've almost capsized several times, but when we reach the other side of the island the wind drops. We're almost back when there's a sudden squall with a lot of wind, and it's beginning to get dark by the time we complete our round trip of Bora Bora. A warm shower at the yacht club revives us, and I'm totally exhilarated by our trip on a super-fast open boat.

The next morning I enjoy breakfast on board *Tomboy* before I toss off the mooring lines and wave farewell to everyone as Guppy and I start our passage for the island of Niue.

Bora Bora–Tonga: 1300 nautical miles

DAY 1: *27 June*

The wind and the waves looked so promising when I left, but I'm cursing the weather again. The short, choppy waves are beginning to irritate me. Things seem to improve in the afternoon, or is it just that I'm getting used to it again? There's a gentle breeze from dead astern, which isn't the best sailing wind for a ketch, and *Guppy* is doing about 4.5 knots. It's not exactly the speed I'm used to from her, but I'll have to be happy with it. I'm once again asking myself why I feel the need to go back to sea just when I've met some nice people on a beautiful island. To bob about like a rubber duck and be thrown around only to arrive at yet another beautiful island? I always have this love/hate relationship with sailing. Ninety per cent of the time it's nothing special, but the remaining 10 per cent makes it all worthwhile. Especially the thrill of arriving somewhere and the attraction of what is waiting just beyond the horizon; these factors continue to drive me westwards.

There are three islands on my route. The first, Maupiti, is behind me, and the other two are two too many for my liking. That's because they're both atolls and so low that you only see them when you are almost on top of them. There's another yacht in the distance that's sailing in the same direction. *Guppy* tries to catch up with the other yacht but doesn't really succeed, and now that I want to sleep, this yacht is constantly in the radar alarm zone, which keeps me awake. And it's not responding to my VHF calls, so we can't even have a chat …

I've developed a sore throat and it's getting worse and worse tonight. I don't get any sleep, as *Guppy* has decided to slowly but surely overtake the yacht in front of me, which means that I'm on

189

watch. By morning I'm feeling really tired, and I now have a cold to match my sore throat, which is making me feel really ill. I try to sleep, but this doesn't work, and neither does reading. I'm not hungry either. The SSB-net comes over loud and clear at half past four and I check in. The yacht that *Guppy* eventually overtook during the night has disappeared from sight behind us and so has the last atoll that I just passed.

The following wind is still weak, but *Guppy* is generally sailing in the right direction and the sails aren't flapping around too much. The flapping happens in light winds when *Guppy* rolls heavily from side to side, too fast for the sails to follow. This results in the sails flipping over briefly and, as they fill with wind again, flying back with a heavy slap, which is very bad for the sails.

I use the satellite phone to call my sister, Kim, to wish her a happy thirteenth birthday. The connection is not good, but I get to sample a bit of the party. I realise that I've been absent from the Netherlands for a while. Kim uses a few new slang words and sounds quite grown-up. I say goodbye and try to get some sleep; that's if the sails don't slap too much. The wind is letting me down at the moment.

DAY 2: *28 June*

I'm feeling terrible. My throat is a little less painful, but I'm really ill. I haven't had a cold this bad in three years, and can't believe it's possible to catch a cold in the tropics. I think I caught some 'flu on Bora Bora. I know that it will pass, but why does this happen at sea when I need to be alert? Even though I'm dead tired, I can't sleep. The wind has dropped away entirely and the water has changed to an endless blue, undulating seascape. The sails begin to flap and I decide to take them down before they get damaged. I start my faithful little engine, and *Guppy* now leaves some ripples in her wake. We're not going fast, but at least she isn't rolling so terribly.

Well, it doesn't really matter whether I'm sick here or in Niue, except that I'm now getting irritated by the sound of the engine and the battle with the sails.

At 16.00, I log onto the SSB-net and talk to Henk, a Dutch solo sailor whom I met briefly in Panama. He's on his way to Tonga. After talking to a couple of other sailors, I know that I'm not the only one who's becalmed. Well, I've accepted that it's going to be a longer trip, and so long as the calm doesn't combine with a heavy swell, it's fine. Nature teaches you to be patient. Everyone on the SSB-net tells me to get well soon. They can hear that I'm ill, because I'm croaking like a frog.

DAY 3: *29 June*

Some wind at last today! I can sail again and I've reached 3.5 knots. But just as my hopes are rising, the wind drops away entirely and *Guppy* is bobbing again with flapping sails. ARGH! Right, drop the sails and on with Mr Yanmar. An hour later the bilge-water alarm goes off in the engine compartment. A leak? Alarmed, I dive straight into the engine compartment and check the propeller shaft, valves and cooling water pipes. Nothing. After a further half-hour inspection, I discover that the stainless-steel exhaust of the Yanmar has rusted through. I thought that stainless steel didn't rust … I now have to squeeze myself into an impossible position behind the engines to bind the exhaust with Rescue Tape, and that seems to do the trick. The automatic bilge pump is not working for some reason, and when I take it apart I find that it's clogged by a huge cockroach!

In the afternoon, I read for a couple of hours and enjoy a bit of food for the first time in ages. While slicing the pineapple, I accidentally cut my little finger. The yellow fruit is soon covered in red blotches and looks gross. But pineapple with spots is edible, and the rest is solved with a plaster.

As always while sailing, I've completely lost my sense of time. Towards sunset, I'm sitting in the cockpit enjoying half a French loaf with a fried egg while the sky turns slowly from orange to purple. A little weight loss wouldn't be a bad idea. Thanks to all the lovely meals I've enjoyed with people I've met on the way, I've put on weight. Hey, I've just noticed that my nose isn't blocked anymore and I can smell the wonderful, fresh sea air out in the middle of the ocean. I've never noticed that before.

DAY 4: *30 June*

Not a breath of wind, but I'm feeling a little better at last and have managed to sleep well for the first time in days. I'm once again interested in my surroundings; in whether there's wind or no wind, and in checking *Guppy*'s speed. It's as though the past few days never happened. It's all so hazy; as if time stood still. But I'm back in business. My crossing is going fairly well and I expect to be on my way for about another eight days. I really love being on my own sometimes, and enjoy sailing long distances more and more. Although I don't exactly know where to yet. I first wanted to sail to Niue, which is about another 700 miles, but I'm now seriously considering sailing on to Tonga, which is 200 miles further on. I'll have reached the halfway mark at Tonga and that will be a fantastic milestone for me. But what if it stays calm? *Guppy* doesn't have enough diesel to motor the whole trip, and I've had enough of hearing it drone on. Maybe I'm worrying for nothing …

I feel some wind when I go up on deck. At last! I immediately set the big coloured code zero, but a little later it just hangs listlessly again. There's a squall in the distance and I wonder whether I should take down the code zero. I decide to leave it where it is. The squall approaches fast and suddenly there's wind. Shit — this is no good, and a sure sign of much more wind to come. I immediately start pulling the sock down over the code zero, but I'm too slow and the squall overtakes me in a matter of seconds. The rain pelts down and the wind sweeps the deck with storm velocity. The sock slides to the top and the code zero unfurls with a snap. *Guppy* heels over sharply and her gunnels and portholes are submerged. She begs me to take down the enormous, wind-filled sail. I'm battling with the wildly flapping code zero, but am winning, bit by bit. *Guppy* rights herself and I stuff the saltwater-soaked code zero down the front hatch. The wind drops again after the squall, and I think I'm going to go nuts. I beg for some wind and my prayers are answered immediately. I now have wind, but for how long?

Towards evening the sunset that slowly changes the sky from orange to purple makes up for everything. My wish for no more annoying swells on this crossing isn't fulfilled, however, and *Guppy* is rolling over a long, waxing swell. It's not that bad so long as the sails don't start to flap and there's enough wind.

DAY 5: *1 July*

The wind is swinging and falls away only to come back a little later. The constant battle with the sails, combined with little sleep, have put me in a bad mood. Fortunately I'm on my own so no one needs to suffer. Towards the end of the night there are more squalls that continue for the rest of the day. And then, suddenly, there's a very heavy squall of more than 45 knots which I notice too late, and once again it's a battle with the code zero … I'm struggling to get down the flapping sail again, but manage to get it inside in one piece. Now there's a constant wind of about 15 knots, which means that *Guppy*'s speed is running at up to 6.5 knots.

I've started a new book, *The Girl Who Played with Fire*, one of the Millennium Trilogy series, and am now in a different world. I'm slowly coming into contact with a group of yachts on the SSB radio. All the yachts are travelling in more or less the same direction. I left most of my sailing mates behind after leaving Hiva Oa, and have constantly had to make new friends and leave them again since then.

It seems like there are two yachts on their way to Tonga with the same travel plans. All the more reason to go straight to Tonga and meet them in person. I text Dad via the satellite phone, and he responds cheerfully by telling me about his day. Kim is staying with him, together with a friend, and there's a weekend party at the yacht club. They've all been sailing, and they're now on Dad's boat having fun as usual, which makes me feel a little lonely. But reading Dad's cheerful texts also perks me up. He's done so much for me that I sometimes feel bad leaving him alone with Spot while I sail happily around the world; even though my life's not always a bed of roses.

Guppy enters the night on a long, big, southerly swell with a 20-knot wind from the south. Super sailing weather with a steady speed of 6 to 7 knots.

DAY 6: *2 July*

There's still some wind, but it continues to play games with *Guppy*. This keeps me busy, constantly changing the sails and adjusting the course. As soon as I've got the sails set right, the wind drops, with the result that *Guppy* starts to roll and the sails start to flap. The rolling causes a lot of wear and tear, and I'm having to fix some tape around the sheet that runs through the spinnaker boom again to prevent it from fraying, as well as using tape on the sails that are slapping against the rigging. But that's sailing!

Up until now, this crossing hasn't been the fastest. Nor have I seen another boat or even a flying fish so far. The day has flown past and I've finished the close-on 300-page book about the woman who played with fire. I've now started the last of the Millennium Series, *The Girl Who Kicked the Hornets' Nest*.

I'm not the only one who's becalmed and am grateful to be sailing at all. This is what I discover from the conversations with a number of yachts on the SSB. 'I think I'll be here forever and slowly get cooked, sigh,' says one. We give each other some encouragement and float on. The closest boat, Henk's *Sogno d'Oro*, appears to be 140 miles ahead of me. I continue to chat with Henk, who's also on his way to Tonga and plans to sail around South Africa in his small 26-footer, just like me. He's used up nearly all his diesel and hopes to have just enough to enter the harbour in a while. When the conversation dries up, I switch off the radio. Peace ... quiet ... I'm on my own again.

DAY 7: *3 July*

I wake up from the splash of a bow wave and fly up on deck. WIND! Yes — wind at last! It's an easterly wind of about 20 knots and has *Guppy* racing at about 7 knots. I don't make much progress through the third part of the Millennium Series today. I've been reading too much and am tired of print, anyway, so I spend my free time either chatting on the SSB or making tasty food. In the meantime I occupy myself with the sails and the course to make *Guppy* go as fast as possible.

Gup and I have definitely decided to give Niue a miss and head straight for Tonga. Other sailors on the SSB who've been there before say that the anchorage is very rough, and in Tonga it appears that you are in a lovely, quiet bay and not in the open sea. It sounds lovely, and I'm also dying to see the dateline from close up at last. I've planned my route to bring me close to the Palmerston atoll so that I can catch a glimpse of it, but it starts to get dark before I reach it, and the only thing I see is a light in the far-off distance. And I've managed to spoil a good night's rest as I won't be able to shut my eyes this close to the reefs ... *Guppy* is no longer sailing that fast. In fact, she could have been 100 miles further if I'd taken the trouble to get rid of all the growth on her hull when I was in Bora Bora.

From Tonga, I'd rather have sailed straight on to the land of my birth, New Zealand. It's so close, yet so far. If they'd let me leave at the age of 13, I could have taken it in my stride, but I now have to skip it due to time constraints. I still want to try to be the youngest person to have sailed solo around the world.

DAY 8: *4 July*

I'd like to give the wind a good kick in the butt if I could. It's playing games with me, and I can only make the best of it and try to make some progress. I wake up in the middle of the night and *Guppy* is sailing too much to the south. The wind has swung to the north, which is good. I switch on the deck lights when I go outside as I need to take the spinnaker boom off the genoa. I try to open the boom eye but it doesn't work. Under the dim lights, it takes me a while to figure out what's wrong. The spinnaker boom is entirely stuck to the sheet with the tape that I'd used to prevent it from fraying any further. I try to cut away as much of the tape as I can while I'm hanging overboard and being tossed every which way. I finally manage to release the boom using a winch. In the course of the night the wind backs further and further to the west until *Guppy* is close-hauled and I'm unable to hold my rhumb line.

Towards morning, I'm still sailing close to the wind and doing 6.5 knots in a strong 25-knot wind, making *Guppy* plunge like a submarine more than anything else! Massive waves engulf us at regular intervals, but she just shakes them off every time and carries on regardless. When I go below to look for something dry to wear, I notice that my entire cupboard is soaked in saltwater. Great, that's going to mean a load of washing later on.

Guppy is forced to sail further and further south, which means that I'm unable to get past Niue; even worse, I'm making straight for it. I spend the whole day staring at my compass and adjusting my course. Just when I think I'm going to go crazy and be forced to drop off to sail below Niue, the wind slowly swings back. I'm still close-hauled, but I'm gradually able to get back to the correct course, and by sunset *Guppy* passes 5 miles to the north of Niue. *Sogno d'Oro* lies just 55 miles ahead of me and we've started to fantasise, over the SSB, about the hamburgers and cold milkshakes that we'll be enjoying after we anchor our boats in a couple of days.

DAY 9: *5 July*

Guppy continues to sail close-hauled, rolling up and down like a rocking horse, but the wind eases off towards midnight, keeping it nice and constant, which means that I finally get some sleep and wake up feeling reborn. *Guppy* and I are making progress; Niue now lies far behind and I only have another 240 miles to go to reach Tonga. Wonderful! I make something to eat and switch on the SSB. I hear that *Sogno d'Oro* lies only 20 miles ahead of me and *Guppy* is gaining on her. We decide to maintain VHF contact from this point on. In the afternoon, the wind drops slowly and I start the Yanmar. *Sogno d'Oro* continues to bob about to save her diesel, and by 17.00 I catch sight of the little 26-foot Midget.

We drift peacefully while Henk, who's an elderly guy, plays the accordion in a very laidback way. I try to throw over to him the bar of chocolate that I'd promised him days ago, but it bounces off the deck and is sacrificed to Neptune. Henk wants to throw over a tin of food that he wants my opinion on. Taking care that the two yachts don't get too close in the ever-present swell, I balance on the aft deck and manage to catch the tin. Before nightfall, we put more distance between our boats, and, after a fat squall with much wind and rain, the slower Midget's little light has disappeared from sight.

DAY 10: *6 July*

I've been underway for exactly 11 months and it feels fantastic. I'm sleeping well again, and the wind is doing exactly what I want it to do for a change. I can even sit outside decently this morning without having to swallow saltwater. Despite the headwind, *Guppy* is sailing well and has made a fair average distance for the day. It looks like I'll arrive in Tonga the day after tomorrow, where I'll have reached the exact halfway mark of my voyage! I plan to stay no more than a week and then continue to Fiji. With a bit of luck, I should be able to complete my voyage by February next year. I haven't really stopped to think about having covered all this distance. I always tend to look forward rather than back, but it's a strange thought that only a year ago I'd been involved in one court session after another. I'd had no idea nor even a spark of hope that I would ever get away and be sitting in the middle of the Pacific Ocean. But I finally found a judge with sense — and here I am!

Sogno d'Oro now lies 20 miles behind me. *Guppy* will have to sail a constant 7 knots to reach Tonga by daylight. I don't want to arrive in the dark, and, seeing that it's impossible to hold the speed up to 7 knots in this wind, I lower the mizzen and mainsail and sail on only the genoa. *Guppy* slows down to 4 knots, but that's still too fast. If I continue like this, I'll arrive in the dark anyway.

DAY 11: *8 July*

This is a weird day. In the space of one second, I skip a whole day to find myself in 8 July. I try to figure out exactly where the dotted International Dateline runs, and, according to my calculations, I am sailing across it right now. There's a good wind blowing, just when I don't really need it because *Guppy* is going too fast! It's only another 35 miles, but I definitely don't want to reach Tonga in the dark with all its reefs. *Guppy* is now sailing with only a half-furled genoa and is still running at 3.5 knots. A tsunami warning has been issued for the Pacific Ocean between New Zealand and Tonga. I don't think it's going to give me any trouble and think it will have passed by the time I'm amongst the reefs. Tsunamis build up in shallow water and the depth under *Guppy* is 3.5 kilometres. I hope to get some sleep tonight and be nearing my new destination in the morning.

DAY 12: *9 July*

I don't really manage to sleep. By midnight, *Guppy* is much too close to land and I need to be alert. I roll in the genoa some more until *Guppy* is running at 2.5 knots. That's perfect and ensures that I will get there exactly when daylight breaks.

By the end of the night, *Sogno d'Oro*, which has been sailing under full sail, also comes into sight. We wait for the first signs of daylight, then sail past all the little islands and rocks. The rising sun spreads its warm light over the morning mists that shroud the islands. The palm tops raise their heads proudly above the rest of the vegetation in the distance, while *Guppy* makes her way through a maze of little islands on an azure blue sea. Tonga, here we are! We tie the boats to moorings in Vava'u, and then it's time to clear Customs. But before I do so, I spend a moment in the cockpit to enjoy one of the most beautiful approaches I've ever experienced.

Tonga

Quarantine, Immigration, Customs ... Once again they're not close together or easy to find. With the exception of the Customs official, they're fortunately all very friendly. All in all it takes me most of the day to fill in forms and collect stamps, but I've got plenty of time anyway.

In the afternoon I enjoy a cold Coke on the terrace of a restaurant while gazing with satisfaction at *Guppy* lying peacefully at anchor amongst other yachts in the distance. Time for a break after a tiring voyage. Strangely enough, I'm not that tired even though I haven't slept all night.

Tonga is really beautiful. In the evening, I have a hamburger at the same outdoor restaurant and enjoy the setting sun and the beauty around me. These people are just as friendly and generous as those on the other Pacific islands I've been to, and I'm already enjoying myself. They drive on the left-hand side and speak English — a luxury after the French-speaking islands. I even have to get used to the fact that they understand me and I don't need to decipher any French anymore.

I have breakfast with Henk at the Aquarium the next morning; the restaurant with the view over the anchorage where I'd eaten yesterday. It turns out to be the sailors' hangout. We gobble up our breakfast of eggs, bacon and pancakes. Yum — I really needed that! Afterwards, Henk comes back to *Guppy* with me. My SSB radio has been playing up, and today gave up the ghost altogether. After turning the whole boat upside-down and working on it the entire day, we come to the conclusion that it must be the electronics and not that easy to fix. We try changing the fuse once again, but it blows instantly. So I've basically spent the whole day discovering something I didn't want to know. I now have no SSB with which to contact other sailors — sometimes 10,000 miles away — nor can I send and receive my email. Argh! That big black box has come to mean a lot to me. This is a sad day in the life of a young solo sailor …

Having turned *Guppy* upside-down in the process, I have discovered things I'd forgotten even existed. In the aft cabin, which I emptied to get to the transmitter, I found the big dinghy. I put it together again and attach my outboard motor to it so that I no longer have to paddle everywhere.

I try to resuscitate the SSB a few more times with Henk's help, as he has the exact same model, but we don't succeed. I'll have to wait until I reach Darwin to get a new one. I give up on it and decide to explore the bay in the dinghy. I once again forget to take my shoes along … and as soon as I get to shore, I pay for my carelessness. Oh no, not another foot injury!

It rains a lot, especially in the mornings and evenings, and today there's even a bit of a storm, but it's all good for my water supplies.

Ever since I mentioned my broken SSB radio on my website, I've had a lot of concerned and helpful emails from radio hams around the world, but despite all the good advice I still can't get it to work.

I planned to scrub the hull today, but it's still overcast and raining, so I decide to wait until the sun comes out. Swimming is for sunny days, and, because I'm so used to the heat now, a water temperature of 28 degrees is a little cool for me. Instead, I dive into the engine room to check the engines, filters, water, oil and electrics, and look for any leaks. Everything seems OK, except for the Yanmar which continues to use too much oil. This is in contrast to the Volvo engine, which never gives me any trouble. I also remove a dead cockroach from the bilge and throw it overboard before it gets stuck in the bilge pump again. I think the pesticide I used earlier has done its work, because I haven't come across a live specimen for months.

It's been raining all day and I decide to collect some freshwater using an old sail I found while tidying up. I've just got the sail ready and have caught half a bucket of water when it stops raining, of course. Well, five litres of freshwater is better than nothing!

The anchorage, which is surrounded by palm trees and lots of vegetation, is beautiful, but as soon as the wind drops it changes into a mosquito paradise and you can forget about sleeping. I'm not the only victim, and I hear a lot of muttering about this nuisance coming from the boats around me.

The public holiday that had begun when I arrived is over today, and everything is open again, so it's time to look for diesel and do some shopping. I also need to complete the clearance procedure. I have to do the 'health' bit and send a form to Fiji. When I get to the health centre, I realise that I've left my ship's papers on board and have to go all the way back. Returning to the health centre, I need to pay 100 Tongan dollars, which, of course, I don't have on me. So off to find an ATM to draw some money to purchase another piece of paper with all those important-looking stamps …

As I'm walking back to *Guppy*, my shopping bags tear and I struggle to get the contents on board intact. But that's not the last of my less successful activities… There's another important thing I left aboard *Guppy*, and I spend a good bit of time furiously looking for the ignition key for the outboard motor. All in all, it's been a testing day, but by nightfall all the cupboards are stocked, my clothes washed and everything has been securely fastened so that *Guppy* and I can set off tomorrow.

Tonga–Fiji: 470 nautical miles

DAY 1: *14 July*

I didn't succeed in getting my clearance papers from Customs yesterday, so I need to go back there this morning. I treat myself to a good breakfast at the outdoor restaurant with the view of the bay and check the latest emails. Icom America has offered to sponsor a new SSB radio and send it directly to Fiji! I'm so happy about that and it gives me even more reason to set sail immediately.

After five days in the beautiful bay of Vava'u, *Gup* and I are off again. It was a fairytale experience to lie in amongst this group of small green islands. I would have loved to stay longer, but I need to continue my world voyage as the seasons won't wait for me. So it's time to head for Fiji which lies about four days' travel from here.

Behind me, Tonga shrinks as we sail away, and I see *Sogno d'Oro*'s little brown sail moving from side to side. Henk and I leave at the same time, but *Guppy* is much faster. As the SSB is out of order, I no longer have any contact with the outside world. But this does have its advantages, as I pick up my rhythm quickly and enjoy the peace and space around me even more.

The crossing to Fiji shouldn't present any problems. Somewhere midway there are a couple of reefs and islands, but the weather conditions are fair with lots of sun and enough wind. I'm really curious about Fiji. I spent a month there with my parents' boat when I was just one year old. I still have a number of photographs from that time. There's one of my dad with me in a baby carrier on a horse trek in the mountains. In another photograph, I'm floating in a dinghy. My parents tell me I was able to swim before I could walk; insofar as you can call doggie-paddle swimming, of course. I don't remember a thing, but I think it's going to be special to see these places with my own eyes.

The wind is cooperating fairly well, but, alas, starts to ease and then comes from behind. This makes *Guppy* roll terribly, making life difficult on board. *Sogno d'Oro* had disappeared from sight within a few hours yesterday, and now Henk is also out of VHF reach. I'm cut off from contact with other sailors and peace has returned, so now I have time to read and write. By day's end, Fiji is 340 miles ahead of me, but there are numerous atolls and reefs on my path which means hours of being on the lookout and little sleep tomorrow ...

DAY 2: *15 July*

I'm still waking up tired in the morning, but can't work out why as I've slept fairly well. The sun is glowing like a copper plate above the horizon and it heats up quickly. There's little wind, and *Gup* and I have to exert ourselves for every mile gained, but I'm having fun doing stuff like breaking open and eating the coconuts that I've brought from Tonga, reading and pruning my banana bunch.

Towards afternoon, the speed drops drastically and the sails begin to flap. Dismayed, I switch on Mr Yanmar to spare the sails. Luckily, I've learnt to relax and not get annoyed anymore when we motor or are becalmed. There's little you can do about it, and it's always better to work along with nature than to fight it. It's getting dark. Suddenly I see something in the distance ... Ripples? The ripples become little waves, and before I know it there's a good 15-knot wind blowing. The sails are set, and with a good beam wind *Guppy* is soon making for the atolls at a speed of 6.5 knots.

DAY 3: *16 July*

To my great amazement, I see a hill rising out of the water in the distance, at the very spot where I expected to see an atoll. I rush to the chart and discover that I couldn't have studied the obstacles on the chart all that well yesterday. But it doesn't really matter if it's a hill or an atoll: both are in our path and are merciless for any boat that ventures near them. I just need to avoid an island, a reef and various fishing boats, and I can make straight for Fiji. In the meantime, I pass the 180-degree line of longitude, and *Guppy* and I once again find ourselves in the Eastern Hemisphere.

Unfortunately, the wind is dropping and *Guppy* is now running at only 4.5 knots, which means that I'll be arriving in the dark.

Fortunately it's full moon and, according to the chart, there are leading lights to guide us between the reefs. Even in daylight you usually only see reefs when it's too late. So *Gup* and I have decided to take a chance.

DAY 4: *17 July*

With the city lights shining brightly, it takes a lot of effort to distinguish the leading lights that guide you through the channel in the reef to Suva. When I finally discover them, they are actually blue and very weak. It then starts to rain and they are hardly visible anymore. They're just bright enough to guide *Guppy* safely through the reefs. The bay is full of moorings, with a number of unlit anchored ships. *Guppy* sails very slowly and I have to constantly walk to the foredeck to check with my search light so as not to bump into something. She manages to glide past all the obstacles without any damage and now lies peacefully at anchor. I'm now going to spend the rest of the night sleeping blissfully without interruptions.

Suva

I take a look at Suva when I wake up the next morning. It looks like a sizeable city. It's cloudy and the bay is full of big cargo ships. I may as well inflate my dinghy and start the obligatory clearance procedure. It's apparently not that easy on Fiji, so I'll probably be busy for a couple of hours.

While I'm inflating the dinghy, I'm told by the neighbouring yachts that I'm not allowed to go ashore before Immigration and Customs officials have come to me. OK, then I'll just wait ... The Customs launch eventually arrives in the afternoon with a mountain of paperwork, but they're very friendly and wait patiently while I fill in the unbelievable heap of forms before they apply all the fat stamps.

By the time we've finished in the late afternoon, I see *Sogno d'Oro* come puffing in. The Customs officials don't want to clear him in at this stage, which means that I'm not officially allowed to board, but

I'd promised Henk some pancakes on his arrival and bring him some anyway. I know what a treat it is when you've made a crossing and don't have to cook for yourself.

The next morning I meet a local boy at the yacht club and we visit Suva together, go to the cinema and drive around the city in a bus. Fiji is great, but it's really busy with all the people and traffic and I have to get used to it. They also drive on the left, which means I really need to keep my wits about me when I cross the road.

A bus ride here is quite an experience. Music blasts forth from enormous speakers and there's no suspension to speak of. I almost hit the roof several times! It's really something; especially if you're used to a speed of 5 knots. So different, but also fun to have the luxury of cinemas, shops, buses and even a McDonald's. It will only be a short stop, because *Gup* and I will be on our way as soon my vane is pointing in the right direction.

When I look at the photographs taken by my adventurous parents, I notice that there are more of them taken on Fiji than I thought. While I am looking through them, I stumble on one of my mother with lovely long hair at the fruit market in Suva with me in the pram. I decide to see if the fruit market still exists. When I get there, I discover the stall that is featured in the photograph. Not only that, the whole place still looks exactly the same! Of course, I don't recall a thing, but it's strange to be back at the exact same spot 14 years later.

I increasingly feel like making a detour to visit my birthplace, Whangarei in New Zealand, but really don't have the time now. It will definitely be on my route on my next voyage around the world. And that counts for lots of other beautiful places that I visited too briefly or not at all.

Icom America has sent my new SSB radio directly to Fiji and I've just received a message from the yacht club that I can pick it up at Customs at the airport. It got there two days later than expected, but it's arrived! Henk offers to help me install the complex radio. After a good day's work, I'm able to email again and talk to people all over the world. It works like a bomb, and callers in Tonga even ask me to turn it down a little because I'm coming over too loudly. Awesome! A well-functioning SSB at last.

There's a beautiful old square-rigged three-master, the *Alvei*, which is anchored next to me. I'm soon on friendly terms with the crew, and they invite me to sail with them for a few days on this special ship. They're on their way to the north of Fiji. The north end of the island is supposed to be lovely and, because I don't have enough time to go there with *Guppy*, I don't say no, of course. I ask Henk to keep an eye on *Guppy* for a few days and secure her with some extra anchor chain. I spend the rest of the day swimming and doing chores on *Guppy*. Henk and I go to McDonald's for a hamburger in the afternoon; the first one since Tahiti. I then board the *Alvei* as they leave early the next morning.

I wake up in the middle of the night and wonder where on earth I am. At 05.00 I'm shaken awake by the firing-up of the mega-big two-cylinder Sabb motor. After half an hour's hard work weighing anchor, we sail out of the bay. It's my second time on a square-rigged ship, but what a world of difference! The crew is much less experienced than the one on *Stad Amsterdam*, and of course it's much smaller, too; but they have much more fun, even though all the equipment is incredibly old-fashioned and the ship is a great deal smaller. We set two sails, but roll them up again almost immediately as the wind drops and turns against us. After cruising on the old Sabb the whole day — a sound you can listen to all day — we arrive at Baque, an island that lies a few miles north of the main island of Fiji. The crew is very relaxed and I'm getting used to life on board here fast. The sea is beautifully clear, and we snorkel around a small reef.

After two days I'm supposed to be taken to the main island, which is 10 miles from here, by a local boat, as the *Alvei* is not going back to Suva. But this boat is not running and I'm literally stranded on an almost uninhabited island until someone decides to sail to the main island. The island is beautiful and, together with three of the crew, we decide to find a waterfall. With some help from the locals we meet along the way, we finally find an awesome waterfall high in the mountains. We were advised not to follow the river back down, but do so anyway. We soon discover why: the river runs through cliffs and various caves. There are some more waterfalls along the way, which we clamber down over slippery rocks. We get back to the village by nightfall, totally drenched, muddy and tired, but an experience richer.

While we are on the beach trying to crack open a coconut, I see a small fishing boat being loaded a little further up. I run to meet it and ask if they intend sailing to the main island.

'Absolutely, and there's a place for you if you'd like to come along,' I'm assured.

I say goodbye to everyone, grab my belongings and jump on board the small wooden boat. It takes more than three hours to cover the 13-mile crossing, and we moor off a fishing village. The locals tell me that the bus stop for Suva is on the other side of the village. After an hour's ride with the usual blaring music, I reach Suva where *Guppy* lies peacefully at anchor. It's wonderful to be back in my familiar surroundings after being absent for a while.

I check the weather forecast via the SSB and see that it's looking good for the next five days, and so I decide to get *Guppy* ready for departure. The next morning Henk is standing at the railing at 06.00. He's also looked at the weather and seen that the next five days are perfect. A lot of wind on the quarter and then it will drop ... The trip to Vanuatu could be done in five days. I want to leave immediately and that means getting to work. I gobble down a sandwich, collect my documents and am on my way to Customs. There's a strong wind and I'm soaked by the spray and drizzle even before I get to shore in my dinghy. Once I get to Customs, the female official appears to have gone out, so I spend an hour checking the latest updates in an internet café. When she gets back, I try to fill in the forms as quickly as possible, but it still takes me two hours and many stamps before I'm finally done.

I'm yearning to leave, and almost run back to *Guppy*. I'm longing for the open ocean, the wind and the sea air ... I want to sail again! But the cockpit looks like it's exploded with all the clothes, tools, spare parts, jerry cans and other things that are lying around. What the hell, that's what I've got the aft cabin for ... and I add it to the mountain of stuff that will be securely wedged in there for the passage. I then heave up the anchor as quickly as possible and turn *Guppy*'s nose towards the open sea.

Suva–Vanuatu: 600 nautical miles

DAY 1: *27 July*

Once I'm on the open sea, the water is nice and rough and *Guppy* is asking for a reef in the mainsail. The waves are washing over the deck, and a fishing boat which left at the same time as I did turns back to the safety of the harbour. But *Guppy* is in the mood for more and thunders on regardless; more under than above water. She is sailing high into the wind and straight into the oncoming waves to round an offshore island. I'm soaked to the bone and everything is wet and salty again, but anything is better than no wind! Passing the island, I can ease the sheets and sail on a beam reach. The wind is now on the quarter, but there is no way I can sit and read outside. *Guppy* is blasting through the confused seas with gusto. I've had some tiring days and want to catch up on some sleep. I fall asleep almost immediately to the wonderful sound of water rushing past the hull while the radar keeps watch.

It's been a long time since I've had this much wind during a crossing and *Guppy* is going fast. With a bit of luck we should arrive during the daytime. That will be a pleasant change from my night-time arrivals in Fiji and Tonga. Not that I need to sail around all sorts of reefs this time, but still. It's also nice to be able to see something of your surroundings as you're approaching, and have the time to enjoy your destination as soon as you've cleared Customs.

This morning I'm sitting outside and enjoying the sunrise for the first time since my departure. The problem with so much wind is that the waves like to jump over *Guppy*. She's performing well and bravely climbs up and down the waves, but it makes reading or writing impossible. Eating is not much fun for my stomach and I don't manage more than a few carrots. But I can sleep well, and somehow it's always fun to look at the churning waves. At 16.00 Henk, who has also left and appears to be 30 miles behind me, calls me. Towards evening a cargo ship comes into sight. I call the ship to ensure that it has seen me. He answers me politely and confirms that he has.

207

DAY 2: *28 July*

I've been at sea for two days now and am about 300 miles from Vanuatu. Once again we're running downwind and the wind has dropped considerably. The result is that *Guppy* is rolling a lot on the huge swell, with everything that isn't securely fastened landing on the floor. It's not too bad, except that my bowl of cornflakes has joined the rest on the floor and coated everything. Grrr! Let me try a sandwich. I swap the jib for the boomed-out genoa and am happy that the hatches can stay open again. It's good to feel the sun and enjoy the fresh air. I eat my sandwich and continue reading *The Long Way* by Bernhard Moitessier. He took part in a non-stop sailing race, and then, when he'd gone all the way around, decided not to finish but to continue to Tahiti instead. The book was given to me by someone who thought I might do something similar.

In the afternoon, I shake out the reef from the mainsail. Let's hope the wind doesn't drop any more or I'm likely to arrive in the dark again. It's another 270 miles, which will take me two days, I think. Besides the cargo ship last night, all I see is the infinite, undulating, blue landscape. I haven't seen any fish or dolphins since my big crossing. I've now definitely passed New Zealand. A pity and it hurts a little to be sailing past my country of birth at a distance of 1200 miles, but I've promised *Guppy* that we will definitely be going there together sometime. The sun disappears behind the clouds and the wind freshens, making *Guppy* go up to a lovely speed of 6 knots by evening.

DAY 3: *29 July*

I have a wonderful night's rest without waking up once; not even when the Echomax alarm that picks up ships at a distance of more than 40 miles goes off. I only need to get up three times to adjust the course, because the wind has veered to the quarter. The breeze prevails, but, unfortunately, the sun disappears behind the clouds. Rainy, grey, sad clouds which produce a few teasing drops but not enough nice freshwater. After an hour's sleep, I chat to Henk who's 96 miles behind me. I'm still having a little trouble with the SSB because it's a newer model, and from time to time I'm unable to find the right frequencies.

When I do manage to find them, I haven't a clue how I did it … I listen to an SSB channel without really knowing what they're talking about for a while, but it's nice just to listen to people chatting thousands of miles away.

Guppy still has 120 miles to go before she reaches Port Vila, and there's a good chance that I'll make it by daylight. The only problem then is that I'll arrive at the weekend when it's difficult to clear in without having to pay extra. I'll probably have to wait until Monday to go ashore. *Guppy* and I have a good relationship, so we'll be alright.

DAY 4: *30 July*

I can't sleep tonight as I have a feeling that something is looming over me. At 04.00 a mass of squalls with heavy thunder and rain sweeps over *Guppy*. Party time! It's an unbelievable spectacle with *Guppy* surfing before the wind and waves. She may be able to handle the strong wind better on this course, but we are now sailing in totally the wrong direction. I adjust the sails so that we can return to the correct course, but then the wind changes again and we are once more on the wrong path … At 05.00, I join the SSB channel as I'm awake anyway and my fellow sailors are happy to hear from me.

Finally it's getting light but the wind drops — *slap, bang, slap*. Oh no, not again! I decide to furl in the genoa, which is flapping from side to side, and start the engine. As I step into the cockpit, I almost fall over a bird that's casually sitting on the seat staring out to sea. It looks totally exhausted and remains where it is, right in my path. I give it some bread and water, but it doesn't respond to the food. Hmm, sea birds should like fish … The only fish I have is tinned herring fillets in tomato sauce, but it turns its beak up at this, too! I leave my offering where it is in case it changes its mind.

A slightly bigger wave makes me shift my position and my hand lands in something soft. The entire cockpit is covered in bird shit, and I've managed to trawl my lifeline through it, too. Argh, this means that this mess is inside the cabin, too … I've just nicknamed the bird Messy!

Although I know that I'm really close now, the land isn't visible because I'm surrounded by squalls. I steer *Guppy* into the bay at Port

Vila in an afternoon drizzle and drop the anchor. Messy is not that interested in land and decides to stay on *Guppy*. As expected, I can only clear in on Monday, and I now look forward to a quiet evening with calmer winds and a beautiful view of Port Vila.

Port Vila

After the previous night at sea with squalls and thunder, I think I'm going to get a good night's rest, and dive into my salty, clammy bed early in the evening. After two hours, I'm still awake and decide to get up. It's lovely in the cockpit with the city lights in the distance. I strum my guitar the whole night through, accompanied by the sound of the waves washing on the beach. At one stage I compose a really nice piece of music, but then I fall asleep.

I wake up early again to find that I've managed to forget last night's lovely composition and notice that Messy is still with me. I meet my Dutch neighbour, who's been here on his boat for so long that he really isn't Dutch anymore. I decide to join him at a beach party this evening where I meet some new people. Needless to say, at the party I have to try the local kava from Vanuatu. Once, but never again! This one is even stronger and more disgusting than the one I tasted in Fiji. After a nice evening, I walk back to *Guppy* and see *Sogno d'Oro*'s lights in the distance from the beach. It's late and I think that Henk would prefer to sleep. There will be time enough tomorrow when I will also have to do the Custom clearance rounds.

Clearance seems to be fairly easy here, except that I have to pay for each bit of paper and every stamp. This always annoys me, and so does the weather, because it's started to rain again and my washing, which was almost dry, is now getting soaked while I'm in town. But never mind, there will be another sunny, dry day. After completing clearance, I wander through the town, and in the evening I have a drink with other sailors and island residents at a kava bar. I've dragged Henk along and he's still trying to figure out whether he likes it or not. I find kava disgusting but enjoy the company. Some people drink too much and then their legs don't work that well. Kava has a kind of numbing effect — your head remains clear, but your body no longer responds to your brain.

When I get back to *Guppy* in the evening, Messy has disappeared. I can now start cleaning up all the bird shit.

I wake up with the wind whistling through the rigging, and it's quite chilly for someone who's got used to a warm climate. There are always boats arriving and departing at every anchorage. Some have left, including *Sogno d'Oro*. I give Henk a few days' head start and am thinking about clearing out and leaving on Monday.

There's a 35-knot wind howling through the anchorage while I'm fighting hard with the internet again. It's either disconnecting constantly or so slow that I really can't work with it. But there's a solution for everything and even the internet can't beat *Guppy*-power ... I walk to another café a little further on, which I'd discovered also has internet and which has just opened. I try to get an internet connection and do my best with all the settings on the computer, but fail. After asking the staff to check whether there's a problem on their end one more time, they discover that they'd forgotten to switch it on! I finally manage to get my blog on the site and run through my emails.

Now that I've been here for a few days, I'm getting to know more and more people, including a local family who has lived here for generations. They ask me if I'm interested in a tour of the island. Of course I am! It's great and includes a drive up a high mountain with an awesome view. I can see *Guppy* lying below between all the colours of the water, which range from light to dark blue. Towards evening we drive back and I enjoy a meal with them on their patio before they take me back to *Guppy*.

It's exactly a year since my departure from the Netherlands, but it feels like I've been away for much longer. I've got so used to life at sea and moving from one island to the next that I haven't missed the Netherlands for a moment. Especially not the Child Welfare and Child Protection Board or, rather, the Board of Tricks and Deception and Youth Destruction! Although it would be great to see Kim, Spot, my parents and my friends again. I'm feeling down because I've just found a USB stick with photographs taken a year before my departure; the year the authorities and the secret service AIVD tried everything to destroy me. The Hurley 800 in which I would have done my voyage had been confiscated and my new *Guppy* was standing under the bare trees, totally stripped and without portholes. I'm as white as a sheet and look like a ghost, and I can still recall exactly how I felt at that time. How much I longed to be where I am now and thought that it would never happen. Fortunately, I never gave up. It seemed so close yet so far out of reach then. I'm so thankful for everything Dad did for me in that period; and without my lawyer, Peter de Lange, I'd probably be in protective custody right now ... But I'm free and that year now seems far away; as if it were in another lifetime. Something that never happened. A vague dream. But as soon as I see these photographs, I feel all the pain I had then; as if someone were twisting a knife in my heart. So why don't I just throw these photographs away? Because of the trauma the authorities caused me; because of my stepfather, who, together with the authorities, influenced my mother's opposition to the voyage. I don't want to be reminded of it, but at the same time am drawn to and sometimes have to see these photographs; only to promise myself never to look at them again. I neeeeever want to feel that way again. Will I ever be rid of the pain that I feel? All the traumatic things that happened crushed me, and the wound still hasn't healed. I feel it aching when I see the photographs. It still hurts when someone asks me about that time or when I read something about it. I weep all morning and feel awful. I'd despair if there were any paparazzi here now. There is so much to remind me of that black hole I was in. Even now, the Dutch authorities continue to bother me and try to put me in as bad a light as possible. That's why I've come to a decision during the last crossing that I'm never going back to the Netherlands.

I'm sailing to the Caribbean to fulfil my dream of sailing around the world, and then I will sail on to New Zealand to try to build a new life for myself. There are still many nights at sea for me and *Guppy*, and I will sail wherever the wind takes us; far, far away from that dark little country behind the dykes.

In the afternoon, I'm walking through town when I find something that I can focus on, something that will make me forget my present mood. I find a 12-string guitar on my walk back. Unfortunately, it's quite expensive. I could buy it tax-free and quite a bit cheaper once I've cleared Customs, but they don't want to give me a clearance stamp before I depart. I have an alternative plan, but the shop doesn't go along with it: to sell me the guitar for the full price and then pay me the difference once I have the clearance stamp. I'm just about to accept defeat and walk out of the shop when they change their minds and give me a big discount. They've seen me come into the shop often to look at the guitar and like the idea that I really want it.

Back on *Guppy*, I immediately try out my new acquisition. What a beautiful instrument this is and what an awesome sound it makes! I'm so happy with my purchase and it's not that much more difficult to play than a normal guitar. I get *Guppy* ready for departure between strumming my new guitar. All I still need to do is to fill up with water and diesel. I plan to leave for Darwin in a few days' time; a crossing of about three weeks. I should get there well before my sixteenth birthday. A milestone! Dad has already let me know that he's keen to join me in Darwin, but before that there are a couple of things that I need to check. The waterlock on the Yanmar is leaking again, in a different spot this time; the stern light has stopped working and it's not the light bulb; and I need to replace the steering lines of the windvane and inspect the entire rigging, of course.

I move *Guppy* to the wharf where she's allowed to stay for a day. I decide to stow the dinghy as I won't be needing it now, and almost fall overboard in the process. I'd built up the big dinghy and had forgotten that it was a lot heavier and difficult to get on board. The dinghy almost wins the tussle, but I eventually manage to get it up with the winch and the halyard. I now face the next ordeal: the aft cabin's where I dump stuff I don't use often, which is why it's, uhm, a bit of a mess. In its present state, there's no way that I can fit the dinghy in there, however much I push and pull. It means I have to tidy it up, again! Is there no end to tidying up? While I'm busy, a journalist comes by. I answer a couple of questions but really have had enough of the media.

After the clean-up, I treat myself to some home-baked biscuits and then cook some rice with chicken and veggies. I still need to master the skill of boiling Vanuatuan rice, but fortunately I'm the only one who has to eat it.

I also decide to spend half a day cleaning *Guppy* underwater from keel to waterline. There's a lot of marine growth there again, and if she's clean she can go at least half a knot faster. Once the sun is high enough in the sky, I dive into the water armed with a putty-knife and snorkel. After three hours of diving and scraping off molluscs, I climb back on board exhausted. I'd done the same in Tonga, but in these tropical waters everything grows so fast. I've had a sore throat and a bit of a headache since yesterday, so I decide to take it easy after all the diving and spend the rest of the afternoon strumming my new guitar and reading.

In the morning I'm at Customs when they open, but I'm sent from pillar to post. Payment is done on the opposite side of the town and I then need to return to Customs and Immigration before fetching the duty-free form from another part of town.

Once I've got all the stamps and official papers, I walk back to *Guppy* and fetch the jerry cans for the duty-free diesel. At the filling station in town, I ask if I can use my credit card. That's no problem, but after I've filled the jerry cans and try to pay with it, it doesn't work and I have to find an ATM to draw money. Once I've paid for the diesel, they decide the jerry cans are too heavy for me and offer to deliver them. They manage to fit them all in the truck and drop me off next to *Guppy*. So nice of them!

I really want to be at sea again and feel the freedom; just *Gup*, nature and me. It's a long crossing of about 2400 miles to Darwin, with the notorious Torres Strait on my route. It also means that I'll be leaving the Pacific behind me, which really is another milestone.

Port Vila–Australia: 2400 nautical miles

DAY 1: *9 August*

There's very little wind and I'm trying to catch every breath with the sails, but we're not doing more than 2.5 knots. The weather is beautiful and I'm able to read in between finding the best setting for the sails to push my sea slug forward. As a sailor, I'm in the business of trying to urge the slowest mode of transport to go as fast as possible. But the wind holds the trump card and wins the battle, which will probably mean a night of engine noise. The one advantage is that I can use the electric autopilot, as there is enough power. The windvane doesn't steer well in these light airs and I need to act often, but so long as the sails don't flap I let *Guppy* bob along.

I completed all the paperwork for the new SailMail in Port Vila. It's an email service for yachts that works via my new SSB radio, and I used it for the first time yesterday to send my blog to Dad. I still need to get used to being able to send an email while I'm out at sea, but it's much easier than sending a text message. However, the blog doesn't seem to have arrived … Hmm, that could be because I haven't been registered yet, which means that I may still have to send everything as a text message via the satellite phone.

It's wonderful to be out at sea again, and my brain slowly finds some peace. My thoughts are still jumbled, but this is a long crossing and there's time enough to get them sorted out before I reach Darwin. It's fun to read Nature's signs and make forecasts. I'm often right, but Nature remains unpredictable.

I've just finished reading *The Long Way* and now take Tania Aebi's book *Maiden Voyage* off the shelf for the umpteenth time. I know it back to front, but it's so well written and I can relate to it so much. There are many differences, too. She writes so well; I don't. My boat is much bigger than hers was and I have a GPS, radar and a working engine. She sailed solo around the world many years ago and has been home for some time. Home is a long way away for me and I'm not at all sure what the future holds. We'll see.

The sun drops into the sea like a big ball of fire. The fire dies and it slowly gets dark. My Dutch flag is drooping and its days are numbered. I switch the plotter to its night mode, switch on the mast light and enjoy all the space around me. There's still too little wind to sail, but we're floating along nicely and the SailMail is working. I can finally email at sea and no longer need to send my blogs via a text message. What a luxury to be able to write my blogs on the PC!

DAY 2: *10 August*

There's a light breeze when I wake up, but it dies as the sun rises. It's enough to drive me nuts! I've had hardly any wind since my departure.

This means that I'm almost constantly battling with the sails, booming out the genoa, furling, unfurling either the spinnaker or the code zero ... Putting a reef in the mainsail to prevent it from flapping too much, then taking it out again, dropping the sail, switching on the engine, then switching it off; with an average speed of no more than 2.5 knots.

If there's no wind, and if she has to, *Guppy* can motor for almost a thousand miles. But sailing is much faster, and I hate the engine noise and need to cover more than two and a half times that distance ... Oh well, there will be wind at some stage. Being becalmed does have its advantages; there's almost no swell and I can spend the night lying in bed without having to brace myself between the sides of my bunk to stop myself from sliding around. I eventually decide to switch on the engine to limit the damage to the sails when they flap. Now that I don't constantly have to keep myself busy with the sails, I can make music again — on my old, faithful guitar as well as on the new 12-string. I also read a lot and keep myself busy with all sorts of chores and repairs. Today I inspect the rudder, and this is how I discover that the bearing house of the steering wheel has broken ... In the evening I watch several episodes of the TV series *How I Met Your Mother* on my laptop. At moments like these, I tend to forget that I'm in the middle of the sea. I haven't seen a soul, besides a flying fish and two seagulls, and *Guppy* thanks them for the great job they did in shitting all over her!

I've been giving a lot of thought to my trip from Darwin. I now know for sure that I want to sail around the Cape of Good Hope and end my voyage on Saint Martin. I could make some stops in the Indian and Atlantic Oceans, but a non-stop trip is also beginning to appeal to me a lot; even though some of the islands in between do seem worth visiting.

I've managed to make brief contact with Henk on *Sogno d'Oro*, which is sailing 340 miles ahead of me. He's experiencing good winds and is sailing well. I'm sure I'll have good winds soon, too. According to the weather forecast, this could be in a little more than 24 hours' time. But we're not quite there yet. Patience, Laura, patience!

DAY 3: *11 August*

Time is passing fast. It's 11 August already and I've had another visit from a bird that couldn't help leaving the usual calling card. It has shat over the entire foredeck and the mainsail, and has now landed on the mizzen from where it is taking care of the whole aft deck. The sun canopy ensures that the cockpit — where I spend most of the day — is spared.

We finally have a little wind and *Guppy* is sailing at 3.5 knots again. I've thought up something to prevent the genoa sheet from chafing against the spinnaker boom. I wrap a piece of cloth around it and fix it to the worn spot with tape. *Voilà!* I need both hands to do this and am holding a piece of duct tape between my teeth. The tape attaches itself to my lip and I pull a little too hard to get it off. It wouldn't have been too bad if a salty wave hadn't washed over me at that very moment. Damn, that stings!

The speed drops slowly but surely to below 3 knots, and now there's a whole flock of birds flying around *Guppy*. Messy beasts, kindly find another landing strip!

I'm a little worried about the helm. It has a strange tremor and there's too much play. Luckily, *Gup* also has a tiller that I can use to steer. The problem is that if the helm gets stuck, the rudder also seizes up. Should I remove the steering cables and use the tiller to steer *Guppy*? Fortunately the windvane is connected directly to the tiller, which means that the helm is not that vital.

It's a beautiful, clear, warm day, but when will the birds finally leave? The sun is setting by the time they make their departure, leaving *Guppy* under another load of bird shit. There's still some wind, too little for windvane steering but enough to sail. There are also some clouds. Does this mean I may have wind tomorrow? *Guppy* is not really gaining fast on Henk's little *Sogno d'Oro*, and I don't really want to know what distance she's covered today. I can only guess that it's been depressingly little. I'm still having fun cleaning bird shit and thinking of a solution for the helm. I think that the bearing around the steering shaft has become corroded and broken. I try to fix it and it seems to work, but it's a very temporary solution. Another problem is that the foot of the genoa is slowly withering under the effects of the sun's UV rays. There are an increasing number of small tears and I try to stitch and tape them together.

In the meantime, I've started making a note of all the important coordinates in the Torres Strait. You never know when they will come in handy. The notorious Torres Strait is a passage between Australia and Papua New Guinea that divides the Pacific and Indian Oceans. It's also the end of the famous Great Barrier Reef. The problem with reefs is that you don't see the actual reef until you're almost on top of it, and the coral heads sink you on the spot if you hit one. It's going to mean being watchful and probably not sleeping for two days. And that's not only because of the reef; it's also a busy shipping route and I'm expecting a lot of cargo ship traffic.

The longer I study the chart with all the reefs and islands and all the currents, the more I realise that this is a difficult stretch of water. It's going to be a challenge again, but one I'll be able to manage, given fair weather. In any case, *Guppy* has another 1300 miles to go before I get there.

DAY 4: *12 August*

I spend the whole night waiting for wind. It doesn't arrive, and I eventually have to switch on the engine when *Guppy* becomes difficult to steer. In the morning, there's some wind at last and I'm doing between 4 and 5 knots. It's cloudy and the clouds look strange. I haven't a clue what it means, but they are low, puffy clouds that are hanging like a blanket all around me. Could this mean more wind? Hmm, not: I now have a 3-knot following breeze.

I switch on the SSB and chat to some of my fellow-sufferers. Most of the ones I know are still in French Polynesia and Tonga. The closest yacht is *Sogno d'Oro*, which is more than 260 miles away and moving further and further afield. Henk is enjoying good winds and sailing at 5 knots. Damn, why is the wind hiding beyond the horizon? Am I going to experience *Guppy* sailing at 6 knots before getting to Darwin at the beginning of September? Shouting, talking, pleading — none of it really helps. There's another 1875 miles to go to Darwin.

Bleep, bleep … Dad texts me that I can expect some wind in about six hours' time. He's following my progress closely and forwarding all the weather charts and updates he can find. I'd checked my own weather charts and needed nobody to tell me that I was floating in the only calm spot between Vanuatu and the Torres Strait.

The western horizon has been dark all day and I'm watching three mega-squalls in the distance. They have been hanging around for hours and I keep a watchful eye on them. A squall can sweep over *Guppy* at a speed of 35 knots within moments, and I need to reduce sail before they envelop me.

DAY 5: *13 August*

There's wind behind the squalls and they create some motion at last. I rush to drop the mizzen, furl in the genoa and continue sailing on mainsail and storm jib. The squalls come over me one by one until about two in the morning, and the wind is changeable. At times it starts to shift and then drops away again … I hoist the mizzen again and unfurl the genoa. It seems to get calmer. *Guppy* stays on course with the windvane and I steal a few hours' sleep. Towards morning, there's a good wind and *Guppy* is running at 7 knots. The bits of tape that I used to protect the foot of the genoa are now hanging in tatters on the rigging, sigh …

There's some sun in the afternoon. I'm increasingly worried about the genoa. There's a new tear and it's getting bigger and bigger. Please, genoa, hold on for at least another 1800 miles!

The start of the Torres Strait is less than a thousand miles ahead of us, and it looks like I'll be approaching it with very little moonlight. A pity, because I can't even see *Guppy*'s bow from the cockpit in the dark sometimes when there's no moon at sea.

DAY 6: *14 August*

There's a strong wind from the quarter and I'm asking myself if I should boom out the genoa on the high side or not. The waves are building up with some annoying cross-seas. *Guppy* is surfing off the top of them from time to time, which is a lovely sight. I'm sitting below reading after a breakfast of cornflakes, when I hear an oncoming roar. At the same moment, poor *Guppy* is thrown completely on her side. I fly through the cabin and make a hard landing against the bookcase on the low side. I hear the boomed-out genoa swing out with a bang, and the cockpit fills with water. When I get to my feet and sprint on deck, I see all sorts of loose bits floating away. I think of what I had out in the cockpit: a towel, my favourite mug, a book, a screwdriver and probably lots more that's now sinking towards Neptune. I hope he enjoys them.

The windvane soon has everything under control again and *Guppy* sails on. While the water runs out of the cockpit, I ask myself what could have caused such an enormous wave. Is it a taste of things to come? I'm beginning to be apprehensive about the Torres Strait where the two oceans meet and where the sea isn't much deeper than 20 metres. I'm going to have to stay awake for at least 48 hours to get past a mass of reefs and islands and deal with a strong current. On the other hand, I also see it as a challenge. At the Torres Strait, I'll be leaving the Pacific Ocean behind me and ending another chapter of my voyage. After brooding over the Torres Strait, I listen to the SSB radio channel and hear *Kiwi* for the first time; a ship that I saw in Tahiti and Tonga. The reception is poor and we don't get much further than 'hello' and 'goodbye'. Other acquaintances don't manage to get through at all because of atmospheric interference, but tomorrow is another day …

It starts getting dark and I make supper. It's going to be a mix of soup with spaghetti and bread. It's surprisingly nice. I go and sit on the chart table, wedging myself against the steps while the music plays. I study the steam rising off the little islands of bread in the brown sea in my spoon and burn my tongue with the first mouthful!

I was feeling listless today but am a lot more cheerful now. It's going well and *Guppy* is almost flying! She is now going at more than 7 knots, which means that the Torres Strait is approaching very fast; something that I anticipate with mixed feelings. I'm leaving the lovely blue Pacific and a huge part of my voyage behind, while a new part is about to begin. I'm very curious about what to expect after everything I've read about the Torres Strait. It's another 700 miles until the first reefs, so I've a few days to give my imagination free rein.

DAY 7: *15 August*

An email from Dad refers to the weekend, but here on *Gup* there's nothing to remind me of what day of the week it is. It surprises me that I actually know it's Monday today. It's a beautiful day with lots of sun, a clear blue sky and a pleasant 28 degrees. The enormous cross-seas are still present, but they don't worry *Guppy*, who cheerfully cuts right across them at a good 7 knots. A cargo ship passes us and it's going to get steadily busier the closer we get to the Torres Strait.

The batteries are running lower and lower and I can't find the cause. What's using so much current? I check everything, including the fridge. I find a forgotten cucumber, or rather what's left of it. I always switch off this power-guzzler as soon as I leave the harbour, as *Guppy* needs the current for her navigation lights and instruments.

I replace a windvane steering line that runs through a block that's too small, and climb up the mast to take some photographs. Looking down from here, I discover that my feathered visitors have left behind even more shit than I had bargained for. The solar panels are covered in a thick layer. Well, I have my work cut out for me because the panels will generate little electricity in this condition and I really need them for the radar and the navigation lights. I can just reach them by balancing on the railing, and I scrub every centimetre clean.

Just as I'm finished and turn around, a big buoy floats past. A buoy?! Escaped from somewhere? Is it dragging a net? Have I sailed through it? But *Guppy* thunders on regardless, and the buoy disappears within minutes. The SSB reception is still bad, but I've at least managed to get the weather forecast after some trouble. An 18- to 20-knot south-easterly wind is forecast for the next two to three days. Hey, that's not bad! I've got back into my daily rhythm and am feeling great. Although I'm not looking forward to the Torres Strait after all I've read about it, I am looking forward to getting to Darwin, as Dad and Jillian will be joining me and I plan to stay there for about three weeks. I'll celebrate my sixteenth birthday there and will no doubt hear all the news from the home front.

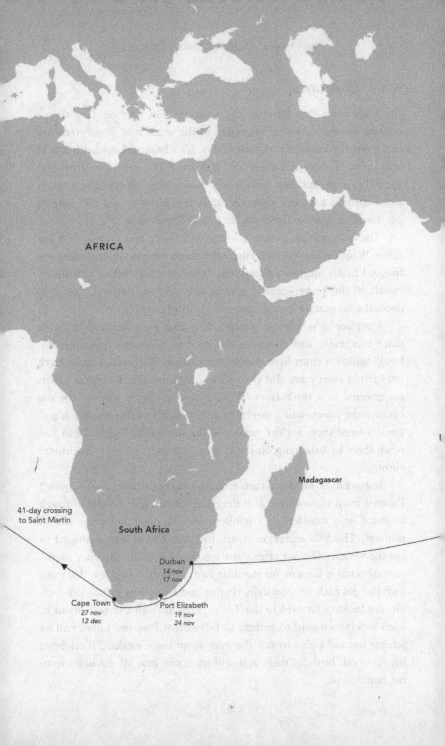

AFRICA

Madagascar

41-day crossing
to Saint Martin

South Africa

Durban
14 nov
17 nov

Cape Town
27 nov
12 dec

Port Elizabeth
19 nov
24 nov

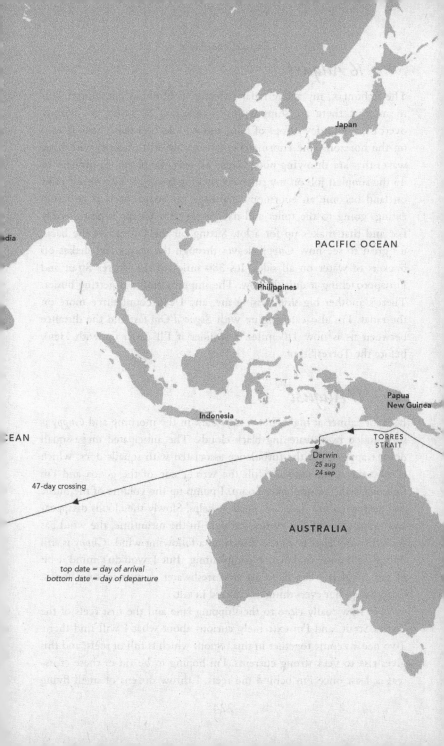

Japan

PACIFIC OCEAN

dia

Philippines

Papua
New Guinea

Indonesia

EAN

TORRES
STRAIT

Darwin
25 aug
24 sep

47-day crossing

AUSTRALIA

top date = day of arrival
bottom date = day of departure

DAY 8: *16 August*

The Echomax, my active radar reflector, is blinking constantly. This means that there are ships within a radius of 30 miles. It's heavily overcast, with a few drops of rain, and it looks like there is more rain on the horizon. The enormous cross-seas are still present, with high waves that are throwing poor *Guppy* all over the place. It's difficult to do the simplest job on my runaway rocking horse ... The easiest tasks on land become an enormous challenge on board, such as cooking, eating, going to the toilet and navigating. But *Guppy* is going really fast and that makes up for a lot. Sitting on the taff rail at the back, it's great to see how *Guppy* cleaves through the waves and shakes off buckets of water on all sides. It's 380 miles to the Torres Strait and I'm approaching it quickly now. The shipping traffic is getting busier. There's another big ship passing me, and I can count three more on the radar. I'm also catching up with *Sogno d'Oro* fast and the distance between us is now 110 miles. I wonder if I'll catch up with Henk before the Torres Strait.

DAY 9: *17 August*

It's a lot calmer at night, but it stays dark in the morning and *Guppy* is surrounded by threatening black clouds. The anticipated mega-squall doesn't appear, but the turbulence associated with squalls does, which is why the wind suddenly fills the wrong side of the genoa and I'm fighting with the spinnaker boom. I pump up the volume of the music and perform a sun dance on deck. It helps! Slowly the clouds disappear and eventually the sun comes through. In the meantime, the wind has shifted to my least favourite direction: a following wind. *Guppy* is still doing 5.5 knots, so I'm not complaining. But I wouldn't mind a bit of rain so that I can have my first freshwater shower in two weeks. Everything, but everything, is covered in salt.

I'm now really close to the shipping lane and the first reefs of the Torres Strait, and I'm extremely curious about what I will find there. Two oceans come together in this region, which is full of reefs, and this gives rise to very strong currents. I'm hoping to be rid of these cross-seas at least once I'm behind the reefs. I throw dozens of small flying fish overboard as I walk to the foredeck to stitch up some of the new tears in the genoa.

Now that the sun is shining and the solar panels are generating more power, I decide to charge my laptop and check my SailMail. I've received three emails and one of them is from my mother. She tells me she has plans to go to Gran Canaria for her holiday and I wonder if she doesn't secretly plan to move there, too. Just like Dad and Kim, she's not really happy in the Netherlands and is restless. It seems as though we are all, each in his or her own way, trying to leave the Netherlands; Mum by moving, and Dad by finishing his new ship, the *Havørn*, with which he is making progress by all accounts. Dad left his heart in the Pacific on his previous world voyage, and as soon as he has completed his ship he'll be going back there for sure. Does it make any sense for me to return to a country that treated me and my parents so terribly? I don't actually want to leave the Pacific behind me so soon; I feel at home here, and it feels bad to leave this beautiful ocean behind me. But here's a thought to cheer me up: so long as I keep travelling in a westerly direction, I'm likely to land in the Pacific again, and next time I definitely won't sail past the country of my birth!

DAY 10: *18 August*

In the corner of my eye, I see another one coming: a flying fish that finds it necessary to land on deck. There are sailors who eat them. They are apparently tasty with a little lemon juice, but they don't look all that appetising to me. Most of the fish I find are so small you'd only be chewing on bones, anyway.

Sogno d'Oro is sailing 22 miles ahead of me and it's only 50 miles to the shipping lane and the first reefs. From there it's another 100 miles before I turn *Guppy* into the real Torres Strait which is a further 170 miles long. But even here I need to be alert. A look at the chart shows me that there are more reefs than water here and they are strewn with shipwrecks.

The wind is back with a vengeance and *Guppy* is galloping at more than 7 knots. I'm running downwind, but I'm managing well with a boomed-out genoa. While it's still possible, I'm trying to get as much sleep and rest as I can, as I think there will be precious little opportunity for that in the coming days. This crossing is actually going much more quickly than I expected.

DAY 11: *19 August*

Sogno d'Oro's light is coming slowly closer, but I still can't see the contours of the boat. We chat via the VHF and eventually say good night. *Guppy*'s speed is 2 knots faster and by morning the little light has disappeared behind me.

At 23.00, I reach the shipping lane. Fortunately, there are only a few cargo ships, but I'm still having to contend with a strong 25-knot wind from astern. The sea is getting shallower here and the currents are coming from all sides, making the waves even bigger. It's only 70 metres deep instead of the 3 miles *Guppy* is used to, and it's getting shallower still ... Bligh's Entrance, the start of the Torres Strait, is still 30 miles off, so I should get there by daylight. Henk is now sailing a few miles behind me, and I see his green boat faintly when I peer hard through my binoculars.

I grab the genoa to stitch it up for the umpteenth time and find something to keep the helm in place. The shaft seems to be working further out of its broken bearing, and I fear that it could drop out at any moment. I've attached the tiller extension, just in case, and have the pliers handy for pulling the split pins from the steering cables.

In the meantime, *Guppy* races into the Torres Strait at more than 7.5 knots. There are reefs everywhere, but I see nothing as it's slowly getting darker. In the last daylight, I see the contours of the first island that I need to round, and then *Guppy* needs to sail close-hauled. Is this going to work or do I need to tack? *Guppy* has a reefed mainsail and genoa, and is cleaving straight through the waves with tons of water washing over the deck. The genoa is having a hard time. The foot of the sail disappears underwater regularly and I'm seriously worried about it lasting the night.

Rtttschhh ... I hear a loud tearing noise. Oh, shit! I don't even need to look. Switching on the deck light I see exactly what I expected — a mega-tear in the genoa. I grab my camera and, before I know it, the

226

sun-weathered genoa tears into strips that flap noisily. There's nothing more I can do except take the torn genoa pieces in and unfurl the small jib, because *Guppy* has to continue sailing through the many invisible reefs. The speed hardly drops and *Guppy* lifts her nose and pounds on regardless. And so we thunder on through the night, passing island after island, reef after reef and light after light.

Now that I'm sailing here, I can't wait to get out of this hornets' nest and back into the open sea ahead with more clearance under *Guppy*'s keel. In some places between the reefs it's really narrow and there are a lot of big cargo ships with crews who don't speak a word of English, which doesn't make navigating or communicating any easier. I've really left the Pacific behind me now; the biggest ocean with its beautiful islands to which I'll certainly be returning. I'm now beginning to wonder about the Arafura Sea and what the Indian Ocean will be like.

DAY 12: *20 August*

At dawn, all the little lights around me change into islands. The wind has dropped a little and *Guppy* is sailing over azure blue water. It's only 13 metres deep here. I take the reef out of the mainsail and get ready for the last hurdle of the Torres Strait: the Prince of Wales Channel.

It's 09.00 hours, I'm in the middle of the Prince of Wales Channel and my fingers are itching to use the spare genoa, but I have my hands full just navigating. I've dug the spare genoa out of the forward compartment that's moving up and down, and have put the huge sail on my bed. It's beautiful weather and I can see Australia on the horizon. It's unbelievable! I've crossed the Pacific Ocean, am almost through the Torres Strait and can see the Australian coastline ahead of me! Tears of joy are running down my cheeks. *Guppy,* I love you!!! On a long crossing like this I usually take it one step at a time, stage by stage, and now I've reached Down Under; well, almost. That really is a long, long way from where I began. If we just carry on sailing west, we'll get to New Zealand eventually. *Guppy* confirms this with an extra-deep dive into the next wave, sending a shower over me that ensures I'm now dripping water and fully awake. Yes, *Gup*, we can do it! With music playing full blast, I sail past Wednesday, Thursday and Friday Islands. I've come through the Torres Strait unscathed, have sighted the Australian coast and have entered a new sea! My head is spinning, and after a sleepless 48 hours I use my last bit of energy to do a little victory dance and ask *Guppy* how it feels. FANTASTIC! I don't care that a carton of apple juice has just flown through the cabin and splashed everywhere, that the dishes have landed on the floor, that my bed is wet and salty, that my genoa is torn and that the steering wheel is about to drop off. Yes! Sailing over a light blue sea is so lovely! Booby Island nears and then passes by, like a lost rock in a bright blue world.

I try to unfurl my torn genoa to replace it with the spare one, but it's one tangle of strips of sail. Hmm … Before I do anything stupid in my weary condition, I think I'll catch some sleep.

After a few hours' sleep, the world looks much better and I tackle the problem with renewed zest, but it still resists my attempts. When I look up, I see another problem. Because there's no tension on the torn sail, the halyard has wrapped itself around the forestay. I shake the spinnaker halyard hanging next to it back and forth, and by turning it at the right moment everything falls into place. A little later the genoa, or what's left of it, lies on the deck. The spare genoa was given to me and should fit, but it has a bolt rope that is too thick and the sail is 20 centimetres too long. Hmm … Now that the weather gods are smiling on me, I could fly the genoa with a beam wind. Considering the potential squalls and strong winds, I drop that idea and decide to continue on the mainsail, mizzen and small jib. *Guppy* is going a little slower because the wind has dropped, but is still making good progress. I'm still tired, despite my few hours' sleep, but I can't manage to get any more sleep. So I do the dishes, clean up the traces of apple juice, write a blog, read and play my guitar. Next my tummy reminds me that I've forgotten to eat for the past 36 hours. I'm slowly losing the tension and excitement of the Torres Strait experience and get back into my daily routine. I now have to share my bed with the sail bag containing the torn genoa. I don't have the energy at the moment to fold the enormous sail properly to fit it in the forward compartment.

DAY 13: *21 August*

It's exactly a year ago that I started on my solo voyage from Gibraltar.
That's a weird thought. After a night's rest, I still feel tired but a lot
better anyway. There's a good bit of shipping traffic and I've already
counted six cargo monsters passing me by. *Guppy* smells of delicious,
freshly baked bread at the moment, and I've made contact with Henk.
He's also managed to get *Sogno d'Oro* through the strait unscathed, and
is sailing 85 miles behind me.

The Arafura Sea where I'm sailing is very shallow. The waves are
short and steep and are throwing *Guppy* all over the place; but then it
wasn't a lot better in the Pacific Ocean with its cross-seas over the past
few days. Sitting on the taff rail at the back, I raise my shoulders and
watch how *Gup* jumps wildly from one wave to the next.

DAY 14: *22 August*

A fishing vessel has been sailing behind me at a distance of 2 miles
all morning. It initially came from the opposite direction and turned
around 2 miles behind me, and has been hanging around ever since.
I'm keeping a sharp eye on it from the entrance of the cabin. I wonder
what they want. They don't respond to my calls, and the fishing vessel
doesn't really belong in this area as the chart indicates a no-fishing
zone. I eventually see the mystery vessel move away. All of a sudden the
radar alarm for zone 1 goes off. Huh, what's going on? A vessel first has
to sail through zone 2, but there was no alarm earlier. The only thing
I can see on the radar is a long stripe, and another one a little later. I
suddenly see what it indicates. It's a low-flying Customs plane.

'Sailing ketch, sailing ketch, sailing ketch,' I hear on the VHF.

That's me. They have heard my calls to the fishing vessel that is
now retreating hastily. This is the second Australian Customs plane
that has flown overhead; something that's normal in these waters. They
ask for my boat's name, passport details and a number of other official
enquiries. It's almost impossible to enter Australian waters unseen. I'd
given my details to the first plane that flew over when I sailed through
the Torres Strait, and I now only have to repeat the boat's name. I have
a pleasant chat with the crew of the plane, and they wish me a pleasant

voyage. The plane disappears as *Guppy* sails on into the night. There's less shipping traffic and I'm able to sleep for a longer period. I'm feeling much better than yesterday, which is good as I have to feel fit for the last stage. There's a huge obstacle course ahead of me: a hundred miles of sandbanks, strong currents and a 7-metre tidal range. It's the Gulf of Diemen ...

DAY 15: *23 August*

Bang, splash — congratulations! I know that you like to turn my life on board upside-down, but give me a break. *WHAM, splash!!!* It seems you won't ... The cross-waves are getting worse; steeper and bigger. At regular intervals, *Guppy* is surfing down from the tops of the waves only to be knocked sideways by a wave washing over her when she reaches the bottom of the trough. The waves even splash over the spreaders. The cockpit, of course, gets the full load, which means I need to keep the cabin entrance closed, and it's hot and humid below. But even though the water is coursing over *Guppy*, she's running at more than 7 knots.

The water looks peculiar; there's a strange brown substance floating on it — whole fields of it. It looks like sand or mud. Could it be sand from the desert in Australia?

I have another 280 miles to go to Darwin, a real mega-milestone for me, and I still can't quite absorb the fact. I've been looking forward to being in the Pacific since I was young and have now left it behind me. Wow!

The wind freshens at night and I drop the mizzen and put a reef in the mainsail. When I crawl into bed a little later, I notice that the wind has increased to more than 30 knots. Sigh. I climb out of my warm bed and put a second reef in the mainsail. I don't sleep much for the rest of the night while *Gup* chases on at 8 knots.

DAY 16: *24 August*

In the greyish dawn, I alter my course and sail close-hauled in the direction of the Gulf of Diemen, which is known to be a rough sailing area with a 7-knot current to contend with. While *Guppy* thunders on at a speed of 7.5 knots, the groundspeed falls back to 6, then 5, 4, 3 and finally 2 knots. Damn, I'm heading into the current! Hmm, that means having to wait until the tide turns. The Gulf of Diemen is just a bigger version of the Wadden Sea, in the Netherlands, where I sailed with my Hurley when I was 10. I have to spend the rest of the night tacking between sandbanks, and should get to Darwin by tomorrow morning if all goes well. I'm really looking forward to it, especially to the moment when I can finally get some sleep.

Towards nightfall, the tide turns and *Guppy*'s speed visibly increases to 11 knots. I'm not used to this speed and have to be totally alert to find my way between the sandbanks in the pitch dark. It's almost midnight when I need to alter course, which brings me sailing close to the wind. Water is pounding over *Guppy* and me, as I stay on deck to watch everything closely. I'm cold and drenched and suddenly hear that dreadful tearing sound. *Rtsch, rtsch, flap* ... Oh no, my mainsail has torn to shreds! It's flapping like mad as I drop it down to the deck and bind it together while watching where *Guppy* is heading. There are shallows all around and it's very dark. Something like this will, of course, always happen when I'm sailing close to the wind on a small strip between bits of shallow water. It's not the right moment to set the spare mainsail, but *Guppy* is managing to maintain a speed of 6 knots with just the small jib and the mizzen.

Towards morning, the wind drops slowly and the contours of Darwin become visible. I make contact with Customs, who direct me to a jetty in front of the lock at the marina. During the last 8 miles the wind eases further and I switch on Mr Volvo. The sun shows itself above the horizon, and *Gup* is slowly drying while I get the lines and fenders ready. Wow, *Gup*, we've reached Darwin!

Darwin

There's no time to even think about getting some sleep, as Customs and Quarantine officials are ready to clear me inwards. I fill in form after form and answer the questions while the letters swirl through my head and I can't seem to find the right order. It's suddenly hot inside, especially since I'm still in my sailing gear. *Guppy* is lying still, but now the land is moving! The quarantine official takes his time; an hour and a half to fill in forms and to inspect the boat. They end up taking a tin of meat and the refuse with them. I then give a brief TV interview for the media who have been waiting patiently.

I feel as if I'll drop from fatigue when I sail from the dock. Once I'm at anchor, a small boat bearing the yacht club manager, David, comes to welcome me. I let myself be persuaded to come on land for a nice shower at the yacht club, and can't refuse a cold Coke with ice either. This entails putting the dinghy together. I decide to do this on land where it's easier. This should definitely have been the moment for me to have gone straight to bed … I forget to take the outboard with me, of course, and need to be towed back to *Guppy* after my delicious cold Coke and shower. Once back, I find that the outboard doesn't work and the wheels of the dinghy are flat, and that my folding bike is tangled up and its tyres are flat, too. I carry on trying to sort it all out, but my body, which hasn't had any sleep for two and a half days, protests and wins. Tomorrow, tomorrow is another day, I'm trying to tell myself. Yes, but today is not over yet. But for me it is, and I'm going to sleep without interruption; a whole night without tearing sails, without islands, reefs, sandbanks, buoys and ships. What a luxury! But my brain is still working at full speed. Slowly, even this last active part of me falls asleep; a long, deep sleep that I only wake up from 17 hours later. The next morning it feels like a whole lifetime has slipped by since I arrived in Darwin.

At the yacht club, I dismantle my Mercury outboard carburettor and Michael, who can't bear to witness my pathetic attempts, offers to help me. He lives on a catamaran in town and does day trips for tourists. I soon get to meet a lot of people through Michael. There's a festival in the city and, seeing that I haven't been further than the yacht club so far, I think it would be nice to go along. After the festival, he shows me some more of the town.

While I'm wandering through the yacht club, I bump into David, who's busy preparing the afternoon sailing races.

'You can borrow one of the club's old Lasers and take part, if you like,' he suggests.

'Yeah, what the hell, why not?'

The club Lasers are obviously not used often, but after a while I find all the parts and start to put one together. I'm ready just before the start, and only just make it to the start line in time. The race goes very well. In the Netherlands I sailed in a lot of competitions, and it feels good to know that I can still stay up with the leaders when it comes to sailing small boats; and it gives me just as much pleasure as it did in the past. During the second day of the competition, the wind is strong and I'm only just able to keep the boat under control with my light bodyweight. My Laser is leaking quite a bit more than the previous day, and in these waves it lies deeper and deeper in the water while I steadily drop further behind the rest of the fleet. When almost everyone has crossed the finish line and the rescue boat is waiting patiently for me to round the last buoy, I can't manage to keep the boat upright anymore. The Laser is slowly sinking and I capsize again and again, but I'm not giving up. With just a few centimetres of freeboard left, I get over the finish line and sail the Laser back to shore, where I'm laughingly helped to get the sinking Laser back on the beach. At the prizegiving, it turns out that I've come second overall thanks to my good performance the previous day. Wow — I've never managed to come second in a sinking boat before! The prize, a pretty flag, is added to the collection of souvenirs in *Guppy*'s cabin.

Jillian arrives at the airport tonight, and when I make my way to the dinghy ramp in the early morning I see her waving to me in the distance. We take the bus to town to buy a cheap phone and SIM-card. We are chatting so much on our way back that we forget to press the stop button and sweep past our stop. Knowing that our bus tickets are valid for three hours, we remain seated. Surely, it will come around again? Suddenly we are at the airport, the end of the route. We get off and take the next bus back. Once again we are too late to press the button for our stop. We get off at the next stop and now need to walk back to our original destination.

Now that *Guppy* has been moored for a while, I notice that it's getting harder and harder to move the rudder. I'm afraid that *Guppy* needs to be lifted out of the water to solve this problem permanently. While I'm sailing it's not a problem, but as soon the rudder is unused for a while the rudder head starts to rust due to the leaky packing between the bearings. After having travelled halfway around the world and stopped at many harbours and anchorages, she needs a good service and has truly earned one. I'll take the sails to the sailmaker. That will make a big dent in my savings, because everything is really expensive here. It's a heavy blow for the boat's kitty!

Life is suddenly very busy, and it seems as if everyone around me, including *Guppy*, needs me constantly. I'm longing for the sea again, but I first need to get *Guppy* into shape. I'm trying to find the best place to lift *Gup* out of the water. According to David, there are two shipyards that are equally expensive. The one in town is said to be the best and is closer, but it still costs A\$1000 to lift her out. That's not a prospect that makes me happy.

Through the Laser sailing I've come into contact with a group of people of my own age at the yacht club, and they've invited me to join them at The Sandbar. It's a sandbar that's dry at low tide and an ideal place for a party. Half of Darwin sails to this location and it's full of boats. We have a tube behind the speedboat and there's also a kneeboard, but no one is interested in using it. When I want to try it everyone laughs at me, but they soon stop laughing when they see that I can actually do it. I've been doing this since I was six on a special little board that Dad used to tie up behind the dinghy. On the way back I'm hanging onto the tube behind the boat with two others, when the outboard suddenly cuts out and we are launched into the air. I land with my face on one of the tow ropes and two of my teeth bite through my lip. Ouch! Eating, drinking and laughing are not going to be much fun for a while, and that's easier said than done. The rising tide brings the party to a natural end and I'm asked to join another party at someone's home. Here there are snacks that I simply CAN'T eat. Eventually someone feels sorry for me and gives me an ice-cream that I eat very carefully. Wow, it's been great fun and very late by the time I sail back to *Guppy* in my dinghy.

If everything goes according to plan, Dad should be getting on a plane in the Netherlands today to arrive here in two days' time. I'm crazy about him and am so glad he's coming over. With Jillian on board it's getting rather crowded, and we have to find three places to sleep amongst all the spare parts on *Guppy*.

234

Darwin is a fairly big town, but there's nothing but desert around it. It's really hot during the day and I don't have much energy to do much. By contrast, the nights are nice and cool. It's the dry season at the moment. Summer starts in a month's time, and so does the rainy season, and I want to be finished and gone before then. There's still a lot of work to be done on *Guppy*. Jillian is the most untechnical person and not much help, so I'm on my own. Well, Dad arrives the day after tomorrow and he can lend me a hand. I've made some friends at the sailing association, and in the evening I join them at Bogarts, a local pub. I end up talking to someone who turns out to be the pilot of the second Customs plane that flew over *Guppy* in the Arafura Sea. Small world! At 01.00, I'm back at the yacht club. It's low tide and I need to tow the dinghy over the sand and mud for about 500 metres to the water's edge. I forget to push in the safety cord with the ignition key so it takes a while to get the motor started. Jillian is still awake when I climb on board and is going through the film shots I've made of the voyage. We chat for a while and then go to sleep.

By now, I've spent two weeks in Darwin and have done a lot. Dad arrives tonight and I can't wait to fetch him from the airport at 04.00, together with Jillian. Dad is totally surprised to see me there at night and I jump into his arms.

'Dad, I have so much to tell you — it's wonderful here and *Guppy* and, and …' I gush.

'Hey, take it easy. Let's take it one thing at a time.'

We take the taxi back to *Gup* and talk until the sun reminds us that a new day has begun.

Jillian makes breakfast, and together Dad and I take a look at *Guppy*'s problems. Dad reckons that I've managed to fix most of them well. We make a list of the things we still need to do and what we're going to need to complete them.

We spend each day working really hard while the dolphins swim around *Guppy* and inspect her. We walk up and down to Bunnings, the hardware store, and comb the entire town for the parts we need. After two days of phoning around I finally find the right filters for the Volvo engine, but it entails a two-hour trip to the middle of the desert! Someone at the yacht club overhears my phone conversation and says

'Take my car', and throws the keys to me. 'It's the white one around the corner to the right.'

Dad and I walk around the corner to find a beautiful new pick-up with all the mod-cons. Dad is relieved to return the expensive car without a scratch later that afternoon, after which we enjoy a drink at the yacht club. And so the days come and go and soon *Guppy*'s sails are delivered, but the genoa doesn't seem to fit. The sailmaker has done something wrong.

Dad and I start to tackle the Yanmar's exhaust, which still leaks, but first I need to tidy up on board. I've discovered that working in chaos only creates more work, so I clear everything out of the cabin fore and aft and then put it all back neatly. I now have the benefit of knowing where everything is, and have found a place for the things that were drifting around in the cockpit and cabin. There are four over-stuffed dustbin liners standing in the dinghy for removal; filled with unnecessary stuff, according to Jillian and Dad. I must admit that I have a problem getting rid of things.

Henk left on *Sogno d'Oro* a week ago, and slowly more and more yachts are leaving Fannie Bay. A strong whirlwind passes *Guppy*, and the rainy season is almost on our doorstep, but for the moment it's still hot and dry. Dad and I decide that *Guppy* needs to come out of the water after all. There are two tall, rusty poles standing upright on the beach, which is dry at low tide. We inspect the poles and decide that it should be possible.

The alarm goes off in my ear; it's 04.00 and cold. We heave up the anchor and I slowly manoeuvre *Guppy* between the anchored boats, closer and closer to the upright poles on the beach. *Guppy* doesn't like it and wants to go back to deeper water. I tie her to the poles with a lot of fenders to protect her. The water drops, and half an hour later she's 10 centimetres from the sand, then 5 centimetres and …, then yes, she's touching the ground. The water ebbs steadily and, securely tied against the two poles, *Guppy* shows more and more of her hull.

The 7-metre tidal range means *Guppy* is dry in half an hour. Then the sun comes up and the work can begin. First we need to get rid of all the barnacles and other growth with a putty-knife, which is easier to do than we thought. Only then can I apply a coat of anti-fouling while

Dad works on the rudder-shaft packing. After working for nine hours, it's high tide again and we need to watch that *Guppy* doesn't crash into the poles in the wind and swell. We have a quick meal before the tide starts to ebb again and we can apply the second coat of anti-fouling. It's midnight by the time we crawl into our beds, tired but satisfied. I miss the familiar sound of water lapping against *Guppy* and her gently swaying me to sleep. She is standing high and dry on the beach next to my dinghy with the water at least 200 metres away. I'm feeling like a fish out of water! By 05.00 *Gup* is happy and floating again and we anchor her amongst the other yachts. It's the first time in a year that *Guppy* has been out of the water and it was really necessary. But I'm glad it's behind us now, as I get a bit nervous when *Guppy* is on dry land. We've been able to save a thousand dollars which we badly need for the rest of the refit. And so the days fly past.

I give a presentation for the local kids at the yacht club and follow it up with one for the Carbon Club. Then there's a big surprise for me: the chairman hands me a cheque to give to the sailmaker for the repairs to *Guppy*'s sails. The Carbon Club has sponsored the entire bill!

Today I've been invited to join the Dutch Solar Car Team, which is going to run the well-known 3000-kilometre race from Darwin to Adelaide. It's a nice change from working on *Guppy*. The car is made entirely of carbon fibre and is even lighter than I expected. There are an amazing number of factors at work to make the vehicle go as fast as possible, which is really interesting. *Guppy*'s electrical system also runs on solar energy, but the car is something else. It's pure high-tech, and both Dad and I are impressed. They, in turn, seem to be as interested in my voyage as I am in their vehicle. They ask many questions. I get to know a lot about solar car racing, and they get to know all about sailing around the world.

It's 20 September — my birthday! Jillian surprises me with fresh doughnuts in the morning and we decorate *Guppy* with balloons. I celebrate my sixteenth birthday with Dad, Jillian and a few local friends at the yacht club. Suddenly a big cake with *Happy Birthday Laura* iced on it appears. It's not every day that I'm given such a delicious cake, and I now have a good excuse to help myself to a big slice. This is my second birthday on my voyage. Having left Gibraltar when I was 14,

I celebrated my fifteenth birthday in the Canary Islands and now find myself on the other side of the world on my sixteenth birthday. In the evening, we eat at the fancy restaurant in the harbour and light sparklers on the beach.

Jillian is flying back tonight and I say farewell to her at the yacht club. I have one more day left with Dad, and we talk about my trip to South Africa, which I want to complete non-stop. Dad asks why I don't want to stop at the islands along the way. It's difficult to say why; I just love it when it's just *Guppy*, water and me sailing towards infinity. The excitement of the big, new challenge of sailing 6000 nautical miles non-stop. The next day we say goodbye to each other.

'Be careful and look after yourself,' Dad says as his taxi pulls away. After Dad has left, I see David returning with his windsurfer and ask him if I can try it out, but the sail is too big for me in this strong wind …

I'm sitting on the beach with my laptop on my lap, the sun has just dipped below the horizon and the last bit of daylight is draining away. The darkness of my last night in Darwin is creeping in and the waves are lapping on the beach. I'm feeling good; I'm intensely happy. Everything is fixed and *Guppy* is ready. We are going to do it; we can do it! I hear the bustle from the yacht club, there's music coming from somewhere and there's the noise from the dinghies and laughter. The sea is whispering and *Guppy* is swaying gently at anchor in the distance … Why should I leave? Why do I constantly have to go? Because the sea is calling. I want to find out what's beyond the horizon and I want to know if I can do it. I'll follow the ocean until she brings me to the place where I will find my future … New Zealand? Australia?

In the morning, I'm at Customs in town with my ship's papers, filling in more forms. Planned departure date? Hmm, tomorrow. Planned arrival date? No idea; honestly. Next to me someone else is clearing outwards on his way to Indonesia. It's going to be his first major trip, he tells me proudly. And how long have I been sailing? Oh, for more than a year now. All the way from Holland? Well, yes … Then there's silence … until he asks me how old I am. Fifteen, I tell him proudly, and then correct myself quickly. No, sixteen! I still have to get used to it.

When I get back, I check *Guppy* again and again. The water and diesel tanks are full, and *Gup* and I are totally ready. Just one more night and I will be leaving Darwin behind me. My time here has flown. I've met a lot of friendly people and am amazed at the fact that the schools here have sailing on their educational curricula. I'm going to miss everyone and everything here, but that's all part of sailing around the world. Ahead of me there are many, many miles at sea to lure me on to new adventures.

Darwin–South Africa: 6000 nautical miles

DAY 1: *26 September*

After a good night's rest, I'm watching how Darwin slowly disappears in *Guppy*'s wake in the early-morning light. I sail through the shipping lane towards the open sea while the sun rises and it slowly starts to get really hot. There's a container ship coming towards me and then another, but slowly it gets less busy. My mobile phone no longer has reception and I put it away for more than a month's rest. It feels great, and I'm slowly getting used to life at sea again as peace returns on board *Guppy*. The wind could be coming from a more favourable direction, but at least there's wind! Amazingly enough, I'm able to cope with a speed of 2 knots and a course that's far from ideal. If I've learnt one thing, it's not to be in a hurry to get anywhere. *Guppy* bobs about for half the night, taking us further from my charted course, but we're also making some headway in the right direction.

DAY 2: *27 September*

The wind lets me down, so I switch on the engine and point *Guppy*'s nose in the right direction for the first time since my departure from Darwin. The sails are loose and flapping from side to side and I take them down. Wait a minute, why doesn't the genoa want to furl up? Oh no, the only thing I can think of is that the halyard has got snagged around the forestay! It's pitch dark, and even with the use of a spotlight

I'm unable to see what the problem is. Well, there won't be any wind tonight, so it can wait until tomorrow.

DAY 3: *28 September*

I've had a good night's rest, because *Guppy* has been motoring calmly on her little engine because of the lack of wind and a strong swell. Early in the morning I'm standing on the foredeck; the sun is already burning hot without a breath of wind to cool me down. I peer up the mast and jiggle the halyard and genoa until everything falls back into place. I'm sitting in the shade enjoying the sunrise and see an enormous number of jellyfish float by amongst the golden brown dust that covers large parts of the sea here, too. Just when I've cleaned *Guppy*'s entire hull! At this stage, I'm not too sure whether I'd rather carry on sailing or be sitting in Darwin with an ice-cold Coke …

While I'm making breakfast I notice a rotting smell that gets stronger when I open the fridge. Oh no, not again! I've once again left something in the fridge which I switched off two days ago. I can't have the fridge on at the same time as the navigation lights and instruments, as this uses too much current. The last time it was a cucumber, and this time it's some slices of ham that are the villains.

I'm trying to distract myself from the prospect of sailing 6000 miles without wind by finishing the book *Fashionista* and then starting on *Déjà Vu*. All of a sudden I feel … yes, WIND! The flag fluttered! And it's coming from the right direction. Unbelievable! I set the sails and *Guppy* does over 3.5 knots. For the first time since leaving Darwin we are SAILING in the right direction! A hundred miles further on, there's a labyrinth of reefs and oil rigs, but that's for tomorrow, and I hope to finally leave most of the windless area behind me. I immediately feel a lot better. Let's hope that the wind stays, because it's certainly good for my mood. I play some music and start to write again, something I haven't done for three weeks. My flute playing is improving, and it's a lot easier on a moving boat than trying to play my beloved guitar. I try to play the tune from *Silas*, a German children's series that I was crazy about as a child. Playing guitar is more fun, but my guitar has enough scratches from all the flying lessons it's had on *Guppy* … In the afternoon, the wind slowly but surely lets me down again, while I retreat as far as possible into the cockpit to stay in the shade. Towards midnight, I start the little Yanmar that keeps me company for the rest of the night with its *putt, putt, putt* …

DAY 4: *29 September*

Beep, beep, beep. I'm woken by the alarm for the umpteenth time. This time it's not a ship, but an oil rig that slowly comes into sight on the horizon as it gets lighter. *Guppy* approaches it painfully slowly, and there isn't a trace of wind. At night the stars are reflected in the water, which makes it look as though we are gliding through space. Clouds are now reflected in the light swell. The oil rig is disappearing behind *Guppy* when I feel some wind. It slowly strengthens to a light breeze and, at last, the sound of the engine makes way for the lapping waves that are being parted by *Guppy*'s bow. Sadly, the wind is not coming from entirely the right direction, but for the moment I'm happy that there's any wind at all. I'm still not quite into my rhythm and am annoyed with the lack of wind, but I'm hoping to leave this area of calms when I leave Australia behind me. I want to get some real sailing done now!

Sunset tells me that another day has passed. The clouds and stars are no longer reflected in the water, but the ripples are not really convincing. The wind has dropped to about 5 knots and the windpilot is not doing a thing. So I've switched on the electric autopilot. Well, there's still some wind and *Guppy* is running at 2.5 knots for the moment. The diesel tank that feeds the Yanmar is already half empty, and that's a bad start for a trip of almost 6000 miles. I really hope that I can continue sailing from now on.

I finally manage to get hold of Henk on the SSB. The reception is very bad, but I'm able to gather that he's about 1200 miles ahead of me.

DAY 5: *30 September*

Guppy has continued to sail through the night, and almost in the right direction too. But the wind is dropping and there's a very irritating

241

swell that manages to bring *Guppy* to a complete stop with every second wave. ARGH! So I switch on the engine and we *putt-putt* along slowly. Wind, please! Haven't I waited long enough? It really annoys me that I've already used up so much of my diesel supply at the beginning of this trip; but if I don't use the engine, the wind and current will take me right back to Darwin. I don't have a choice; I must get out of these calms as quickly as possible.

I've put the clock back an hour and the wind has freshened a bit. I'm still not able to follow the desired course, but the most important thing is to get *Guppy* sailing. Now the wind drops again and I think I'm going to go nuts; if I'm not nuts already. I'm drifting straight towards a reef, but it's 40 miles away and it should take a while for *Guppy* to get there at this speed, so I needn't worry too much. I'm sure the wind will either shift or drop before we get there.

I spend most of the day reading and thinking about my voyage. The SSB radio chat starts in five minutes' time; let's see if I can reach a couple of boats. It's always good to hear from other people, even if I don't know them personally, and it will take a while before we have more to talk about than just the wind and our location. Every human contact is welcome at this stage. I manage to speak to three sailors, besides Henk, whom I chat to almost every day. They all mention the lack of wind and we share our frustrations.

DAY 6: *1 October*

Yay, the wind continues to blow! Unfortunately from the wrong direction, but at least there's wind. *Guppy* is running at 5.5 knots, but on a course that's too northerly. I really can't be too bothered at the moment; I'm just happy that there's some wind. *Guppy* is sailing close to the wind and heeling at an angle of 45 degrees, so life on board is a little more difficult, but I can handle that. We are going well; *Guppy* is cleaving through the waves again and leaving a trail of foam behind her. All the weather reports forecast wind from the south, which gives me hope. In the meantime, the wind is still coming from the west and that is precisely the direction in which I want to go. I'm happy and, if only we could now go in the right direction as well, life would be perfect.

In the morning I do some work on my book, but give up after an hour and just enjoy the fact that we're sailing again. I bake some biscuits and offer one to Neptune in the hope of humouring him. The biscuits have turned out a treat; maybe the best I've baked so far. They are finger-licking good. Amazing, actually! I've sacrificed my last two eggs to bake them. Seeing that I forgot to buy eggs before leaving, and that these came from the refrigerators at the supermarket, I needed to use them up quickly. I was left with a choice of an egg for breakfast, pancakes or biscuits. It's a toss-up between pancakes or biscuits, but I finally opt for biscuits. I'm not the greatest cook and *Guppy*'s pounding motion doesn't help matters. While I'm sitting in the cockpit enjoying the waves and biscuits, a ship comes into sight. It's an old wooden fishing vessel; it's coming straight for me and not responding to the VHF calls. I eventually alter course around it and see no one on the bridge or deck. Two hours later, I come across a similar ship and there's no lookout on this one either. A good thing that I'm more alert than they are! Or do they know that yachts will give way if you're going full steam ahead in their direction?

The wind still isn't coming from the south, which should have been the case by now according to the GRIB files that I've got from the SSB. Sigh. We are still sailing close to the wind, on a course of 270 degrees. Alright for now, but I would be happier if I could sail on a broader reach and preferably on the correct course!

DAY 7: *2 October*

It looks like Neptune is enjoying my biscuits! The wind continues to blow and *Guppy* is holding a course of 260 degrees and sailing close to the wind. I ease her to 270 degrees because she sails much better on this course. That's good enough for now, and the wind should shift at some stage to take *Guppy* on a more southerly course. I'm cheerful and enjoying everything around me. There's a long, heavy swell, but *Guppy* is too small to be affected. She just rolls over it like a rubber duck. Up she goes and down she goes. At the bottom of a trough the wind eases, but once back on the crest *Guppy* heels over again. In the meantime, a rumbling tummy wakes me from my daydreams: I'm beginning to get hungry and have an appetite for good food. And that's good news as it means that I've finally found my rhythm. All it needed was some wind. I go below to make something to eat.

Another 5000 miles to go and I suddenly wonder what will happen in those 5000 miles. What will I experience? A lot of wind, storms, calms, and will I get bored? What will my arrival be like? All questions which only time will answer, and that's a good thing. What would it be like if we could see into the future? There would be no more challenges and life would probably be pretty boring. There's no such thing as a perfect life and never will be. You have to experience the bad moments to be able to appreciate the good ones; but I'm hoping that *Guppy* and I can look forward to a good crossing.

In the afternoon, I eat some more of the delicious biscuits I baked yesterday. With some canned New Zealand butter they are a real delicacy. I'm standing with my back to the mainsail, which has been heaved in tight, and gazing out to sea while *Guppy* sails close to the wind and ploughs through the waves. She is sailing at more than 6 knots. We're still 20 degrees off our correct course, but that doesn't matter. The sun drops below the horizon like a big red ball while I enjoy watching the waves.

I've switched off the tracker because there's a lot of piracy on the Indian Ocean and this website is easy to hack. I'd rather not let the whole world know where I am at the moment. I text my location to Dad twice a day and that's enough.

I've seen nothing since the two rickety fishing vessels I saw yesterday. Not even any flying fish, dolphins or other sea life. Just a few birds that are gliding around *Guppy*; but I'm not really fond of birds. They are certainly pretty to look at, but, however good they look gliding through the air, climbing over the crest of a wave and playing with the sea, they always manage to shit all over the boat. They also have a mean look in their eyes.

DAY 8: *3 October*

Beep, beep, beep. The radar wakes me up at 03.00 … There's a light in the distance, and half an hour later another one and then another one. There are no navigation lights, and I'm beginning to wonder if they are actually boats because I'm not getting any response on the VHF … The wind springs up: this could be a squall. It's a bit scary and I can't figure out what those lights are. I avoid the mysterious lights all night while squall after squall breaks over us. After many hours of nervous irritation, it slowly gets lighter and the black clouds disappear. The night's mystery is solved when I look at the last white light through my binoculars and see that it's a fishing vessel. I think *Guppy* has been sailing through a whole fleet of them. I count eight spots on the radar and none of them seem to be moving. I wonder what they are doing 800 miles from the nearest coast? As if there aren't any fish swimming close to shore!

The sun shines brightly when I wake up from snatching some sleep. The wind has shifted and *Guppy* is finally right on course with a broad reach which gives us speed. She is running at 7 knots on a 260-degree course; a little higher or lower doesn't really matter at this stage of the crossing.

DAY 9: *4 October*

Flap, clunk, flap, clunk … Huh? I'm suddenly awake; *Guppy* lifts right up and prances on the turbulent waves. The wind has dropped entirely and has left *Guppy* with wildly flapping sails. The moon and stars disappear behind pitch-black clouds and there's a squall close by that's clearly visible on the radar. I'm almost certain that there's some wind behind the next squall, but my patience continues to be tested. I can't sleep due to *Guppy*'s staggering up-and-down motion and the anticipation of a squall. I sit at the chart table with one eye on the film *Elf*, and one on the radar waiting for the squall to hit us. The film is about someone who's brought up by elves and then returns to civilisation. It's all pretty vague, but a good laugh and that's exactly what I need right now.

The rising sun is colouring the sky orange again when the squall, carrying a huge amount of rain and a shifting wind direction, hits us. As usual it turns into a battle with sails and the course, after which my beloved constant wind returns and *Guppy* can continue on her way. Good, time to catch up on a few hours' sleep as I'm dead tired.

During my inspection round of the deck in the afternoon, I discover that the storm jib drum has lifted 2 centimetres. That shouldn't be possible and would mean that something has broken or something is wrong with the bearings. It still furls up without a hitch, and I don't know what's wrong. Hmm, something to keep an eye on. Otherwise *Guppy* is bearing up well and moves on with dignity, while my life follows its normal course.

DAY 10: *5 October*

I haven't been reading much these past few days, but time flies past. I chat with other sailors on the SSB and am playing the flute a lot. My guitar remains in the cupboard because nothing that isn't secured is safe. I'm looking at potential arrival places: Durban, Port Elizabeth or directly to Cape Town. Between Durban and Port Elizabeth a strong current flows in the opposite direction to the prevailing winds. The pilots warn sailors about the extremely high waves that make it impossible to make any headway with a yacht in these conditions … Hmm, I'll see. Before I know it, my tummy reminds me that it's evening again. I'm going to cook a nice meal for myself tonight: brown beans with mushrooms and string beans. It will make a change from spaghetti. The last two times I made spaghetti I didn't get it quite right. The first time was five days ago when I mixed in some pesto. I'd forgotten that the jar of pesto had been open for a while and couldn't remember for how long — BIG MISTAKE! It didn't taste quite right… The second time I cooked it in salt water, but that should have been half saltwater and half freshwater as I usually do. I'd stupidly forgotten to add the freshwater and it was super salty — YUCK! I ate half, but couldn't manage the rest and fed it to the fish. They probably had less of a problem with the saltiness …

DAY 11: *6 October*

It seems as if the wind is waiting for me to fall asleep … Yes, she's almost sleeping; in a little while … And then it drops away and *Guppy* starts to roll from gunnel to gunnel on waves that are coming from all directions, while the sails flap wildly. I'm wide awake and standing up on deck before I know it. After battling with the sails for hours, I can't stand the sound of the flapping sails anymore. Poor *Guppy* shudders with every flap and it hurts me to hear it, knowing that something is going to break. There's just too little wind tonight to be able to sail with these big waves.

I therefore partially roll up the genoa so that it can't slap into anything and set the mainsail in the centre. Sigh. Mr Yanmar will have to keep me company to prevent *Guppy* from breaching the waves, or we won't be making any progress. *Guppy* is still rolling heavily, but the waves are not tossing her around like a ball that much now. It's my third night with little sleep and I'm feeling a little under the weather, but I'm going to sleep now.

I wake up later that afternoon because *Guppy* is calmer and is listing to starboard … Huh? Wait a minute, WIND! I shoot outside to set the sails. I've had a good bit of rest and the wind is really behaving itself, with *Guppy* sailing at 7 knots. I feel reborn!

In the evening, I chat to Henk on the SSB about everything ahead of us. He's sailing about 900 miles ahead of me and has also been plagued by high waves and little wind. I use the SailMail to access a GRIB file and it doesn't really look favourable. There's another area of calms ahead, but it looks like it may pass below me. Please, let that be so! I change my course a little more westwards, so that I don't move too far south and can avoid the calms. In the evening, I watch the film *Happy Gilmore*, and then dive under the covers.

DAY 12: *7 October*

I'd got my hopes up too soon … The wind is back to normal — that is, no wind, headwind, shifty wind and everything between 0 and 10 knots. Of the 12 days that I've been out at sea now, I've only been able to sail properly for about 24 hours and have only enjoyed one good night's rest. Up until now, this is not likely to be the most pleasant crossing. *Guppy* is bobbing around and is rolling from side to side. The swell is not as bad as it was, but not ideal either. It's dark and grey around me, and it's not likely to get any lighter today. One shower follows the next; it drizzles, but there's not enough rain to collect the water and I end up with four litres of brackish water because everything is still covered in salt. Damn it!

247

In short, a good day to catch up with some schoolwork. I've almost completed *havo 5* (Year 11), but am wondering about doing my exams in a country that has done its best to break me. They still haven't given up and continue to bother my parents, who are constantly receiving threatening letters by registered post about all sorts of things. They continue to do everything they can to stop my voyage before I can complete it. The Dutch media also continue to publish nonsense without any verification. I have been anxious about the possibility of sabotage all along the voyage, so that they can say 'I told you so!' Just like my departure from Portugal, when the Dutch authorities tried to use their influence there to stop me. Fortunately, we had seen it coming and had thought up a plan B; the departure from Gibraltar without the media in attendance. Anyway, they would only have caught on when it was too late, as we hadn't informed the media where I would be starting from. I keep thinking that they might try again when I reach South Africa. What could they do? All sorts of thoughts run through my head: sabotage one of the stays, poison my drinking water? Whatever, I have really had it with the Netherlands! In Australia I replaced the Dutch flag with the New Zealand flag, and I haven't regretted it for a moment.

In the afternoon I climb into my bunk with my laptop and a good film, with the cosy sound of rain falling on the deck. *Guppy* is rolling slowly from side to side and is hardly making any headway. It's so dark during the day that I need to switch on the cabin light. I drift into a different world for a moment; away from the Dutch authorities, the lack of wind and the dark clouds.

In the middle of the night the breeze *Guppy* enjoyed for most of the night falls away. The ocean is almost smooth and she is rolling gently. Every now and then a sail flaps and there's a breath of wind … After looking around in the dark for a moment, I close my eyes and slip back into my dream world.

DAY 13: *8 October*

When I wake up, it's light and the sun is shining. Yesterday's dark clouds have disappeared and there are only a couple of white clouds above us. But let's not get ahead of ourselves, because there are more squalls on the horizon waiting to strike. I'm really glad the sun is shining again, because the batteries are running low. My mood lifts immediately. There's not much wind, though. I try opening a jar of apple sauce that has a rusty lid, but it doesn't open. I eventually grab a screwdriver and end up breaking the glass, which means that I no longer dare to eat the apple sauce. Defeated, I open a tin of pears and have them for breakfast. To my delight there's a little wind, and *Guppy* is leaving a trail of ripples behind her. I'm not entirely certain that the wind is here to stay, but surely there'll be good winds sometime?

I have some stowaways on board again. This time it's ants! Not really a surprise, as there were a lot of them in Darwin. Fortunately, it's a tiny species that doesn't bite. Every now and then one of them runs across the kitchen counter. Anyway, their presence ensures that I keep the galley clean and do the dishes in good time. I'm not really keen on an entire ant colony. While I prefer them to cockroaches, I'd rather just sail solo.

At night, the shifty wind and slapping sails drive me nuts. I've had it with adjusting the sails and changing course constantly. I really need a good night's rest, so I furl up the genoa, set the mainsail in the centre and put little Mr Yanmar to work. In the middle of the night there's a squall for an hour, and usually I'd use the wind to sail a bit. After some hesitation, I let it go and decide that while it won't make much difference to motor for another hour, it will make a huge difference to the amount of sleep I get!

DAY 14: *9 October*

The sun's heat wakes me up, and *Guppy* is sailing over an almost flat sea at a speed of 3 knots. The warmth is lovely. There are hardly any showers on the horizon, and today could be a really nice day. There's a little wind from the north. I switch the engine off and peace returns as *Guppy* sails on.

My hair is beginning to irritate me; it's always full of knots, hangs over my eyes and is very salty. I don't have enough freshwater to wash it regularly and I really have to use water sparingly if I want to reach Durban. What about the rainwater? Well, it has drizzled and I've managed to collect half a bucket of brackish water over the past four days. The sails, the sunscreen; everything is covered in salt! Saltwater washes over *Guppy* with each squall, but I'm happy with everything around me. The bird that has perched on the mast all night with its bum lit up red and green by the top light, the calms, the squalls and the slow progress; it seems as if it were always this way — or will it change? I spend half the day gazing out over the sea and dreaming of South Africa, the Atlantic Ocean … and then? Brazil? Saint Martin? And on to the Panama Canal again? I'm really looking forward to leaving the Indian Ocean behind me. I'm eating too much as it's a good way of passing time and I have enough food, but I hate the feeling of being constantly full. I resolve to eat less and pay more attention to my books.

A big liner passes me. It's amazing; I've seen a ship every day for the past four days on the endless ocean. And even here I still come across an old wooden fishing vessel from time to time. I was glad to leave Indonesia behind me, because I was following the movements of these boats closely every time I came across them. Now that I'm 800 miles from Indonesia, I come across another old wooden fishing boat. On the SSB I hear that there was a pirate attack near Madagascar so I'll be glad not to encounter any more of these small, sinister boats.

DAY 15: *10 October*

Finally, some wind, but it's so dark and grey outside that it looks as though the clouds will envelop *Guppy* at any moment. There's a 4-metre swell and I've been having squall after squall breaking over me for the past two weeks. The wind isn't constant for more than an hour at a time, which entails adjusting the sails and the course regularly. I dive into a book so that I can forget everything around me, but every time I get up there are dark clouds, drizzle and little wind. During my crossing from the Galápagos to the Marquesas Islands, I'd covered 2600 miles in the same time it's taken to cover only 1500 now. This ocean hasn't done me any favours, and I'll be glad to leave it behind me. The most irritating thing is that even though I'm surrounded by rain clouds and showers, I'm not managing to collect a drop of rain for a shower or to replenish my water tanks. *Guppy* is running at 3 knots and bobbing along like a useless rubber duck on the high swell. At the top of the waves, I have an infinite view of endless grey sea that changes into drizzle on the horizon. I have to accept it because I can't change it anyway, and things are bound to get better.

DAY 16: *11 October*

When day breaks, a few squalls pass by, causing the wind to come first from behind and then head-on, just to give me a hard time, before falling away altogether. This isn't much fun with the high swell and the cross-seas … *Guppy* is rolling very heavily and the sails are flapping in all directions, but once the squalls have disappeared on the horizon I feel it — WIND! Wonderful wind. *Guppy* flies forward and is making real speed for the first time since Darwin. It's going well and she's jumping over the waves at a speed of 7 knots like a young foal, and looks as though she's enjoying it as much as her skipper.

A glance at the solar panels shows me that there is work to do. I can start cleaning them all over again as it seems to have become a regular shithouse for all my feathered friends. Not good, and I'm pissed off about all the lost current that I need so much. Seeing that I've hardly had any sun, *Guppy*'s batteries have not been charging optimally, which means that I can make only limited use of my radar and beloved SSB radio, which both need a lot of electricity. A pity because my SSB offers me something else to do other than staring over the grey sea and skies.

Towards afternoon, my mood improves when the weather starts to clear gradually. I'm proud of *Guppy* as I watch her cut nicely through the sea. We have covered so many miles and experienced so much together. I think back to my first crossings, years ago in my little 7-metre *Guppy*. At the age of 10 I didn't have a clue what lay ahead of me, but that never stopped me from venturing into the unknown. After the first plunge into the deep end, many more followed, but I never regretted my decisions. I'm glad Dad gave me the freedom to discover things for myself, but never before he was certain that I could handle the situations I would be confronted with. This voyage of mine has already taught me so much. When I left the Netherlands I didn't have a clue what I wanted to do in the future, just like any other teenager, and now I have loads of plans. I want to go to New Zealand, finish my schooling there, and then do something in the sailing field. But most of all, I've come to know myself very well. I have consciously faced the fear of the unknown; confronted myself and conquered anxieties and loneliness. I've become stronger mentally and feel on top of the world. I know I will get to South Africa richer for the experience of having crossed 6000 miles of the Indian Ocean.

DAY 17: *12 October*

No bird shit today, and no squalls either, but a strong wind and something to go for! It's still cloudy, but the sun breaks through from time to time and that cheers me up. The wind gives me a broad reach and I've boomed out the genoa. The sheets are still getting chafed by the spinnaker pole and I invent a new solution. A sort of safety rope. I make a short loop in the eye of the genoa and fix the spinnaker boom to this. This line is sure to tear, too, but that's not serious. It's holding so far, but then I think of all my other attempts — the duct tape, Rescue Tape, the patches bound around … But theoretically this should work. *Guppy* is in her element and races through the waves.

I'm too late to see it coming … A massive wave breaks over the cockpit and soaks me to the bone. I've had my shower, but it leaves me even more salty. When I go below to change into some dry clothes, I feel *Guppy* balancing on the top of a wave and, before I know what's happening, I'm flung through the cabin, along with everything else that's loose. Everything in *Guppy*land is back to normal … Welcome back, wind!

DAY 18: *13 October*

In the meantime, the wind has got a little too frisky… Braids of white foam are flying over the water and the seas are mounting. In contrast to the Pacific, the waves are steep and high with a swell that's coming from a different direction to the wind. *Guppy* is being blown forward at a speed of 8 knots while massive waves wash over the deck. The companionway has to stay closed, and I see walls of water chasing past when I look outside. But *Guppy* is handling it well; I'm proud of her and know that she will continue to thunder on until the sea calms down again. All I have to do is keep watch. I've been at sea for 18 days now and this has been my longest crossing so far in terms of time; and I'm not even halfway yet.

Sitting on the chart table with one foot on the cabin steps and the other firmly against the cabin wall, I switch on the SSB. *Guppy* is occasionally surfing off the waves at speeds exceeding 10 knots, and is rolling dangerously from side to side. I have to reduce sail, put a second reef in the mainsail and possibly set the storm jib before night falls, because otherwise it is simply too dangerous. I'm busy thinking about all this when I receive a call from *Sogno d'Oro*. We've been talking for a few minutes when *Guppy* starts to surf faster and faster off a wave.

'Oh, shit!' is all I can say.

A huge breaker crashes over *Guppy* from the side, taking poor *Guppy* down a mountain of white foam to land on her side at the bottom of the trough with a mighty bump. Looking through the Plexiglas door, I see the sea wash into the cockpit. Still holding the microphone in one hand with the other on a handgrip, I'm hanging horizontally to the companionway and am looking at the oncoming water in shock. Slowly, *Guppy* manages to right herself while I survey the chaos inside and the water that is slowly running out of the cockpit.

'I, I, we — *Guppy* has just been knocked down,' I stutter into the radio. 'I'll call you back in half an hour.'

I switch off the SSB, click myself into the harness and wait for the right moment to venture on deck. In the meantime, the windpilot has got everything under control again. Almost everything that was in the cockpit has been swept away. The sprayhood has been totally flattened on one side, and I'm standing up to my knees in water in the cockpit … I take in the remaining bit of the genoa that's still attached to the spinnaker boom. With water flying over me, and cursing myself, I insert the second reef in the mainsail; something I should have done hours ago. Several lines are trailing in the water behind *Guppy*, and I bring them back on board. Half an hour later, everything looks to be under control again. There doesn't seem to be much damage to the mast or equipment. Cold and soaked to the bone, I get back to Henk and explain what's just happened. *Guppy* is more stable now that she is going slower, and I'm more comfortable about facing the night. We chat about life on board. Things that are so easy to do at home are a real challenge on board. Just going to the toilet is a major task, and you have to wedge yourself into a certain position just in case an unexpected waves launches you through the boat … But what must be done must be done; including eating liquid food that flies through the cabin the moment you let go of it, and losing stuff you left on deck. Reefing on time, but not too early, in case *Guppy* becomes a toy in the waves — it's all part of it.

It feels as though *Guppy* has been on a rollercoaster all night. I hear the breakers gathering height in the dark, but only see them when they crash over *Guppy* with force. The cockpit is underwater regularly. All the hatches have to stay shut tightly, which makes it very stuffy inside. I'm impressed by the waves here; not only are they really huge, but they are particularly steep. Each big breaker could knock *Guppy* down again, but she's handling it well and is running at 7 knots on a small piece of sail.

DAY 19: *14 October*

It's already light when the wind starts to drop a little. By noon it's just 25 knots and the waves are becoming longer. The breakers have disappeared. I shake out a reef and unfurl a good bit of the genoa. The situation is improving steadily and I suddenly feel exhausted. I've been on standby all night watching the turbulent conditions from behind the Plexiglas door. Before turning in, I check *Guppy*'s position and see that we've made good progress in the past few days.

DAY 20: *15 October*

The wind has totally died and we start the umpteenth grey, wet day. I can't even remember the last time I saw the sun. Everything is timeless here. If I didn't make a diary entry every day, I would lose my sense of time altogether. What does it matter if you're at sea for 20 or 25 days? Even though there's a big difference between one and five days. I'm still very tired, miss the sun and sometimes feel like running. At the same time, I'm intensely happy here on *Guppy* on the waves that have calmed down now. There are times when I'd like to be on land, but there are always more moments on land when I wish I was at sea. The sea continues to draw me onwards, and so does my curiosity to experience what lies beyond the horizon.

DAY 21: *16 October*

I'm woken up by the sun for a change. It warms me and *Guppy* all morning and things get a chance to dry, but now slowly but surely the sun disappears once again and so does the wind that has been blowing *Guppy* along nicely for the past few days. The speed drops to below 3 knots, leaving *Guppy* to float aimlessly. It drizzles from time to time. The sea is an endless dale of grey waves over which *Guppy* glides up and down. But, as always, the wind will return at some stage. It's all or nothing, and it's actually quite pleasant to be able to walk over the deck without a wave washing over me, and to be able to sit in a dry cockpit.

DAY 22: *17 October*

Drizzle and more drizzle. There's still little wind and the grey horizon ends 500 metres further off. Eating has become an important part of my day; something to look forward to. I try to make a special meal out of the large stock of long-life products. This will require a little imagination … I watch a film from time to time and read a lot. Now and then it rains a little harder, which means I've managed to collect 10 litres of lovely rainwater. I'm happy, even though there's little wind. *Guppy* has just passed the halfway mark and we have another 3000 miles to go before we reach South Africa. When I open one of my laptops to download my email via SailMail, I notice that it hasn't survived the wave crash we had earlier when it flew through the cabin. The screen has a huge crack in it! Fortunately, I have other laptops on board and have installed the SailMail programme on one of them as well.

How is it possible to be at sea for three weeks without having two consecutive days of good wind? *Guppy* floats into the night surrounded by spooky whitish-grey veils of rain. Everything is wet and damp on board. But *Guppy* is still moving forward, and the sails aren't slapping. It may be miserable weather outdoors, but it's really cosy inside.

Triggered by an approaching rain front, the radar alarm goes off in the middle of the night. Wham! A few minutes later, there's suddenly 35 knots of wind and *Guppy* is up to her portholes in water and begging me to reef the sails. All the stars have disappeared behind a big black cloud and the rain pelts down. I furl in the genoa halfway in the streaming rain, reef the mainsail and sail with a broad reach until it gets a little calmer. It's all over an hour later, and I now have a 20-knot wind. I've lost my bucket of lovely fresh rainwater in the squall. A pity, because it was still half-full and good for a nice freshwater shower. Oh well, shit happens ... I should have tied the bucket down or put it away!

DAY 23: *18 October*

At first light, *Guppy* is still sailing with a good broad reach and, although there are some strange cross-waves, she's running well at more than 7 knots. While I'm making breakfast in the galley, a big wave comes from nowhere and almost throws *Guppy* on her side again. Its twin follows and washes over the entire boat. The plastic flap in front of the entrance hasn't been able to keep the wave out, of course, and a good deal of water washes inside and over me. Dripping water, I try to find what's left of my breakfast ... In the cockpit, the water washes over the seats while the windpilot brings *Guppy* back on course to continue undeterred. While I'm mopping up the water that drips from the steps, I notice that they have worn and decide that I'll sand them down and varnish them in the coming days. The wood of the cabin steps has been wet for days, and this saltwater doesn't do them any good. But there isn't much I can do about it at the moment. I've had countless grey days. I read an entire book, forget to eat, and log in my position. Before I know it, the day has passed.

DAY 24: *19 October*

A sunny day at last! That's good for the batteries and for me. The wind and waves also offer good sailing conditions. *Guppy* and I enjoy it while it lasts, and are making good progress. I've managed to cover a good many miles on this journey so far, and I enjoy looking back at all the lovely places that *Guppy* and I have visited. I'm feeling great and decide to bake some bread. A little later, the entire cabin is full of the delicious aroma of fresh bread. Yum, this is a real treat at sea! I can open the companionway now that the rain has stopped and the waves seem to have calmed down. It's great to be able to let everything dry and to feel the warmth of the sun.

DAY 25: *20 October*

The sun is shining on my face when I wake up. I move immediately on deck to discover that the wind is still good, and finally everything on deck gets the chance to dry. I'm glad that the solar panels are doing their best to charge the batteries. I never sail without the radar, mast light and Echomax, so I really need to charge the batteries well after all the rainy days we've had. This is also good for my morale; the sun feels so wonderful! Funny that I should say this now, because I was cursing the sun while I was on the Equator … All in all, I've made good progress over the past few days and everything is taking its course on board, but sometimes things do break and I repair them; such as a broken fastening, a worn line or the water pump. I've also repaired the jib drum with some improvising, and hope it holds. And so the days pass.

DAY 26: *21 October*

The wind is easing, but *Guppy* is still making steady progress. After a good start this morning, the sun disappears, alas. There's just a watery sun now and it's fairly cold, but *Guppy* sails on at a good 3.5 knots, so I can't complain. I'm going to use this calm day to check everything and carry out the necessary maintenance. I grease the rudder bearings, cables and discs again. While I do this regularly, I have neglected doing so over the past few days because it wasn't possible with the waves washing over a staggering *Guppy*. My extra lines for the genoa aren't really working as well as I'd hoped; they are wearing faster than

I'd anticipated, which is why I've come up with something new. I've attached some stainless-steel rings in the hope that this will work. It's hard work bending the sprayhood frame back into shape, and it takes me a few hours before I can look at my work with satisfaction and get an approving wink from *Guppy*. Eventually, it's back in place and looking pretty good. I then hear *boink* and a dragging sound behind me on deck. The boom vang has dropped off because of a broken locking pin. This is why the thick pivot pin is also missing. I soon find a spare one and try to repair the troublesome thing. But there's too much tension on it, which means that I need to get the mainsail down in order to get the pin in. I replace the pivot pin and then the split pin, and now *Guppy* can sail under full sail again. Let's hope the wind doesn't drop entirely so that *Guppy* can continue to make progress.

DAY 27: *22 October*

During the night the wind changes its mind, and towards morning it's calm again and I've dropped the mainsail to stitch up a hole and do some other mending. I have the feeling that I'll be at sea forever, but it feels good. A feeling of peace has come over me. We are just floating around, but that's just fine.

There's a splendid sunset with the sky looking as though it's had big blobs of white, orange and blue thrown at it. Some are thick and bubbly, and others soft and fluid, and all of it is reflected in the sea which doesn't have a ripple. It's enchanting to look at. Lying in the cockpit, I gaze at the sky until it turns black with pin pricks of light that start to glitter overhead. *Guppy*'s speed is about 1.5 knots; not something to write home about, but I don't really mind.

DAY 28: *23 October*

I'm woken in the middle of the night by the sound of slapping sails and busy myself trying to get as much headway as possible out of the wind, which is constantly changing. But when there is no wind, there is no headway. There's nothing I can do about it, however much I try trimming the sails, and that's really frustrating. A few hours later, I'm treated to a massive downpour. I'm sitting inside and don't feel like going out into the dark, cold night to enjoy the freshwater.

I feel good and am thinking about everything. There are moments when I miss my family and friends and feel like giving them a hug; or going out for an evening with people I know instead of having to make new friends all the time, whom I then have to leave behind just as I'm getting to know them. But that's what I've chosen, and I've really grown since my departure in that respect. (And I'm not talking about my height. At 1.63 metres, I'm not really tall.) I've acquired a better view of the world and a better idea of what I want to do with my life. I have so many plans that I sometimes worry about how I'm going to pack them all into one lifetime. But the most important plan I have at the moment is to return to my country of birth, New Zealand. I like Australia, what I've seen of it so far, and I'd certainly like to return there. People's attitudes there are very different compared with the Netherlands. Australians and New Zealanders have a 'can do' mentality, making the impossible possible and going for your dreams. In the Netherlands, people are put into little boxes and those who say 'can do' are given a hard time. I know one thing for sure, and that's that I don't fit into one of those little Dutch boxes! I want to fulfil my dreams; something that's normal in New Zealand and Australia.

In the morning there's hardly a cloud in the sky and the sun casts a magic glow over the water. I take a nice freshwater shower from the bucket that has filled with rainwater overnight, and realise that it's not only the air but the water, too, that's a lot colder here. Whoa, this is a really cold shower! Brr … But the sun makes up for it all, and I'm enjoying the space around me. I play music all day long, and check the weather reports on the SSB from time to time. There's not much promise of improvement, alas, but at least *Guppy* is making some headway. Towards nightfall, there's enough wind to keep her on course and make some progress. The stars are awesome tonight; more radiant than they have been for some time. Mostly it's been too overcast to see much of the unknown world above. Now that *Guppy* is sailing without any assistance from me, I can sleep through the night without having to battle with the sails every 15 minutes.

DAY 29: *24 October*

I'm now 'channel controller' of the small radio net we have on the SSB. There are just four boats I still have contact with; *Dakota* is in Mauritius and, besides *Artic*, another solo sailor, the rest are behind me.

It's more overcast today, but this is compensated for by some wind. I'm seeing speeds of 4 and 5 knots again. *Guppy* maintains her course throughout the night, which is hard to believe. I keep waking up, thinking that the wind has dropped and that *Guppy* is sailing in the wrong direction because the wind has swung 180 degrees. Every time I can hardly believe that she's still sailing well and on exactly the right course. It feels like the wind is playing a joke on me. Because I've been so restless in my sleep, I spend more time daydreaming and lying in the cockpit today; something to enjoy as long as there are no waves coming over.

DAY 30: *25 October*

It's midnight when I'm woken abruptly by squalls with strong gusts, and rain, rain and more rain. Towards morning the wind is coming from all directions; strong, then weak and then from the opposite direction, and so I have my hands full with the sails while it continues to pour. I've put all the buckets out to catch water for a nice shower later. In between the squalls, I'm playing Solitaire inside. When the cards start flying through the cabin, I know it's time to take a look outside …

Guppy is not making much headway, and hasn't covered the mileage I'd actually hoped for. I've lowered my expectations and am hoping for an average of 4 knots — which I managed yesterday. That would mean that *Guppy* has another 20 days before I see the South African coast. But it would seem that I have little to say about these things since the weather and the wind are in control.

It appears that I've stocked up with more than enough food — something that is so difficult to gauge when I'm standing in the supermarket. Do I have enough of this and that? Fortunately, I've polished off all the sweets and biscuits. I consciously don't take too many of these snacks with me, as they are always the first to be eaten.

I know myself too well. Two weeks ago, I didn't feel like cooking anything and lived on two-minute noodles and biscuits. Now I often eat cornflakes for breakfast, and today I do so with freshly collected rainwater and milk powder. In the evening there's spaghetti, beans or some other tinned food on the menu. In between, I eat some tinned cocktail sausages or some soup, and that does me fine.

I can gaze at the sea for hours, or just think about all the countries I've been to and the people I've met, and I'm never bored. I rarely think back to the period with all the court cases just before my departure. I've finished the 'The Netherlands' chapter and would rather never think about it again. I'm feeling good at the moment, and have at last been able to distance myself, bit by bit, from the awful lead-up to this journey. I no longer have panic attacks when I'm confronted by the media, and I even manage to answer their questions in a normal manner. I can even laugh about all the guest-book messages and other reactions on the internet, even if they are negative. A lot of people support me and that's nice to know. I no longer have the feeling that it's me against the world and that I need to prove something. After all, I'm doing this for myself. It gives me a real kick to think that people enjoy following me on my voyage via my blog; especially when I notice that other people have been encouraged to pursue their own dreams now that they see how a teenager from a simple family is managing to do so. At least that's something I've achieved!

DAY 31: *26 October*

I've had some problems downloading my emails and haven't been able to receive or send mail for two days. I hope this improves when I get closer to South Africa. *Guppy* is sailing close-hauled and I'm unable to maintain the right course any longer, which means that we are sailing too far south, but at least there's some wind. Anyway, today has been the least cloudy day up until now, with just a few small greyish clouds and a burning sun. My batteries have been fully charged again and I'm using the extra power to charge everything that can be charged. Long live the sun!

DAY 32: *27 October*

At last I'm able to access my emails and I'm pleasantly surprised by an email from my mother, who writes that she misses me and would have loved to have come to South Africa. Kim is fine and doing well at her high school. Otherwise, life in the distant town of Harlingen, in the north of the Netherlands, doesn't seem that exciting. Which isn't the case on *Guppy*, who is ploughing through the waves in a 25-knot headwind with waves that are building up, and an approaching new storm. I'm not feeling that well for most of the morning, but I'm a little better after a few hours and am getting used to the pitching and stamping of the boat. *Guppy* is sailing with a reefed mainsail and storm jib, and is 20 degrees off her ideal course. Now that the waves are coming at an angle from ahead, I'm able to leave the companionway open. Suddenly I feel the boat hover, and then there's an enormous thud as a massive wave rolls over *Guppy*. The water rushes in between the sprayhood and the conduits near the entrance. *Guppy* doesn't seem to notice, shakes off all the water and continues on her way. It might be sensible to close the hatch at this stage if I don't want to have a saltwater shower inside.

DAY 33: *28 October*

I'm sitting on the chart table and have wedged myself in with one foot against the steps and the other against the side of the cabin so that I have my hands free to write an email to the home front while *Guppy* jumps up and down, hardly making any headway. The rollercoaster is in full swing, but fortunately we haven't done any somersaults yet. I'm amazed at how good I feel, but I can't see the sense in being flung around like a rubber duck in a gigantic washing machine and getting wet and salty while sailing in the wrong direction at a speed of 3.5 knots. At least the sun is shining! Maybe I'm losing it a little, because I'm feeling great — even laughing when a huge wave washes over me as I'm taking down the thrice-reefed mainsail. The wind gauge hasn't dropped below 40 knots since last night, and *Gup* is now sailing only with the storm jib. Sailing this close to the wind in 8-metre-high, phosphorescent waves with the sound of whistling rigging is truly awesome … This is when you realise just how powerful nature can be. And *Guppy* just thunders on. This is so incredibly cool! Sometimes *Guppy* climbs to the top of a wave, only to make a metres-deep, stomach-wrenching plunge before picking herself up again and bravely climbing the next wave. I'm sure the pleasure would soon fade if this were to go on for days, but so far, so good. Besides the saltwater from the toilet bowl that washed over my clothes cupboard on the other side of the boat, a broken windvane line, and a short time later a broken shackle, it's all going well.

DAY 34: *29 October*

The wind picks up even more during the night when I go on deck to look for the light of the first ship I've seen on the radar in two weeks. However hard I look, I can't sight the ship. I only have a couple of seconds to look for the ship every time *Gup* balances on the crest of a wave, before facing a wall of water in the next trough. The spray blowing over takes away all my visibility. On the radar, I see that the ship passes *Guppy* neatly, and I stay on deck for a while to enjoy the flying waves, the stars and the sliver of moon while the wind is whistling in the rigging. The sea is growling and bellowing, but it's fantastic. I've got *Guppy* and I know that she can do it. The deck is constantly awash with water, but I'm enjoying the moment and know that I will cherish this for ever when we come through fine. At the same time I realise how powerful Nature is and what a teeny, tiny dot *Guppy* actually is in this immense ocean. But she continues to take on the sea and wind, diving into a wave, shaking the water off as if nothing's the matter. And, yes, there's little I can change about the situation, so I may as well see the fun in it and wait until things improve. You can love the sea or hate her; but you can never trust her. And that's probably exactly what makes it all so interesting.

Guppy is still sailing close to the wind, but her course is improving slowly. I seem to have got used to the violence and the overwhelming noise, but sleeping is going to be tricky tonight. I'm learning how to avoid getting bruised and, besides an amazing bump on my head, I only have a few big bruises on my legs, so it's not that bad.

263

DAY 35: *30 October*

The weather improves towards morning and the wind drops to about 30 knots, which feels like a light breeze by contrast. *Guppy* is sailing on a beam reach with a double-reefed mainsail and storm jib while the wind is getting more and more favourable. She is pounding a little less and beginning to pick up to a good speed. For the first time in three weeks I see a cargo ship; and that's not only on the radar. It's far off and travelling in the opposite direction, but it's a sign of life in this vast, empty ocean. A little later, I see a dolphin jumping high above the waves. So lovely! I keep looking to see if there are more coming, but the stunt is sadly not repeated. This is the first marine creature I've seen since Darwin, and it makes my day. *Guppy* has another 1500 miles to go and, if the weather charts are anything to go by, it's not exactly going to be a holiday. Probably I'm going to have to wait a while for that first cold Coke …

DAY 36: *31 October*

During the night, the wind drops even more and I'm worried that it might disappear altogether, which won't be much fun in this heavy swell, but there's wind two hours later and I manage to get some more sleep. Mother Nature seems to want to make up for the storm front and all the violence that she's thrown at *Guppy* and me, and rewards us with wonderful sailing weather. The waves have subsided and there's a 20-knot wind and a very long swell. *Guppy* is cutting through the waves with a beam wind at a good 6 knots; a speed that I'm more used to from her. I'm enjoying the sun in the cockpit and spot another ship. There's more shipping traffic now. When I step inside the cabin I'm confronted by the enormous chaos the storm has wreaked and am keen to establish some order. It's high time, too, as the rough weather has made everything salty and dirty, with wet clothing and things scattered throughout the cabin. Now that the boat is stable enough for the dishwater to stay in the basin, I spend hours scrubbing *Guppy* and making her liveable again. The ants seem to appreciate my efforts, too. I hadn't seen them for days, but they are now coming out of all the nooks and crannies. They don't have long to live when I see them, but their numbers don't seem to diminish. I find them in the strangest places, and they even run over my keyboard and my charts. But I don't really mind them, and they are a whole lot better than cockroaches!

At 23.00, I see the light of a ship in the distance. The Echomax peeps almost constantly, which means that there are more ships within the 30-mile zone. Once the ship has passed, I set the radar on a 6- and 4-mile range and go back to sleep.

DAY 37: *1 November*

When I wake up in the morning, I hear a fizzing sound along *Guppy*'s hull, which is how she tells me that she is going nice and fast. From my bed, I see that the sun is rising from the right spot, telling me that we're not only going fast, but in the right direction too! There's a beam wind, which every now and then shifts to become more on the wind, and it feels great. I'm able to stick to my course and that makes me happy. *Guppy* is going like the clappers for the first time in a long time and we manage to sail more than 140 miles in 24 hours, but the wind continues to shift and change in strength, which keeps me busy. I'm asking myself if I should put a reef in the sail, but as soon as I do this the wind drops again. Hmm … *Guppy* begins to roll because I don't have enough sail up in this high swell and I need to remove the reef. This carries on all day, and it's exhausting keeping *Guppy* constantly on course this way; with not too much, but especially not too little, sail up. Nothing has changed by evening. Every time I get into my bunk, the wind drops or changes direction. Hard as I try, I don't get more than about three hours sleep in total. I hope it's better tomorrow so I can catch up on the lost hours. But we're making progress and approaching South Africa fast now. Just 1250 miles to go!

DAY 38: *2 November*

The predominant northerly wind disappears during the night and is replaced with rain and shifting winds, which means even more work. I have to adjust the course and trim the sails constantly, but my efforts at least keep *Guppy* moving and prevent the sails from flapping. There's a pelting burst of rain which flattens even the waves, and I take a lovely, but cold, freshwater shower while I'm filling pans and buckets with heavenly water. It ends in drizzle, which I've had so much of on this ocean. The rest of the day is dark, rainy and very overcast. I even have to switch on the light when I want to read inside in the middle of the day. I'm feeling tired and try to catch up on as much sleep as possible in between the many sail changes and course adjustments. During one of my catnaps, I'm woken up by the course alarm after only 15 minutes when the windvane is unable to maintain its course. When I look at the log, I see that *Guppy* is going at half a knot; I hear the flapping sails and feel how she is rolling. Hmm, it looks like I'm going to have to exercise a lot more patience …

I battle with the sails all night while I'd rather be sleeping, but the wind has its own ideas about that and keeps on shifting. At times it drops away only to come back later, throwing in some thunder and heavy showers. Halfway through the night, I can hardly keep my eyes open and decide to take down the sails to prevent them getting damaged when the wind shifts or dies. I start Mr Yanmar, switch on the autopilot and hope to get a few hours' sleep.

DAY 39: *3 November*

When I wake up, it's lighter and the wind seems to be more constant, but it's coming from ahead. I set the sails quickly, even though it means sailing 40 degrees off my planned course. But at least *Guppy* is moving and the wind is fairly steady, so that I manage to sleep for a few hours. I wake up in the afternoon feeling totally fit. The clouds have disappeared and *Guppy* sails on happily, while the sun actually shines!

DAY 40: *4 November*

I hear *doink, boink, doink* when I open my eyes; no wind, sigh. I'm up early and do my inspection round. I try to use the bilge pump to get rid of some water and discover that it doesn't work. After struggling with the pump for a while, I get it working again. I also top up the oil-guzzling Yanmar. When I go to my cupboard to look for some clean clothes, I notice that many more of my clothes are wet and salty. The ones that were wet from the salty toilet water had been laid out to dry … But the sea seems to have found yet another way to come in during the last storm. I use the sunny, calm day to dry everything, and this keeps me usefully employed while *Guppy* floats along very slowly. My cheerful mood is interrupted when I find a packet of spaghetti that is full of bugs! Alarmed, I immediately dig into the rest of my food supplies. All the other packets that I bought in Darwin are infested with bugs, which means that almost my entire supply of spaghetti is spoilt. After a futile attempt to filter out the good spaghetti, I throw everything overboard. This is a total spaghetti disaster! The supplies that should have lasted for weeks, have been reduced to a few packets … I still have enough rice and tinned food on board, so there's no shortage of food, but I'm rather fond of my spaghetti meals and will now have to make do with rice … I recall the last time I cooked rice — a total disaster which put me off eating rice for some time. I do, however, manage to get it right this time and it's more than edible, so my culinary skills must be improving.

DAY 41: *5 November*

ARGH, the wind really doesn't know what it wants, and there only seems to be a choice of either a lot of wind or no wind at all. Towards evening, there's finally a lovely breeze that freshens quickly. The wind is soon up to 30 knots, on a broad reach which has *Guppy* accelerating like a galloping horse at 8 knots throughout the night. In the morning, the wind drops more and more and comes from ahead, until *Guppy* is sailing close-hauled at 25 degrees off her ideal course. Looking at the weather charts, I expect the wind to fall away altogether, but we've managed to cover quite a distance overnight and only have another 800 miles to reach South Africa. *Guppy* will make landfall in just over a week. That will take some getting used to after a month and a half of only waves, horizon and clouds. Something else I need to get used to is the number of ships that are increasingly appearing around me; mainly cargo ships, but also some fishing boats. While I'm enjoying my breakfast in the cockpit, I'm gazing at the heads of foam on the

waves when I suddenly see a tall white one … After a good look at it
through my binoculars, it appears to be a sail. When *Guppy* gets closer,
I discover a yacht below the sail — the first one since leaving Darwin! I
jump for joy on the cabin roof and then dive below to call them on the
VHF. No response. The hours pass and the boat gets closer and closer
until I hear '*Crackle … crackle …* sailing vessel, *crackle …*' from the VHF.

They have just discovered me! I have a good chat with the Irish
couple on board their 12-metre sloop, who think they are just as fast
as *Guppy*. It makes me happy to think that there will be a boat in the
vicinity to talk to for a while, but *Guppy* soon appears to be much,
much faster, and by evening the Irish boat is 20 miles behind me and
outside the range of the VHF … Well, they shouldn't have told *Guppy*
that their 12-metre yacht was just as fast as *her*. :)

I've found some more packets of spaghetti that have only a few
bugs in them, and manage to fish the bugs out of the pasta once it's
cooked. There's a beam wind of about 20 knots and we're coursing
ahead. There's a high swell and the waves *Guppy* is cleaving through
leave a bright green trail of light in the dark night. Lying on my back
in the cockpit, I lose myself while gazing at the moon, the stars and the
unbelievable power and beauty of the sea. There have, of course, been
enough days when I've had to shelter indoors and wouldn't have dreamt
of going on deck just for fun. And when I did have to go on deck, I
cursed every sideways slip and every wave that washed over the deck.

I go below to download my emails via the SSB, and see that there's
one from my little sister, and this, together with the good wind, makes
my day. It always cheers me up to receive news from the home front.

Hey Laura.

I've also emailed Dad and have a reply from him, but I
still need to read it.

I understand why you don't want to return to the
Netherlands …

I'm glad that you're enjoying yourself so much, and it
doesn't really matter where, but I would like to see you again
very soon :) <3 Have you seen any more dolphins? Or sharks :)

Check my Hyves when you have access to the internet :)

I'll bring a giant pack of spaghetti and a calm sea with me when I come over.

Are you still sleeping in that corner under the cockpit? Or have you moved?

I've moved to the first floor. I live there now :) and the attic is now the guest room.

Well, happy sailing and cursing the waves.

No one hears you at sea and you can really shout, a good way to chill. If I try anything like that on the street here, they'd stop me and put me in a nuthouse :)

xxx your little sister, i miss you,

i love you <3 <3 <3 <3 <3 <3 <3 <3

DAY 42: *6 November*

My forecast that the wind would drop has, alas, come true. At about midnight the wind disappears completely and *Guppy* is rolling madly on the subsiding swell. Sleeping is practically impossible, and towards morning the blue sky suddenly turns pitch black and we have a mega-squall bursting over us with hard rain and much wind. Fortunately, most of it passes behind *Guppy* and, after doing a 360-degree swing, the wind is now coming from the south-south-west, which means I have to sail close to the wind but this time with the sails to starboard. The squall has really got *Guppy* spiced up... When we heeled, a pot of pepper lost its lid and it flew through the entire boat. *Achoo!*

DAY 43: *7 November*

At last, a night with some good sleep! There's a lovely southerly wind that's helping *Guppy* along at 6.5 knots. The wind has dropped a little and we're going well. What I like most is that it's constant, so that I don't have to go on deck all the time to adjust the course or the sails. There are many cargo ships about in the morning; three are in sight, of which one is on a collision course. I call them up and ask if they have seen me: 'Yes, no problem. We will go around you.'

Ten minutes later the ship is still coming straight for me and so close that I can read its name through my binoculars. This really is too close! They call me, asserting that I am too close and that I need to alter course. Well, yes, I'd come to that conclusion myself. Sailing at a speed of 6 knots, *Guppy* is not able to make way for the fast-coming, terrifying impact, so I answer: 'How about *you* altering course?'

'What? Us?!' Followed by a brief silence, and then: 'Oh, okay. Yes, we will alter course.'

The huge ship sweeps past me at a distance of half a mile and disappears on the horizon within 15 minutes. A little later I come across a large steel buoy; the second one in three days. What are they doing here? It has a lot of rope, nets and other stuff attached to it. *Guppy* has been lucky enough to avoid them so far.

DAY 44: *8 November*

On 8 November, I get this email via the SailMail. An article from the media:

> Solo sailor, Lucas Schröder, has withdrawn from the Conny van Rietschoten Trophy nominations 'because of Laura Dekker'

Speaking from Salvador de Bahia, Dutch solo sailor Lucas Schröder says he has withdrawn as a candidate from the Conny van Rietschoten Trophy 2011 selection. The sailor does not want his performance (the 10th place in the Mini Transat 2011) to be compared to that of the 16-year-old solo sailor, Laura Dekker, who is sailing around the world and who, according to Schröder, is still 'controversial'. The whole text reads:

> 'On my arrival in Brazil last Tuesday, I heard that I had been nominated for the Conny van Rietschoten Trophy. Of course I am very honoured to be nominated and learnt about my fellow candidates with due respect. I was, however, surprised that Laura Dekker had also been nominated in my category. As you well know, her project is rather controversial. By

putting me on the same platform, my own sailing projects and performances will, inadvertently, be associated and compared to those of Laura. It is also unavoidable that Laura's nomination for the most prestigious sailing trophy in the Netherlands will be viewed as a stand on the matter by the sailing world. This makes it so awkward for me that I request you to no longer consider me as a candidate for your trophy.'

The Conny van Rietschoten Trophy is presented to 'a Dutch sailor who has distinguished him- or herself by an outstanding competitive performance or someone who has made a valuable contribution to the sport of sailing'. Despite his statement, the exact reason for Schröder not wanting to compete with Laura Dekker when it comes to this prize is not entirely clear. Is it purely because she is said to be 'controversial'? Laura's solo voyage is no longer that controversial, and now that she is over the halfway mark of her expedition, her name is increasingly mentioned alongside those of other top sailors — especially abroad. You might query whether the fame that she won at an extremely young age with her love for sailing could be expressed as 'a valuable contribution to the sport of sailing', in the light of her personal circumstances. But that would lead to an academic debate and there is no denying that Laura Dekker's solo voyage around the world at an extremely young age has drawn more attention to her sport in the regular media than that of all the performances by other Dutch sailors put together. However much the more regular competition sailors may regret this, it all has to do with the structure and nature of this sport.

Hey Muis,

You can't have any idea about what's happening here … We have been receiving piles of threatening registered letters from the authorities again. Fines that will be exacted if you don't appear at school immediately, etc. They still want to try to stop you; by whatever means possible … It seems that they are not happy that their game with the documents in

Portugal wasn't successful and that other countries have not wanted to cooperate with them up till now, as you know … The authorities have got Lucas Schröder on their side to achieve this, as you can read above! … It looks as if the state does not want to allow you to finish and certainly not achieve any success. We didn't want to tell you any of this, but the situation is getting more and more serious now that the Dutch authorities think you may complete your voyage. You have been worried about the threat of sabotage to *Guppy* by people working for the Dutch security services all along your voyage. All of us, including our lawyer Peter de Lange, suspect that this threat now needs to be taken seriously more than ever. It's our opinion that you and *Guppy* will have to be protected 24 hours a day in Africa. For this reason, I will be coming to South Africa together with the people from the security company that supported you in the Netherlands. We really are sorry about all this, but fortunately Peter de Lange will help us through to the end. He will be making as much as possible public through the media so that it makes it more difficult for them to continue their games. That's how we finally won last time. We will make it all public, including the fact that the state is still trying to stop you through legal means, etc. Granddad and Granny will help where they can, and Peter de Lange will be giving these matters his attention for the whole day tomorrow.

Sorry my dear, I love you so much. You really don't deserve this.

XX Love from a very sad Dad

I knew that despite the efforts of my small support group — comprising Dad, Granddad, Gran and Peter de Lange — to keep these matters to themselves, there had been big problems for months. We were aware that all our computers were being hacked again and again, and that our telephones were being tapped. When we discovered this at the time and reported it to Child Protection, they simply informed us that these were standard supervision procedures! I had picked up the fact that they were taking legal steps with the schooling from media reports. And the dirty old tactic by the authorities of using the media to set the nation against me had again been going on for months. After I left the Netherlands, more than a year ago, I thought I had rid myself of this *nasty* game. Hadn't I won my court cases? Case closed.

At the time, in 2009, the Dutch authorities had also made the *Guinness Book of Records* liable for any possible consequences of record attempts by minors, which resulted in the *Guinness* scrapping these records. All this in the hope that I would give up. But that didn't bother me that much. I had been busy with the preparations for a very long time before I realised that I might also break a record. Surely you don't undertake a voyage like this to feature in a book? My life has been disrupted since the age of 13 when I was unwillingly cast into the public eye by the Child Protection Board. The one moment I was enjoying a fantastic childhood, and the next I was in the midst of a bureaucracy nightmare. With one goal; to destroy me and shut me up. I was thrown into the deep end without any time to get used to having to stand on my own two feet; and after almost drowning, I learnt how to swim … I learnt that adults, especially state officials, were not to be trusted. They have a wicked amount of power! When people think there is a way of making money out of you, then you've really had it. Every time I had the opportunity to earn something from my voyage, it disappeared before my eyes. This was done by people who'd been in the game for some time and they left me with debts and even greater problems. It all happened so quickly and I, just like Dad, didn't understand what was really happening. Managers who knocked on our door were only in it for the money. I was the target for paedophiles who posed as sponsors. And all this thanks to what the authorities said about me in the media. Who can I trust? I've been pursued and followed by the Dutch authorities and the AIVD (Dutch Secret Service) for two and a half years now …

Why? Simply because I threatened to slip through the fingers of the Dutch authorities? Why can't I just sail around the world like hundreds of other people? There is no law that prohibits it. Why do I need to fail? It's clear that the state's Child Protection and Child Welfare organisations have lost face, but why do they have to win this battle?

So that they can say: 'I told you so; all we wanted to do was to protect her, but she didn't want to listen.' Is it SO important to show the Dutch youth that this is not tolerated? Is it SO important for Dutch schools to brainwash the young into not having any ideas of their own? At school you're taught that the Netherlands is a democracy, but in reality it appears to be a totalitarian state. I've got a headache from brooding over it all and trying to find solutions. Will there be more court cases? Do we have to start all over again? My lawyer Peter de Lange is doing his best, but will that be enough?

I'm not going back to the Netherlands, anyway. I'm ashamed of the country where I grew up and I made my mind up a while ago to continue sailing to New Zealand. Fortunately I was born there, but I am concerned about Dad who now has to deal with fines and all sorts of other things. While I'm no longer a resident of the Netherlands, Dad still has guardianship of me until the age of 18, and he still lives in the Netherlands.

The risk of sabotage has been on my mind from the start of my voyage and I would prefer to sail on non-stop to Saint Martin. I'm safe at sea and no one can harm me there. At sea, all I have to fight against is nature, an honest battle in which I know all the ups and downs; but on land there are people … People who can deceive me and people who can sabotage *Guppy*. I don't want to believe it, but the evidence is everywhere. I want to think that it's all a bad dream; that it's not really happening … I'm feeling helpless and disheartened. I don't know what's going to happen now, but I do know that I want to continue as quickly as possible. That I would rather be at sea until the bureaucratic storm has blown over, so that I can live safely without being constantly in fear of the country where I grew up.

DAY 45: *9 November*

Guppy and I are being tossed around fairly vigorously tonight by a beam wind of 25 knots. Good sailing, but the strange confused seaway is very irritating. I get little sleep, which means that I'm not very cheerful this morning. After brooding over the fact that I'm now approaching land fast, whether or not I'm happy about it, I decide to go up to the cockpit to get some fresh air. What a wonderful— *WHAM!* Splash, drip, drip … ARGH, grumph, hrumph, bloody wave! I swear at the sea, the waves, the wind and everything I hate at the moment, but it makes me feel a lot better. Staying moody doesn't improve the situation anyway.

Guppy is going like a spear under full sail at a speed of 7.5 knots. At this speed, the coast is approaching very fast, but with 300 miles to go I really don't feel like going ashore. I could sail on for weeks; I'd prefer to just carry on and skip all the harbours. And I would do if I didn't need to stock up on diesel, water and food. The days just slip by and I've got used to the constant movement, the interrupted sleep; and — even though Mother Nature hasn't made it easy for me — I have never felt more in tune with my surroundings. Wonderful peace with only the waves, the wind, *Guppy* and the horizon. No people who all want something from you; no bustle, cars, internet, media, etc.

DAY 46: *10 November*

I'm almost there! It's really only a short distance now and each hour seems to get longer … Of the 6000 miles that I had to cover from Darwin, there are now a mere 100 to go. The wind is using the opportunity to show me who's the boss one more time, and has been variable all night with speeds from 0 to 25 knots. When day breaks there's a constant wind, but it's head-on! Land is so close, yet so far away … *Guppy* doesn't worry about that and is sailing easily, close to the wind in dark, dismal weather, without making a fuss about the grim skies and the headwind. Slowly but surely it's dawning on me that I could be in South Africa tomorrow, and I'm suddenly looking forward to a night of uninterrupted sleep in a bed that's not rolling and isn't wet and salty, and even a nice shower and fresh meat, fish and vegetables. I actually rarely eat fish, but after seven weeks at sea I'll eat anything that doesn't consist of spaghetti, rice or tinned beans! On the other hand, I really want to stay at sea …

When you have a thousand miles to go, it doesn't really matter where and how fast you sail, but now I'm constantly checking the course and speed, and the calculations for *Guppy*'s arrival time are flying through my head. The shipping traffic is increasing, and there are more and more symbols, lines and numbers on my chart. The wind is not doing what the weather charts had promised and we are going far slower than I'd expected, which really irritates me for the first time in a long while.

DAY 47: *11 November*

During my last night on this crossing, there are many ships around me. The wind has shifted and is coming from the south at a speed of 25 knots. The closer *Guppy* comes to the strong northerly Agulhas Current, the steeper and higher the waves are becoming. Halfway through the night, I'm able to receive the first African radio stations and see a lot of lights along the shore until there is a thick fog that takes away all visibility. It's cold as one squall follows the next and rain washes over *Guppy*. The radar faithfully reflects the shipping traffic, but I can't see it. And so I lumber on while adjusting the sails and the course. At a distance of 10 miles, I'm still unable to see Durban except on the radar ... and still nothing at 5 miles from shore. Suddenly the fog thins out, and at a distance of 3 miles I think I see something! A sigh, a laugh and a celebratory dance; but it doesn't really sink in, no, not really. I've been at sea for too long. Often I'm overjoyed to get to my destination and can be cheerful for days. This time I'm glad, but nothing more than that, because the feeling of peace and being at one with nature has now come to an end.

The skyscrapers appear out of the mist one by one, and an industrial harbour comes into sight. Another mile to the harbour entrance. I call Port Control and they notify me that a big cargo ship is just exiting. I decide to wait to let this giant glide past me first. I then guide *Guppy* between the breakwaters and get into calmer waters, and look for the yacht marina which lies just a few miles further beyond the big harbours.

Durban

After being on the Indian Ocean for 47 days, *Guppy* and I have arrived in Durban. I have to concentrate hard to be able to walk to the harbour office and not fall in the water. The land is moving — everything is moving! I fly back to *Guppy*; my familiar surroundings. After a while I try again, holding on to the railing as if I'm walking for the first time. It's unbelievable how I've managed to lose my sense of balance. After my third trip up and down the jetty — because I manage to forget my boat's papers, of course — it's going better. Clearing in is easy. The Customs official nearly faints when I tell him that I've just sailed from Darwin on my own. He doesn't believe me and I have to show him my website before he stamps my documents, shaking his head and muttering all the while. At the yacht club, I take a lovely warm shower and then buy some fresh food for tonight. I'm gripped by a big spring-cleaning mood in the afternoon; wash all the salt off *Guppy* and clean everything. *Guppy* smells wonderfully fresh again, and I'm slowly getting used to being on land. It's incredibly busy, and how people can talk! It's all a huge adjustment.

The harbour has a very strict 24-hour security watch, but I would prefer to be out at sea again. When I wake in the morning, the wind is howling through the rigging and the wind gauge in the harbour shows a wind speed of 35 knots, which means I can't think of leaving at the moment. In contrast to being at sea, there is so much happening every hour that it's hard to keep up. At sea the highlights were eating, sleeping, a big wave, or spotting a funny cloud or a ship. I was happy and content with these small things, and they made my day. Day after day ... But it's all different now. Eating and sleeping are side issues now. A wave? A strange cloud? Get a life, girl! Who gets a kick out of a funny cloud? No, here I'm running from pillar to post and post to pillar, and everyone is throwing questions at me. Fortunately *Guppy* is always there and I'm able to find refuge from the madness. Or am I already crazy?

Only now do I realise how this crossing has changed me. My view of the world has changed. I'm no longer in a hurry; life carries on no matter where you are. I've learnt to be content with the small things and not to need more and more. You can spend your whole life looking for the ultimate happiness; work yourself to death and become unhappy. Or you can work your whole life and then want to travel, but by then be too old and your body no longer works as it should; or you have kids, a house, a car and a job, and you have to say 'Sorry, but we can't do that.' Why not? I've come across people with children who have left their so-called security far behind and are now sailing around and feeling much happier. It's also a lot cheaper living this way. I've got to know myself and have discovered that I'm a totally different person to the one I would have become under the Dutch legal system. I know what I want, have goals and desires, but, more importantly, am glad and very happy about what I've achieved.

Guppy is pulling hard at her mooring lines when I wake up, while the wind that continues to shriek through the rigging is blowing even harder than yesterday. I speak to my New Zealand neighbour a little later while I'm busy putting out more fenders and lines, and am spontaneously invited to join them in the mountains for a few days. They are sailing around the world in a 40-foot steel boat, *Iemanja*, with their 10- and 8-year-old children, and are on their way to Germany. It takes me 15 minutes to grab my gear, lock up *Guppy* and let security know that they need to keep a sharp eye on *Guppy*. I'm ready to swap the sea air for the mountain air.

A little later, I'm sitting between the two kids in the back of the car they've rented. We quickly leave the busy city behind us. The hills become mountains, and the air gets colder. After a few hours' drive, we get to a nice camping resort close to the Drakensberg where they have rabbits, horses, chickens, geese and dogs running around. In short, an enormous menagerie, and the two kids keep me busy, too. It's funny to notice that they are real boat children: they use the water sparingly when doing the dishes and are frugal with everything they use even when it's no longer necessary.

We go on a horseback tour and enjoy everything around us. After a few days of relaxing and hiking, we are on our way back. It was lovely being in the mountains for a while, but I'm relieved when I see the ocean appearing in the distance beyond the hills. I wouldn't like to live far from the sea, but I also think mountains are beautiful ... Maybe I should live on top of a mountain with a view of the sea — or at sea with a view of the mountains!

Back on *Guppy* everything seems OK, and now that I've had my mountain adventure I immediately look at the weather charts. There's a favourable wind forecast for the next two days, and that's something rare here that you need to take advantage of. Although it's late, the fuel dock is still open and I decide to top up with diesel so I can make a swift departure. I'm so happy with the good wind direction that I want to leave immediately, and am about to make a start when I decide that it might be wise to have a good night's rest first. Sleeping and sailing along the coast just don't go together ...

I was still ambling through the mountains on horseback this morning, so it might be asking a little too much to be at sea the same night.

Durban–Port Elizabeth: 420 nautical miles

DAY 1: *17 November*

At first light I steer *Guppy* out of the harbour. It's beautiful weather for a change, and once I'm in the strong Agulhas Current *Guppy* is running at a constant 10 knots. Thanks to the 5-knot current, she immediately breaks all previous speed records. As the coastline flies past, a whale thinks it's funny to take a huge dive just 10 metres in front of *Guppy*'s bow. I almost jump out of my skin when this enormous beast, which is bigger than *Guppy*, showers us with half the sea! I immediately switch off the autopilot and dive inside, but by the time I manage to find the camera I see only a dark mass disappearing under *Guppy*'s keel. For hours afterwards, I think I spot a whale between every wave, but fortunately that's not the case. At night I see the lights along the coastline passing by and occasionally need to adjust *Guppy*'s course to pass a fishing vessel.

DAY 2: *18 November*

Towards morning, the favourable northerly wind suddenly drops away and a little later there's a 20-knot wind from the south. With the 5-knot current from the north, these are not ideal conditions. The current causes the waves to build up fast. *Guppy* rises on a wave and then crashes into the next trough; time after time and wave after wave. *Guppy* is close-hauled and is only making 2 knots forward through the water, but with the current she's running at 6 knots. I had checked the weather forecasts carefully and there had been no mention of a southerly wind. It's impossible for a yacht to make any headway with a strong southerly wind, and, thanks to the Agulhas Current, south-westerly storms are able to stir up 20-metre waves and have taken quite a number of ships to the bottom of the ocean. Lost in thought I gaze at the sea, which is getting rougher by the minute. The violence continues all day, but the wind begins to drop by evening and the big waves are disappearing as quickly as they appeared. All that remains is a long, southerly ocean swell.

I hope to reach Port Elizabeth tomorrow morning. I don't really enjoy sailing along the coast single-handedly and there is little chance to sleep when you have to be on the lookout for ships, rocks and other hazards while holding your course. This is the second night and I'm beginning to long for more than 10 minutes' sleep. It makes me appreciate how easy it was to sail on the big, wide, empty ocean.

During the night I begin to feel more and more nauseous. I try to sleep a little with the radar alarms on full alert, but feel that I'm becoming more and more ill. I must have eaten something bad. I spend the whole night vomiting and feeling sick.

DAY 3: *19 November*

After a long and tiring night, Port Elizabeth comes into sight as day breaks. Although I'm still tired, I'm slowly beginning to feel a little better, and a few hours later I'm steering *Guppy* safely into the harbour. It's an old harbour and looks as though it's been seriously damaged by a storm. After looking around a bit, I find an old fishing boat that I think *Guppy* can come alongside and tie up to.

Port Elizabeth

I fall asleep immediately and feel a lot better when I wake up a few hours later. In the afternoon I'm allocated a spot at the yacht club, which they are busy rebuilding after the last heavy storm. The last few bollards are being fixed onto the jetty when I arrive. The rest of the harbour looks dilapidated. The narrow, rusty jetties are half-submerged and everything is moving up and down due to the constant swell in the harbour. It's all creaking and squeaking, but *Guppy* is lying safe and I fall asleep immediately.

After a long, good night's rest, there's an early knock on the hull. It's John from *Iris*, the neighbouring boat that came in a few hours after me yesterday. They ask if I'd like to go to the Addo Elephant Park, a 50-kilometre drive from here. Yes, of course! *Guppy* is well guarded here, and we walk into the city to hire a car to take us to this enormous park. The number of animals that are walking around in the wild is incredible. All of a sudden, we're in front of a herd of elephants, followed by all the animals from *The Lion King* — warthogs, rhinos, ostriches, antelopes, kudus, buffalos, zebras and many more species. I'm enchanted! But the highlight really is the elephants. They come really close to the car and are incredibly big. Towards the afternoon we see a herd of at least a hundred elephants at a waterhole. Very impressive, and I'm thrilled that I went along.

When we get back, there's a strong wind from the south and people are very busy trying to keep the rickety jetties afloat in the harbour. There's a strong swell, too, and the boats are straining at their lines. The wind velocity increases steadily and it's impossible to walk straight across the jetties. Everything is creaking, squeaking and pitching, and *Guppy* is tugging hard at her moorings. A glance at the wind gauge shows that the average velocity over the past half-hour has been 47 knots; and this in the harbour. It continues throughout the night and I'm attaching extra lines and fenders, just like all the other yachties.

For the moment, the wind doesn't look like dropping or changing to a favourable direction, so it seems that *Guppy* and I will be kept here for a few more days. In the meantime, I'm amusing myself well with the other yachties, who are also waiting for better weather.

The next morning I meet someone of my own age who wants me to go sailing with him in his boat. Although the wind has dropped to 30 knots in the meantime, there's still way too much wind to manage a small boat on your own, and we therefore decide to try it together. It's a very fast open boat, and I really feel like exerting myself. The boy is a fairly fanatical sailor and, despite the strong wind, we put up the spinnaker while running with the wind, which gives me a huge kick. It's awesome to be constantly planing! At one stage we're unable to hold the boat any longer and do a complete somersault.

Without noticing, we've spent half the day sailing up and down the harbour while no one dared to leave. We've lost track of time, and it's 18.30 by the time we put the boat away. Oops — I was expected at an early Thanksgiving dinner at the yacht club at 18.00 with some other yachties. My hair is still dripping when I hastily join the gathering 40 minutes late; perfect timing, as everyone is just placing their orders and the party is livening up.

Port Elizabeth–Cape Town: 470 nautical miles

DAY 1: *24 November*

At last an easterly wind has been forecast, after all the stormy westerly winds which had made it impossible to sail. So I cast off the mooring lines, and *Guppy* leaves Port Elizabeth to head west. Four other yachts follow my example. Once out of the bay, the sea is very rough and there's a 25-knot headwind and big waves. *Guppy* is eager and scampers out, heeling through the waves, pretending to be a submarine. I'm accompanied by a big pod of dolphins that jump high above the waves with all kinds of acts and then plunge back into the sea. It's really super to watch. *Guppy* soon increases her lead on the other yachts that are all either the same size or bigger than *Gup*. Once out at sea, it all goes really well and the wind drops a little. I have to make a course adjustment to round the Cape, and now have a beam wind. Once I've adjusted the course on the windvane, I feel like a nice mug of steaming hot chocolate. I get to the bottom of the steps and see — water. Because the deck has been constantly awash, water has found its way in to wet my books, cupboards, bed and sleeping bag. To find the cause, I unscrew a panel in the ceiling. The centre bollard on deck has taken such a beating from the storm in the harbour that it has pulled the bolts halfway through the deck, and because the deck is constantly underwater a good bit has now seeped in. The few hours of rough sailing have exacted their toll and, in order to save what I can, I throw most of my stuff to the other side of the cabin where everything is now one big, wet, salty mess. Hmm … In the meantime, *Guppy* is still sailing nice and fast, and the other yachts are mere dots on the horizon. It feels great to be out at sea again and to have rounding the Cape of Good Hope as my goal.

The wind drops considerably during the night and, despite the busy shipping traffic, I'm able to sleep fairly well. In the middle of the night I spend hours at the back of the boat gazing at the phosphorescent wake. There's an enormous quantity of phosphoresence in the water and not only is the wake alight with it, but the wave crests also give off a bright green glow. I've rarely seen it this beautiful!

DAY 2: *25 November*

Towards morning, the wind drops and *Guppy* now glides on slowly at a mere 3 knots. But this does give me the opportunity to bring some order to the inside and to apply some sealant to the bollard now that the deck is no longer underwater. Hopefully this will temporarily solve *Guppy*'s leakage problem, as there are 30-knot winds forecast for the day after tomorrow.

We are nearing Cape Agulhas, the most southerly point of South Africa. The better-known cape, the Cape of Good Hope, lies further north. Towards the afternoon I pass Cape Agulhas in the distance, and for the first time since my departure from the Netherlands I'm on a northerly course. *Guppy* is bearing down on the Cape of Good Hope in a strong 25-knot wind; it's very cloudy and the visibility is poor, but this is actually how I've always envisaged it. It feels great to be rounding the Cape. It's a stage of the voyage that I was dreading for some time, but at the same time have been looking forward to, and especially strived to reach. I suddenly see a helicopter appear through the clouds and circle over *Guppy*. Hmm … There's a huge camera hanging from the helicopter, but fortunately the film seems to run out after about 15 minutes and the helicopter disappears into the clouds.

When I access the weather charts, I see no reason for rejoicing: I'm heading for a rough night with a 35-knot wind and 5-metre waves.

Good thing that I managed to get a lot of sleep today, so *Guppy* and I can simply go for it!

DAY 3: *26 November*

It's slowly getting darker and the wind speed is increasing by the hour. *Guppy* is sailing with only the storm jib and a double-reefed mainsail. It really needs a third reef, and I'm waiting for a good moment to go on deck. Yes, now! I throw open the hatch, jump out and quickly slam it closed behind me before the next wave can slip in. It's pitch dark, and I can hear the raging waves breaking and see the phosphorescent, churning mass of water. There's no way of seeing how high the waves are or when they are coming in my direction. Apart from the light of an approaching cargo ship, it's really very dark. The overhead waves and the biting cold make it a real battle to get the third reef in place. I'm back below half an hour later, dripping water and frozen to the bone. The wind velocity continues to rise, and I'm thinking that this is not the promised 35 knots. *Guppy* starts surfing more frequently. She is going way too fast and I don't want to wait for her to broach and be thrown totally flat, so I decide to take down what's left of the mainsail. I'm wet, my hands are frozen and stiff, but I have to take down the sail whatever it takes! It's unbelievable: *Guppy* is now sailing with only the storm jib and she's still flying towards the Cape of Good Hope at a speed of 8 knots. I stay on deck in the dark for a while to listen to the force of the sea and to bolster *Guppy*'s and my own morale, until an unexpected wave breaks over the aft deck and the cockpit … I wait for the right moment before diving into the shelter of the cabin again, leaving puddles in my wake. I make a warm mug of two-minute noodles and slowly get back to normal body temperature. It looks like this could be a long night …

While I'm sitting in the cabin with all the hatches battened down, the raging forces around me sound like 10 Boeings all taking off at the same time. The wind is howling through the rigging, the sea is roaring and the wind gauge now shows wind velocities of over 55 knots. *Guppy* is still sailing with only the storm jib, but she's increasingly surfing off the waves and it's getting dangerous. It will be light in a few hours and

I should be past the Cape of Good Hope by then. There's still a lot of shipping traffic, and I'm glad I managed to get the bollard sealed. Then I feel *Guppy* being carried up high by a big wave. No, *NO!* She's surfing faster and faster; water is rushing past the portholes and the whole of *Guppy* is beginning to vibrate — 10 knots, 11 knots, 12! The crash sends me smashing into the chart table while she broaches and falls flat in the trough. *WHAM!* The oncoming breaker submerges *Guppy* under an enormous swirling mass of foaming water and everything flies through the cabin. Shit! Was a few square metres of sail really too much? While *Guppy* slowly rights herself and the windvane incredibly brings her back on course, I put my sailing gear on over my clothes for some protection against the ice-cold wind. Clicking on my harness, I climb into the cockpit. While doing this, a waves flashes past me and slips inside. Damn! I furl up the storm jib until it's the size of handkerchief. *Gup* is now sailing at 5 knots on this little patch. And so I wait for daylight as the wind continues to accelerate. By the time it should have been light already, it just stays dark.

Towards morning the gusts of wind are up to 65 knots and the tops of the waves are flying horizontally across *Guppy*'s deck. The average apparent wind velocity is 54 knots, while *Guppy* is almost running with the wind! The sea has changed into a raging mass of white foam. It looks like the contours of the huge Table Mountain are coming into sight. The wind and clouds come off this mountain and form whirlwinds close to the coast. I'm sailing around the mountain and the winds are increasingly coming off shore, which means that the waves are slowly diminishing in size. I suddenly hear a weak '*Guppy*, *Guppy*' on the VHF.

'Yes, this is *Guppy*,' I reply. 'Dad?'

'Hey, Muis, how are you? I'm so glad to hear your voice. I'm standing on top of a mountain and we think we can see you from time to time.'

'You could be right, Dad. *Gup* is spending more time underwater than above it. You know, Dad, she really is fantastic and I—' *Bang!* *Rinkle, tinkle, boink, toink …*

Shocked, Dad asks what's happening when he hears the clamour in the background.

285

'Oh, nothing, *Guppy* almost got flattened by a wave and the cupboard with the pots and pans has just opened and the contents have now spread throughout the cabin … You know how it goes on a boat.'

And so the conversation continues for a while, and I get to hear that my friend Jillian the documentary-maker is also there. It's wonderful to hear Dad's voice and great to know that I'll be able to hug him in a few hours' time.

Guppy is heeling at an angle of 60 degrees and sailing on the tiny bit of furled storm jib. I try to furl in the last bit, but can't manage to get it done. Shit! Hmm … There's nothing else I can do but scramble up to the foredeck through the mass of water that's streaming over the deck, holding on to anything I can. The drum is broken and there's no way I can furl it in any further. Several options shoot through my head, but there's only one that might work, and that is to drop the sail.

'Damn, I hate you, wind!' I shout over the water while I'm undoing the halyard.

Shit. The sail can, of course, only be brought down if it's entirely unfurled! There's nothing else I can do, so I go aft, let go the reef line and the sail opens with an ear-splitting roar. *Guppy* is almost flattened by the wildly flapping storm jib. I'm standing on the deck, which is awash with water, with my feet against the railing and I am pulling with all my might to get the unruly sail in. Within minutes, the wild bit of sail is reduced to a wet bundle of canvas that I bind securely to the deck. I'm totally soaked and stiff with cold. The water is a mere 7 degrees here, and the strong, cold wind makes me feel as though I'm close to hypothermia. I keep on thinking 'only a few more miles', while my frozen, red hands clutch the helm. I push the throttle of the powerful Volvo engine to full speed and head, straight-angled to the wind, towards the harbour breakwaters. Guppy lies over on her bare masts, the gunnel is almost underwater, and we are only doing 1.5 knots despite the roaring Volvo. The wind is making a deafening howling sound in the rigging, and the water, which is bucketing over me, is making it very difficult to see. Suddenly the sun breaks through the clouds; shining exactly on the spot where the harbour entrance should be.

My eyes are smarting from the saltwater and I can't see a thing anymore. I use the plotter and radar to guide *Guppy* towards the breakwaters and safely through the harbour entrance. Only then does it calm down and I can see where I've landed: in the middle of the Volvo Ocean Race boats. I'm allowed to moor at their dock, and slowly I get some feeling back in my hands and toes by warming them in the sun.

Cape Town

Dad and Jillian jump on board and we hug each other. They get a shock when they enter the cabin. Water is dripping from the ceiling, everything is salty, and nothing is where it should be. There are some books in puddles of water, and an upside-down pot lies on my bed. The floor is covered in stuff that was once put away in cupboards. The cushions are sodden, and the ceiling has been removed so that I could keep an eye on the bollard. They shake their heads, come on deck, and then take me off to the boulevard. I'm still very cold, and we find a place on a terrace where we can sit in the sun and be out of the wind. After eating something warm, I'm starting to feel human again. I look around me, and only then do I fully realise that I'm in Cape Town! *Guppy* and I have rounded the Cape, arriving in one of the heaviest storms that Cape Town has seen in a long time. It looks great here. I'm berthed near the city with a view of Table Mountain. In the afternoon *Camper* arrives with the New Zealand Volvo Race team, and we immediately make contact. I get to see the inside of two boats and listen attentively to all the stories, while they seem to have a lot more interest in my voyage. It's very busy on the wharf and many people seem to be more interested in *Guppy* than the Volvo Race boats ...

I need a quiet spot to recover from my journey, and decide to move *Guppy* to the Royal Cape Yacht Club the next day. Here she can be guarded 24 hours a day, and *Guppy* gets a special place in front of the harbour office, where she is privileged to lie between her fellow boats. I visit the Volvo boats daily and often speak to the land crews. I spend hours watching how the land crews are getting these racing monsters shipshape. I'm allowed to help on *Camper* when they take down the mast for inspection, and I get to know the whole team. We set off to meet the French team on *Groupama* on Alan's speedboat. Alan is a helpful Capetonian whom Jillian and Dad met a few days before I arrived, and he has taken them under his wing. *Groupama* is becalmed, and it will take at least another three hours before she arrives.

The Volvo boats fascinate me more each day, and I don't hesitate for a second when I'm invited to take part in the Pro-Am races at daybreak. Wow, this is fantastic! There's a 15-knot wind, and *Camper* is shooting through the water at a speed of 25 knots. I hang over the railing to admire the canting keel, and help with changing the sails. This is one of the coolest things I've ever done! As with all the best things in life, it's over far too soon.

Cape Town is beautiful and at 05.00 I climb Table Mountain together with Dad and Jillian. It's quite daunting, as we've chosen the quickest and therefore the steepest route. Our efforts are rewarded when we get to the top and enjoy a wonderful view of Cape Town and the blue ocean beyond. I gaze at the southern horizon where I came through that storm with *Guppy*, and to the northern horizon where my finish lies some 5800 miles further on. The next day we drive to False Bay in a hire car to meet John on *Iris*. We then continue to the Cape of Good Hope nature reserve, where we are surprised by wild ostriches and a lovely rugged landscape.

We walk through the city a lot and always seem to end at the Volvo race boats. The centre is pretty, clean and always fun, and the temperature is pleasant. After all the really hot countries I've visited, I'm enjoying the fresh sea breeze and the mild sun. I can wear some slacks and a jersey for the first time in ages, and I'm slowly getting *Guppy* into shape again. I clear up all the mess and repair the bollard and the storm jib drum together with Dad; check the rigging and take her out of the water briefly, because the propeller doesn't want to open properly — which happened at the very moment I wanted to reverse in the harbour. Luckily *Guppy* has two engines, and by starting the Yanmar quickly and putting her into full reverse I was able to prevent *Guppy* being blown into the other yachts by the wind. Once ashore we discover that the folding propeller's feathering movement has been completely worn away, and there's no other option but to buy a new propeller. While Dad is busy with this, I spoil *Guppy* by giving her hull a polish and applying a new coat of anti-fouling. After a few days of hard work, she's ready for her next big crossing. I don't want to take any more risks, and am planning to sail non-stop to Saint Martin.

During the last few days before Dad leaves, we use the hire car to do some grocery shopping. Jillian flies back to New York, and the moment has come for me to give Dad a last hug before waving good-bye to him.

After the start of the Volvo Ocean Race's next stage, I watch the yachts slowly disappear over the horizon and it's time for me to leave all the friendly people at the Royal Cape Yacht Club and all the yachties I have come to know. The next day, I thank the people who have looked after *Guppy* so well, and leave beautiful South Africa.

Cape Town–Saint Martin: 5800 nautical miles

DAY 1: *12 December*

With Cape Town slowly vanishing in the distance, I'm sailing with *Guppy* towards new adventures on the 5800-mile stretch of ocean that still separates me from the end of my circumnavigation.

There's a 20-knot easterly wind that is only just allowing *Guppy* to hold her course by sailing close-hauled, but the wind keeps veering further, finally becoming a headwind and strengthening until *Guppy*'s gunnel is underwater and I decide to reef. I can no longer hold the desired course, and *Guppy* is heading too far northwards. She is sailing at 6 knots, and I had anticipated that this first 500 miles wouldn't be easy. After this, I hope to find the trade winds, but *Guppy* first needs to get through this bit.

There's still a lot of shipping traffic, which means that I need to stay alert. The last ship picked up by the radar is now 2 miles behind *Guppy*, and I now want to get some sleep as I'm dead tired. A few hours later the radar wakes me again because it thinks it's found a ship, but in the end it's only a heavy shower that passes us 6 miles off.

one girl, one dream

DAY 2: *13 December*

The few hours of sleep have done the trick and I'm feeling well. As always, I need to get into the rhythm of being at sea; especially now that *Gup* has a 25-knot wind to contend with and is sailing close-hauled with tons of water washing over her. Everything is being put to the test, including me. But I'll soon get used to it: the breaking waves, the salty moisture, and living on a boat that's heeling at a 45-degree angle.

DAY 3: *14 December*

We end our third night at sea having spent hours stamping our way forward with the storm jib and reefed mainsail. At first light, the wind starts to drop and by afternoon there isn't a breath of wind left. The wind has skedaddled entirely.

Guppy is rolling heavily in the high, short swell that remains. I notice that I've spent too much time ashore and am no longer used to the rough movement of the boat. I bump into the corner of the chart table and slip down the steps, and soon I am covered in bruises. Every flap of the sails hurts me, but lowering them isn't an option because it will cause *Guppy* to rock even more. Leaving them will mean a lot of wear and tear on the sails, though. The reefed mainsail is hauled tight, right in the centre; the genoa is half-furled and also taut. The windvane is flapping about aimlessly in response to *Guppy*'s movements. Hopefully there will soon be some wind …

DAY 4: *15 December*

Guppy is rolling very heavily, which means that I spend most of the night rolling from one side of my bunk to the other, however well I manage to wedge myself in with cushions and sail bags. Totally wasted, I'm woken a few hours later by the sun … Wait a minute, did I say 'sun'? SUN! The sun is showing itself for the first time since my departure, and I see some ripples on the water, which means there's wind on its way! I'm suddenly wide awake and fly on deck to set the sails. First the mizzen, then the genoa and after that I take the reef out of the mainsail.

There's just enough wind to fill the sails, and *Gup* and I are on our way again; this time in the right direction.

I feel that I'm getting into my sea rhythm again, and, now that *Guppy* isn't rolling as much, I'm enjoying the warm sun in the cockpit. My stomach suddenly reminds me that I've forgotten to feed myself … The sun has cheered me up and I prepare some food for myself while listening to music at full volume. The wind freshens during the course of the day and by evening *Guppy* is really enjoying herself. Unfortunately, the wind doesn't hold for long and eases after midnight.

DAY 5: *16 December*

Guppy's speed drops dramatically again: 5, 4, 3 … and finally holds at 2.5 knots. The wind is variable until it is finally coming from behind, making the weak breeze seem even lighter. Otherwise, it's a lovely morning, the sun is shining and the sails are standing quiet. The windvane is keeping *Guppy* faithfully on course in the light wind. At least we're going in the right direction at 2.5 knots, which is more than I can say for the past few days. Now that I'm not constantly being thrown to and fro and I'm not salty, wet, tired and having to save what I'm able to save, I'm suddenly faced with endless time for myself. Something I need to get used to. I catch up on some sleep, have a normal breakfast, and then decorate the little Christmas tree I was given in Cape Town with some little lights. It looks as though *Guppy* is slowly reaching for the warm trade winds, and that's something I'm really looking forward to after the rough weather of the past few months.

When I'm woken by the timer, I see the contours of the cabin lit up by the red and green control lights. Lying in my bed, still dry and not salty, I listen to the familiar sounds from *Guppy*: the sound of the waves lapping against the hull, which tells me how fast she is going, the familiar creaking of the mizzen, the swaying of the spinnaker boom. I don't have to go on deck to know that all is well, that the wind has dropped a little and that *Guppy* is moving at about 3 knots and holding her course, as the movements haven't changed. But I get up anyway and do my usual inspection. Everything is as I thought it would be: *Gup* is sailing, softly swaying, under a beautiful starlit sky. Satisfied, I spend another half an hour on deck before crawling back into bed. I cherish these wonderful moments.

DAY 6: *17 December*

There's just enough wind to fill the sails during the day. I trim the sails from time to time to improve the speed, but generally I'm just enjoying the incredibly flat, endless expanse of blue water and the peace that it brings. Towards evening, the wind freshens as usual and *Gup* is sailing a little faster again.

DAY 7: *18 December*

The sun appears on the horizon like a big red ball and the last trace of the night disappears. *Guppy* is gliding along nicely on the little breeze there is. Time is flying, and I can't believe that I've been at sea for almost a week. Fortunately I still have quite some miles to cover, and at this speed there will be time enough to enjoy the peace and the sea around me. I spend the day reading and eating the fruit that's ripening fast, trimming the sails when there's a breeze, or just sitting on deck, now and again and gazing towards the infinite horizon. I'm enjoying it all, although it's nothing more than water. I'm intensely happy on *Guppy*.

A lovely wind surprises me in the evening, and this time it's stronger and freshens further during the night. The waves grow bigger and *Guppy* surges ahead on a broad reach.

DAY 8: *19 December*

When I plot my position on the chart in the morning, it shows surprising progress. *Guppy* really has covered a good distance through the night. But now that the wind has increased, the sun has disappeared. I walk to the aft deck to change my course on the windvane, and notice that there's a film of oil on the swimming platform. It has covered everything! The wind has spread the oil over the aft deck and it's running down from there. It's clearly coming from the outboard engine that is fastened to the railing. Hmm, I need to use the swimming platform to be able to change course. The swimming platform is wet and slippery at the best of times, but the chance of slipping on it and landing in the water in its present condition is 99 per cent! And so a simple task like adjusting the course by a couple of degrees becomes more complex. Carefully I try to see where the oil is coming from without standing in it. The traces of oil lead to the drain plug. It seems to have come loose through the boat's vibrations and has caused the oil spill. Now that I've found the cause and secured the plug with the right spanner, there's the less attractive chore of cleaning up without wasting all my dish-washing liquid.

DAY 9: *20 December*

Today I crossed the line of longitude that also passes through the Netherlands, which means that *Guppy* and I have now crossed all the lines of longitude around the globe. Quite amazing! Just another 4800 miles to the Caribbean and I will have gone all the way around. Compared with the total mileage that I've done with *Guppy* so far, it now seems frightfully close; on the other hand, it's still quite a distance. I'm still in the Southern Hemisphere.

Yesterday's favourable wind is getting weaker, but I shouldn't complain seeing that I have little work to do trimming the sails and holding my course. I hardly see the sun at all, and it's pretty cold at night. The squid think the same and are continually trying to warm themselves up on board. I don't feel the same about their company ... Throwing dried-up flying fish overboard is a lot simpler than squid. They stick to the deck like glue, and split open when you pull them off, causing even more mess. A sign saying *No Squid Allowed* isn't helping, either! Oh well, if these are my only problems at present, you could say that everything is going well.

So many days, so many hours and so many miles still to go. St Helena is ahead of us. I'm spending a lot of time thinking. Hours spent sitting on deck, gazing at the blue sea and the grey sky where the sun is trying hard to come through. I'm thinking of the future; about what I want and what is going to happen when I arrive. What happens when the voyage that I've been dreaming of since the age of eight is suddenly over? I think about the hours spent daydreaming about the seas, freedom, unknown lands and the horizon as I cycled to school. I even hit a road post once while I was daydreaming; so hard that my chin needed to be stitched ... All those sailing boats that I used to draw in my exercise books. They were my riddles and arithmetic; translated into sailing, seeing unknown lands and tasting freedom. And now? Now I've almost gone around the world. Just another month; it looks so far and yet so close. I don't want it to end; I've worked towards this all my life. What will I do after this? Will I be arrested when I arrive? Through this journey, I've unconsciously forced open so many doors. What on earth am I going to do?

I've never thought further than the next island; never further than the horizon. But I've already been to the next island, and this will mean that I've fulfilled my dream; that I have done what I've always wanted to do. The questions that are often asked now, and keep going through my head, are: What now? What are you going to do next, Laura? I don't know; I'm scared to arrive, scared that it will all be over. I know that I won't be going back to the Netherlands, and I have more than enough dreams, but none of them are quite like this voyage that I have always dreamt of.

I stare at the sea for hours and wonder if I have only undertaken long sea crossings since leaving Darwin because I want to be at sea as much as possible. To be able to enjoy the peace, the sailing and the fulfilment of my dream as much as possible. Or was it fear of the Dutch authorities hounding me that drove me on? The people, commotion and arriving somewhere have become less and less interesting to me. Even if they were friendly people that you didn't want to ignore. Journalists who are positive and whom you don't want to say 'no' to. Invitations that you can't turn down. It's all too much, too busy, and I don't know how to be friendly all the time. Always having to smile and taking care not to say anything wrong that might give people in the Netherlands a chance to put me down. I've increasingly come to look forward to the precious, quiet moments at sea, while increasingly dreading the arrivals. Just like the next one — because this arrival is THE arrival ...

Smiling, I concede that I always knew I couldn't be at sea forever and escape everything. There's no way you can always smile and be friendly to everyone. I'm just an ordinary girl; a girl who's already achieved what she dreamt of doing. When I look back at all my adventures, the storms, calms and unknown islands, my face breaks into a huge smile. There's no one on this earth who can say they've sailed so many miles solo at my age. I've got to know myself, the world, the islands and all sorts of cultures. I've gradually learnt to handle the media, learnt to fight for what I wanted to achieve, and, most of all, learnt that dreams don't deceive. That you shouldn't be scared of the unknown and, most of all, should never say that something is impossible and can't be done, because if you REALLY want something then you'll get it. Look at me. I come from a fairly poor family but have fought like a lion and won. The experience has made me more resilient for the future, and I still have my whole life ahead of me. As for the question about what I want to do now … I honestly haven't a clue. What I would really like to do is introduce *Guppy* to my country of birth, New Zealand.

DAY 10: *21 December*

A new day again. Wow, I've forgotten how hard it is to write a piece for my site every day now that there's a trade wind and I have more time. I'm frowning while I'm sitting on the chart table with my laptop on my lap and my foot braced against the steps. Every day at sea is more or less the same, and it's difficult to find something to write about. *Guppy* is sailing and gently swaying at a speed of 4 knots and— Wait a minute, yesterday I realised that there were two interesting facts. The first was that I crossed the line of longitude which also runs through the Netherlands, and I also crossed the Tropic of Capricorn, which lies 22.5 degrees south, on the very same day that the sun completes its journey south and starts towards the north again. Not that I could see the sun, because it's been cloudy for days. Now that it's getting warmer at last, I don't really mind the clouds.

Actually, I'm amazed that I'm not feeling bored yet. Normally there would always be things to deal with; *Guppy* would be flattened by a sudden squall or something would need to be repaired and sleeping would be almost impossible, with everything inside getting wet and salty. And now? Nothing like that! I'm thinking that everything I've experienced in the past year needs this time to sink in, and that I should just enjoy the peace and space around me. It's wonderful to gaze out over the infinite, undulating ocean. Now that *Guppy* needs less attention and is swaying gently onwards, I'm going to bake some bread, get down to reading some books at last, and try to work on my culinary skills, which are improving fast. There's a 10- to 15-knot wind, enough for *Gup* to glide through the night with the boomed-out genoa and mainsail and for me to have a good night's rest. The cloud cover makes it impossible to see the stars and it's pitch dark, but *Guppy* is leaving a phosphorescent trail behind her for hundreds of metres and that's something I can look at for hours.

DAY 11: *22 December*

For the second time on my voyage, *Guppy* and I are crossing the prime meridian with zero longitude, passing from the Eastern to the Western Hemisphere. The first time I did this was when I was in the English Channel just after I'd left the Netherlands. And now *Gup* is running with a light breeze towards the next highlight: the Equator, with zero degrees latitude, where we'll pass from the south to the north latitudes. But I'm not quite there yet. There's still 2300 miles of the South Atlantic to cross before I reach the Equator. This ocean has been incredibly friendly towards *Gup* and me so far. I'm now in the midst of the trade winds that blow between 10 and 20 knots, and we are making good progress. It's still heavily overcast and the nights are dark — very, very dark. I can't distinguish between the sea and the sky, and this frustrates me enormously as I like to see what's happening around me. But although the clouds look threatening, they just brood there and nothing happens. Not that this reassures me. The clouds and sea may look calm, but I know how quickly that can change.

DAY 12: *23 December*

And Mother Nature does have something in store for us, of course … Dark clouds pile up this morning and then pelt us with rain. Very hard showers with irritating gusts of changeable wind. Looking at the course on the plotter makes me wonder if Mr Windpilot hasn't had too much salt and has lost it altogether. Maybe he's just up in the clouds over all the Christmas and New Year wishes that are coming in on the guest book on my site. I can't imagine celebrating a better Christmas than this one, together with *Guppy* in the South Atlantic Ocean, knowing that there are so many people thinking of me. Even the dark clouds are disappearing. It's been the darkest, most rainy morning since my departure from Cape Town, but the sun has come out and I'm enjoying a wonderful afternoon. I'm so glad it's back, and I'm enjoying its warmth while everything dries.

I've been at sea for almost two weeks and it's Christmas the day after tomorrow. It's lovely to be alone with *Guppy* like this. Although I wouldn't mind having a quick look at Dad and Spot on his boat. We always used to play games around the Christmas tree with candles and a roaring fire. My dog still misses me, and I miss him too. Spot and I explored all the rivers and lakes together when I was younger. He was my faithful shipmate and guardian angel. Spot accompanied me for weeks on my holidays and took his guard duties very seriously. And, talking about Christmas, there are just two presents left in the Christmas parcel I received in Cape Town. I was allowed to open one a day in the run-up to Christmas. Time is slipping away again. It doesn't matter whether I'm at sea for two, four or seven weeks. I pass St Helena at a distance of 70 miles, and could have celebrated Christmas and New Year there, of course, but I'm enjoying the peace and prefer to celebrate in my own way. So the first stop will be Saint Martin!

I think back to the last two Christmases and New Year's Eves. Both were spent on Saint Martin, and now I'm on my way to the same island, but with 27,000 miles more under the keel. Unintentionally I seem to return to this small, friendly island in the Caribbean at the same time each year. Two years ago, during Christmas in 2009, I'd just returned from Saint Martin after being arrested by the Dutch Military Police. I'd been sitting on the beach there, looking at the sea and asking myself if I was ever going to fulfil my dream. A year later, I was sitting on the same beach, this time dreaming about all the wonderful adventures that were in store for *Guppy* and me. I was looking forward to all the miles and lovely countries that we were going to conquer. And now? Now, I'm going back to gaze out to sea and be able to say: '*Gup*, we did it!'

DAY 13: *24 December*

It's nice and sunny this morning, and I think that it might stay that way for a change. I shouldn't have mentioned the good weather, because a little later *Guppy* is suddenly surrounded by curtains of rain and dark clouds again. I gaze at the sky for hours. There are dark, threatening clouds, bits of blue sky, white clouds, grey clouds ... and they are all mixed up. There's an arc of clouds that ends in the water. It's such a stunning sight. In the meantime, the waves are getting more and more irritating. The wind has changed, and now there are cross-seas that are causing *Guppy* to make some amazing moves. The one moment it's calm and I forget to pay attention, and the next — *whoosh* — *Guppy* does a mega-swing on a steep wave, causing a saucepan to make an assassination attempt on me and a packet of rice to drop to the floor and split open. Nice! At least I know what I'll be doing for the rest of the day. Why are these grains of rice so small, and how do they manage to spread themselves everywhere?

At dusk there's a beautiful sunset with so many colours and bright shafts of light shooting through the clouds and glistening on the sea that it looks just like a tunnel of light. I've never seen so many colours on land. Slowly the light fades until only the coloured lights on my little Christmas tree can be seen inside the cabin.

DAY 14: *25 December*

There's a good wind of about 20 knots that's carrying *Guppy* towards the northerly horizon at a speed of 6.5 knots. As a Christmas gift, the sun has shown its face all morning, although it's beginning to get a little overcast again. It's a treat to have a day without heavy clouds and rain. I'm not as enthusiastic about the waves. They're not much higher than 3 metres, but they are annoyingly steep cross-waves. A five-course Christmas menu may be a little too ambitious, and I'm afraid that it may have to end up being something very simple in these seas. Not that this is a problem. It's actually quite nice having such a simple Christmas. No obligatory family visits that I have to make, and all that lovely food that you have to eat even when you are full, and all the endless chatter ... *Guppy* is a great listener and never contradicts me; I can eat when and what I want, and I don't have to go anywhere. The little Christmas tree, the Father Christmas hat, the jolly snowman swinging on the SSB radio and Christmas streamers have put me into a real Christmas spirit!

DAY 15: *26 December*

I've just crawled back into my bunk and fallen asleep when I hear a strange noise. There is something in the cabin that is making quite a racket. I switch on the light and narrowly miss stepping on a huge flying fish that had launched itself at *Guppy* a few seconds earlier. It has landed right on top of the dustbin, coming to a stop next to my bunk. It's trying to fly away but not really succeeding. Throwing back dead flying fish is bad enough, and picking up a live one can only be worse, but this smelly beast has to go back to the sea. I'm cursing it roundly, because it's unbelievably slippery and keeps jumping out of my hands. The whole cabin is covered in scales before I eventually get it back into the water. I hope this slimy adventurer tells the rest of its scaly friends all about its really bad experience, so there won't be any more stupid visitors flying into my cabin. It happens to be the first flying fish that I've seen since the start of the Indian Ocean. A sign that the water is warming up. Yay!

DAY 16: *27 December*

Guppy is sailing effortlessly on a broad reach under full sail with the genoa boomed-out on the high side. It's growing warmer fast now, and I'm having to get used to it again, but that's also really nice. In contrast to the rough seas over Christmas, these have now toned down and are friendlier. I feel like making something nice this morning, and have decided to bake some biscuits. An hour later, the cabin is filled with the aroma of freshly baked biscuits. I spend the rest of the day reading in the sun and sampling them. *Guppy* has been sailing well over the past few days and we have covered almost 2000 miles.

After watching two episodes of *How I Met Your Mother*, I close the laptop, switch on the light and crawl out of the covers for a last inspection before taking an hour-long nap while the radar keeps watch.

I see the moon through the porthole for the first time since leaving Cape Town. It's just a sliver, but what's really exciting is that it means that it's no longer cloudy. There's a beautiful starry sky above *Guppy*. What a pleasure to be able to see the stars and moon again! I haven't a clue about the names of these stars or their position in the universe, but I do know that they've left a lasting impression on me. As always, I crane my neck to look at the sky until my neck aches and I'm cold. *Guppy* is nicely on course and sailing at a speed of 6 knots.

I'm happy; it's been a lovely, sunny peaceful day. I'm thinking about the book I read this afternoon, *Maya's Notebook*, which my gran sent to me while I was in Cape Town. The more I read, the more the story touches me. It concerns a 16-year-old girl who is an alcoholic and a drug addict and has run away after rehab. She's been a drug dealer herself, and is on the run in Chile from people in her past. It really touches me, even though it's fiction. I know very well that it's not based on fairytales. Life can be so unfair. Why are some people strong and others weak? Why was I able to fight so hard against the Dutch state to be able to sail, while others don't pursue their dreams and most just carry on dreaming endlessly? I managed to escape the Netherlands and am now fulfilling my dream in freedom. It makes me hate the injustice in this world even more, where a few bad people manage to spoil life for so many others.

DAY 17: *28 December*

I'm still accompanied by the trade winds and *Guppy* is in her element. I'm baking pancakes at daybreak, and install myself in the cockpit while enjoying my treat. I finish reading the book I started yesterday, and then it's time for some maintenance on *Guppy*. The windvane steering lines have worn and need to be replaced. The blocks, shackles and winches need to be checked, replaced and greased. I then dive into the aft compartment and check the steering cables, where the bearings and discs urgently need some grease. Everything else looks fine. Satisfied, I put all my tools away at sunset, knowing that *Gup* is geared for action.

It's slowly growing cooler and the clouds are becoming greyer and bigger. There are some strange changes of wind direction towards nightfall. Sailing with the windvane, *Guppy* is sometimes 60 degrees off-course, but that doesn't matter. She is going well and I let her run with the wind. After a while, the wind returns to the former direction and *Guppy* is back on the right course. I come into contact with *Winddancer* via the SSB, a boat from New Zealand that I met in Port Elizabeth and that sailed from Cape Town a week after me. She is sailing 915 miles behind me. The days seem to be slipping by much faster, and I'm enjoying everything even more. It's wonderful to be in the trade winds, watching *Guppy* surge forward and having the prospect of sea and peace for some time yet to come.

DAY 18: *29 December*

The curtains of rain that have been with me all night disappear in the morning, and the sun comes to say 'good morning'. Now that the water is a bit warmer, it's a pleasure to take a proper shower from the water in my bucket. It gets rather hot in the afternoon, and it's good to be able to cool down this way. The flying fish are now rare, so the message must have got through to them … Although I do find scales on deck and a totally dehydrated squid in amongst some ropes. It really stinks and the deck will require some scrubbing. The waves have calmed, become longer, and *Guppy* is chasing through them at more than 6 knots, bringing us ever closer to the end of our world voyage; something I'm not sure I'm looking forward to that much …

DAY 19: *30 December*

Irritating squalls keep me busy all morning, and this time don't bring much wind but lots of rain and changeable winds. In the end, the wavy course-line on my plotter looks very interesting. *Guppy* is steered by the windvane and her course follows the wind in this way … Eventually the dark clouds disappear and it becomes extremely hot. In the afternoon, the sun is right overhead and burns without mercy. *Guppy* is almost running with the wind, which means that I can hardly feel any breeze and it's slowly getting too hot, so I spend the greater part of the day sitting calmly in the shade as I get hotter with each move I make. I write a bit for my book and listen to music while *Guppy* sways gently towards the horizon without me having to adjust a thing. There are just 3200 miles left of the 6000-mile crossing to the finish in Saint Martin, but we still have the doldrums and the Equator ahead of us, and *Gup* is approaching them fast.

DAY 20: *31 December*

At midnight the wind dies, causing *Guppy* to roll enormously. A big cargo ship passes me and by morning I've only managed to have three hours' sleep ... At daybreak, the wind is a little friendlier towards *Guppy* and me. By contrast, the confused cross-seas need to be taught some manners! Fortunately, *Gup* is now sailing well again and I can catch up on some sleep, because today I don't want to fall asleep before midnight. Except, uh ... When exactly is it 24.00 hours here? It's probably not a good idea to shoot off a flare, but I am going to amuse myself with the many coloured glow-sticks that I have on board. Let 2012 be a wonderful year!

DAY 21: *1 January 2012!*

I celebrate the turning of the new year with music, glow-sticks, the moon and the stars. The glow-sticks are a good substitute for fireworks and shine for hours. The sky is clear and there's no light pollution at sea, so the starlit sky is breathtakingly beautiful. I've decided to celebrate the start of the year in my present time-zone, which is two hours later than it is in the Netherlands. I spend the first few hours of 2012 enjoying sitting in the cockpit and thinking about what this year will bring for *Guppy* and me. The wind starts to drop and *Guppy* starts rolling heavily. There's more wind towards the morning, and I finally manage to fall asleep. So I spend the greater part of New Year's Day sleeping, just like most teenagers ... The only difference being that I'm lying in the cockpit listening to the rush of *Guppy*'s bow wave and dreaming the day away. I wake up in the afternoon, totally refreshed. The worst heat of the day has passed, and I suddenly feel like giving *Guppy* a good spring clean so that we make an orderly and fresh start to the New Year.

DAY 22: *2 January*

Guppy smells fresh and is squeaky-clean after I polished everything until late in the evening. The wind and waves are getting stronger again, which immediately makes life on board less comfortable. But the beautiful weather and the 7 knots showing on the log make up for it all. It's getting hotter by the day, and I keep cool by throwing buckets of water over myself. The flying fish have shrunk a lot in size. I'm only getting tiny fish on board now, but there are lots of them. These dry up quickly and are easy to throw back into the sea. *Guppy* is sailing extremely well and there is little to attend to. The waves can be really irritating sometimes, causing *Guppy* to do a tremendous side-swipe. An ocean without waves just doesn't exist, so I'll have to learn to live with it.

DAY 23: *3 January*

There's a good 15-knot wind and we are on a broad reach, and now that we are approaching the doldrums I'm happy with that. During the day, *Guppy* is increasingly beginning to resemble an oven. I now sleep during the day and am awake at night, which is a pleasant change with the beautiful moonlit sea and countless stars to look at. The fine winds ensure that *Guppy* and I are making good progress, and we're more than halfway. Let's hope it continues this way; as the doldrums are often calm for weeks, I'm taking advantage of every breath of wind.

At midnight I'm woken by a strange chirping sound … What's catching? Is something broken? When I go out and inspect with my searchlight, I find that the sound comes from the beaks of two pitch-black birds that are perching on the solar panels. They give me a cheeky look with their glistening eyes and carry on singing.

DAY 24: *4 January*

Although the chirping is not off-key, I've had enough by daybreak. When I get close to them, they just chirp louder and won't be chased away. They have, of course, shat all over my solar panels. I'm beginning to wonder what attracts these birds to *Guppy* …

We are running downwind and, as expected in the doldrums, the wind is beginning to weaken. There's just enough to let *Guppy* sail at a little over 4 knots without the sails flapping. The number of miles to Saint Martin has shrunk to 2600. While I'm still trying to figure out why birds are so attracted to *Guppy*, it cools down slowly and the clouds around me grow darker. A little too dark for my taste, but I'll have to see what it brings.

DAY 25: *5 January*

The threatening clouds only bring rain overnight and stay where they are without bothering *Guppy*. The wind is weakening very slowly, but the calm sea ensures that the sails remain full and *Guppy* swings on gently. I do my inspection round, and have just got back into bed when I hear *Splat, flap, flap!* next to me. I recognise that floundering sound immediately. A fish has flown into the cabin again and landed in my bed! Flapping around madly, it bounces around on the floor and I'm able to catch it fairly easily and throw it back into the sea, more or less alive. The black birds are back again with their duet, and keep me company all night. Hmm …

I've reached the ITC-zone, better known as the doldrums, but I still have a lovely wind and *Guppy* is going at a good 5 knots, which I'm very satisfied with in this part of the world. It doesn't improve the temperature, though.

It's only 2200 miles to Saint Martin; the distance is shrinking and getting fearfully close. The end of my dream; the fulfilment of a dream and the start of new adventures and new dreams. I often look back at the voyage and all the things I've experienced. Just before the voyage, I got to know a dark side to this world. During my voyage I got to know *Guppy*. At the beginning I would do what suited her best, and I now feel every change in her; I hear every sound and can walk over her deck with my eyes closed. But I have, especially, got to know myself. From how to make a mess, running out of food and clean clothes, to finding out what I want to do with my life and who I am. By discovering the rest of the world, new countries, new people, habits and lifestyles, I've discovered that the Netherlands is certainly not the place for me. After

25,000 miles of sailing solo now, I still haven't had enough of the sea and long for more adventures. A career in the sailing world would certainly suit me, and that's why it would be best for me to go to New Zealand or Australia. This is why my dream to sail to New Zealand is now beginning to make much more sense. The more I think about it, the more concrete and definite my plans become. Slowly my thoughts turn to the Panama Canal and the Pacific, with New Zealand as my goal. I work on finding out about New Zealand, bit by bit, and store everything I hear and read about that country in my mind.

Halfway through my voyage, I'd decided not to return to the Netherlands because of the umpteenth interference by the authorities. Everything that I've learnt over the past year and a half; what worked out, what went wrong and the problems I encountered, I shared with the rest of the world. After the lies that were spread, the news about me became increasingly more positive, and I rapidly needed to learn how to deal with the media. Sailing at sea and adapting to this lifestyle was a lot easier than standing in the spotlight. It's something I still don't feel happy about and dread having to do each time; sharing my life with the rest of the world that sees me as an example. To have become famous without having wanted to, and to have to accept this from one day to the next, was a very difficult phase that I was forced to go through. It had been a calculated tactic by the authorities after they discovered that I really hated being the focus of any attention. This is something that a lot of people don't know. While everyone was concerned about the storms I encountered, I actually enjoyed them because it meant I had some peace and was at one with nature. I couldn't handle the media and broke down every time they spread new lies about me. From an early age I learnt, by trial and error, not to be afraid of the unknown. I succeeded in filling a gap in my heart that I didn't know I had, and can cherish these life experiences for the rest of my life. The fact that I'm the youngest person to have ever sailed around the world … well, that doesn't really matter to me. I just wanted to do it and now know that it was the right thing to do. Half the world has followed my progress and I'd like to urge everyone to fulfil their dreams and not let their dreams remain just dreams. If you want something really badly, you can always make it happen. I come from a family that never had much money;

I used to wear second-hand clothing and went to school on a really old bike, but I've fought to fulfil my dream and managed to persuade sponsors to help out with getting a boat and enough stuff to achieve my dream. So, give it your all, work day and night, and go for it! When I set out, I didn't know whether I could sail around the world; whether I would miss my parents; whether I could handle the boat and manage to get through the storms; but I have always stepped into the unknown and have never, even in times of hardship, regretted it for a second.

DAY 26: *6 January*

My feathered visitors are singing away again on my solar panels, just as they've been doing for the past two nights. I've discovered that they are put off when you point a camera at them to photograph or film them. They get confused and shut up for a while … A very welcome change! They're slightly more considerate now, too, because they no longer shit on the solar panels but on the aft deck. A better spot, as at least my mini power station can do its work.

In the morning, I see a cargo ship on the horizon for the first time in ages. I've been expecting this for a while, as I'm only 350 miles off the coast of Brazil. It's still early but already very warm, and it promises to be a hot day. The Equator is getting closer and, despite being in the doldrums, *Gup* is still sailing along at 5 knots. Some dolphins come to say hello and dive under *Guppy* to shoot up on the other side, doing a lovely somersault before disappearing as quickly as they arrived. A pity, as I haven't had the company of dolphins for a long time and would have liked to enjoy their stunts for a little longer.

DAY 27: *7 January*

At daybreak it's very cloudy for a change, but after a few drops of rain the clouds disappear and it gets even hotter than the days before. The black birds have spent the whole night at their post, but I think they're still feeling insulted by the camera flash, because they don't chirp a note. Something I really don't mind! At about midday, *Guppy* and I cross the Equator and leave the Southern Hemisphere. It's so terribly hot that I'm sure I could fry an egg on the deck, but the eggs are finished so I won't be able to give it a try ... I don't offer Neptune a pancake this time, but make a fine speech to thank him for protecting *Guppy* and me on my long voyage. I spend the day throwing buckets of water over myself to ensure that I'm not cooked alive ... There's still a 10- to 15-knot wind coming from a south-south-easterly direction, and *Guppy* waddles on steadily with a boomed-out genoa and mainsail.

It gets cloudier at night and the moon and stars disappear to leave me in the dark. It's so dark that I can no longer see the front of the boat.

DAY 28: *8 January*

There's a little light towards morning, but it remains very cloudy. *Guppy* weathers one squall after the next, and sails through enormous downpours. The first few times this happens it's really refreshing, but the squalls are getting heavier and heavier. The weather changes from short, heavy showers to continuous rain; from sudden calms to winds of 35 knots. Then, wind from all directions, which sweeps up confused seas that throw *Guppy* from side to side. I'm asking myself if there's any purpose in adjusting the sails constantly and whether the wind will be back soon. It seems I won't be escaping the doldrums entirely after all, although *Gup* has been making good progress in general, thanks to my efforts.

DAY 29: *9 January*

A calm night with no wind and some showers is followed by a cloudy day with more showers. It hasn't been dry since this afternoon, and I've filled all the buckets, bottles and the water tank. It's raining really hard, which means that I have to keep the cabin closed if I want to avoid having a swimming pool inside, but this makes it really hot in there. The wind is changing direction constantly, which means that I'm doing battle with the sails all day long while being showered with rain ... In the meantime, I've had wind from all directions again, with speeds from 0 to 30 knots. There are even gusts of 40 knots from time to time, which blow *Guppy* every which way. I'm already missing the South Atlantic, and hope to be out of the doldrums soon. Towards evening I'm cheered up by a big pod of dolphins that appears before the bow during one of the many heavy squalls with much wind and rain. *Guppy* runs on through the waves at 7 knots, with the dolphins jumping out of the water as the rain drums down. They give me an amazing performance that lasts several hours. Of all my encounters with dolphins, this is probably the best. An unforgettable experience!

DAY 30: *10 January*

There's an enormous squall during the night with a 40-knot wind and pouring rain, making sleep impossible. At daybreak, it gets calmer and promises to be a lovely day. The wind is steady at between 10 and 15 knots on the beam, and *Gup* happily fizzes on under full sail through the waves. What's more, there's some current in the direction we are going, and we're making good progress. Just 1750 miles to go!

I'm dreading my arrival more and more. I don't really care about the fact that I'm the youngest person who's ever sailed around the world. It doesn't matter to me how many people there'll be to welcome me. For me, the ideal reception would be simple: just my best friends, parents and sister. When you've been dumped really hard by a country, it really takes a lot to be able to forgive, and I haven't managed to do that yet. I had a handful of people on my side, but it felt as though the Netherlands had rejected me. What happened has filled me with an anger that has controlled my life until now, but I'm now fighting this. I just had a dream, one that wouldn't bother anyone. A dream to sail around the world. A girl with a tremendous lot of sailing experience, hope and faith in her ability to fulfil her dream. But she made one mistake, and that was to utter her wish. I regret I ever did that. I wouldn't be sitting here right now dreading a big reception with a lot of media attention, dreading having to smile for the very journalists who spat me out a year ago but now want to be the first to send their reports.

Luckily, there was always one person to steadfastly believe in me. Dad always supported me, believed in me and had the courage to let me go. I wouldn't have come through the bad times without him. Because of him, I've had the chance to win back my self-respect and confidence, by doing what I said I would do.

DAY 31: *11 January*

It looks like we have left the worst of the doldrums behind us. While *Winddancer*, the New Zealand boat that left a week after me, remains 950 miles behind me and is still enjoying the trade winds in the South Atlantic, *Guppy* and I are now sailing at a good 6 knots in the trade winds of the North Atlantic. At the moment, she's the only yacht that I have contact with via the SSB. And that's more than enough for now. I'm trying to enjoy all the peace and space around me to the full. Just another 12 days before my unity with nature is going to be broken. And, unlike Durban, I won't have two days to get used to it slowly. I sometimes really dread the idea of my arrival. Of course I'm looking forward to achieving my goal, but, quite honestly, I achieved that goal some time ago. I've got to know myself, have learnt and seen a lot and got to know colourful people and countries. The Pacific gave me all the unknown beautiful islands I had dreamt of. The Indian Ocean was a rude awakening out of that dream world; the bad weather, storms and calms; but also the long stretches of sailing that I longed for. The South Atlantic gave me a light trade wind so that I could absorb all my impressions. But is this enough? Soon my world, which consists of *Guppy* and all my wonderful memories and life experiences, will abruptly make way for crowds and media attention. I'm glad I still have 12 days in the North Atlantic to get used to the idea, because that commotion and attention never featured in my dreams.

DAY 32: *12 January*

Gup and I have now found the true North Atlantic trade winds, a good 20-knot beam wind that causes the waves to regularly wash over the deck. It's still very hot and I have the choice of either taking a saltwater shower on deck and getting ice-cold in the wind, or sitting below in the stifling heat because I have to keep all the hatches and the companionway closed to keep out the breaking waves. I decide to alternate between both options … *Guppy* is completely in her element and doesn't understand why I want to go much slower. She's chasing through the waves at more than 6.5 knots, and the miles to the finish are diminishing before my eyes.

one girl, one dream

DAY 33: *13 January*

The wind freshens at night and the waves continue to grow. In the meantime, the beam seas have become steep and tall, transforming the sea into a churning pot. The view out the portholes below deck looks more like the inside of a washing machine. A flock of birds has been flying close around *Guppy* and over the tops of the waves all day. The birds look like they're having a lot more fun than I am, as it's not really comfortable at the moment. The waves are slowing *Guppy* down, but she's slicing through them and we're making good progress.

DAY 34: *14 January*

The wind doesn't let up. The waves are longer and more regular, which means that fewer of them land in the cockpit, making life on board a lot more comfortable. *Guppy* is still going like a spear under storm jib, reefed mainsail and mizzen. We will be down to a three-digit distance to Saint Martin the day after tomorrow! The birds have escaped to somewhere calmer, but I'm seeing plenty of flying fish again. A few of them land in the cockpit, and I see a school of flying fish being chased by a predator that looks like a dorado. It's catching up on them, so a few of them are unlikely to survive. Otherwise, it's difficult to spot much marine life with all the white horses on the sea and the waves that wash over *Guppy*.

DAY 35: *15 January*

It's getting calmer and the companionway can stay open again. It's lovely to sit in the entrance, from where I can keep an eye on everything without being hit by a wave. Alas, this is not the case for the flying fish that continue to jump onto and over *Guppy*. I don't know what I've done to deserve this, but they continue to attack me ... I was just trying to enjoy a few rays of sunshine when — *wham!* — a huge flying fish struck me on the head. If I hadn't blocked its way, it would have landed inside again! The waves are still big, but *Guppy* is really enjoying herself and sailing at a speed of 8 knots. It's beginning to look as though my arrival in Saint Martin is going to be earlier than expected ...

DAY 36: *16 January*

The waves are becoming less rough, making life on board more comfortable. Unfortunately, *Guppy* is surrounded by squalls that have been plaguing me all day with sudden strong gusts on the beam or from ahead, but no rain. It means that I'm kept busy all day with the sails and the course. Through my efforts, *Guppy* is still sailing at an average speed of 5 knots. There are just 780 miles left between *Guppy* and the finish now, and I think I will reach Saint Martin on the 21st at this speed. I still haven't absorbed the fact that I've more than sailed around the world. It's such a strange notion that the one thing I've dreamt about since the age of eight has now been fulfilled. My life's journey is now almost behind me and I'm overwhelmed by the feeling that I don't want it to end yet.

The squalls are keeping me awake at night, and the heavens have opened over *Guppy*. I'm glad about that, because it's getting rid of most of the salt that covers *Gup* and I can take a good, if icy-cold, shower. An hour later, *Gup* and I receive another salty wave breaking over us, so we don't really get much time to enjoy being clean.

DAY 37: *17 January*

Towards morning, the squalls disappear and it turns into one of the nicest days since I left the South Atlantic behind me; with just a few clouds, a good wind and some gentle waves. *Guppy* has gained even more on *Winddancer*, who now lies 1130 miles behind her. They've just reached the Equator. I haven't had contact with them for a couple of days as there was something wrong with their SSB radio microphone, but they've managed to fix it. Now we can have our daily chat again, which is a nice change from the infinite seascape around me. *Guppy* still has 610 miles to go, which should take approximately four days in these favourable winds. It's now getting fearfully close, and I'm no longer able to ignore the thought of my arrival that easily.

DAY 38: *18 January*

Now that the end destination of my voyage is coming closer, I regularly think back on the experiences along the way but especially the year that preceded it. The painful recollections sometimes take up hours of my day and hurt badly. Now I've been almost right around the world, entered difficult harbours, avoided dangerous reefs, survived the heaviest storms and taken full responsibility for both *Guppy*'s and my own safety.

DAY 39: *19 January*

It's going to be a beautiful, sunny day with less wind than yesterday, so it will be peaceful sailing. *Guppy* is still sailing at 5.5 knots, fast enough to arrive on the 21st. Another 280 miles to go and I think I'll see the first islands tomorrow. This means that this is the last day of my voyage in which I will start in an infinite trough of waves that undulate all the way to the horizon and end it in the same way. I still haven't really got used to the idea that in two days' time I will be the youngest person ever to have sailed around the world. In the meantime, I'm beginning to look forward to my arrival a little more. Eating fresh food, walking, running and seeing my family. Moreover, my 34-year-old mate, *Guppy*, also deserves some rest after nearly 6000 miles. She's done brilliantly and demanded little maintenance; something I have to thank Dad for. It's thanks to his enormous experience with yachts and these kind of voyages that *Guppy* has been so well equipped for my big voyage.

DAY 40: *20 January*

It's slowly getting lighter; I have 160 miles ahead of me according to the plotter, and the first small island is in sight. Guadeloupe is hiding just below the horizon, but will probably come into sight this afternoon. Just 365 days ago I was on the other side of Guadeloupe and sailing off in the opposite direction, with a string of barrels and nets that I'd just sailed through … Since then, a whole life has passed before me. It feels just like yesterday, but also as if it were centuries ago. At that stage, I didn't have a clue that I would ever come back here; a year later with a whole lot of life experience and over 27,000 more miles under *Guppy*'s keel. But I'm really here and have sailed all around the world. Yes, it's beginning to dawn on me very, very slowly … but I still can't absorb it all.

The finish!

DAY 41: *21 January*

The darkness and amazing starlit sky of the last evening at sea is disappearing slowly, and the lights that have been twinkling on the horizon change into islands. I see Saint Martin in the distance, Saint Eustatius behind me, Saba next to me and Saint Barth right ahead of me.

The scheduled opening of the bridge in Saint Martin is at 15.00 and I will have to sail at a speed of 4 knots to make it. *Guppy* is doing 5.5 knots with the mizzen, reefed mainsail and partially furled genoa. Exactly 366 days ago, I was heading south on the other side of these islands and watching Saint Martin disappearing below the horizon. I recognise the shapes of the islands, and it's slowly sinking in that I once again have Saint Martin lying ahead of *Guppy*'s bow and that it has taken exactly a year to circumnavigate the world.

A heavy squall blows over *Guppy* and she's going way too fast. The islands disappear behind a heavy downpour, and it's frustrating being so near to Saint Martin but having to wait to be allowed to sail in. On the other hand, what are a few hours compared with the 41 days that I've taken to make the crossing from Cape Town? I eventually stop *Guppy* on the leeward side of Saint Barth and wait for a signal from Saint Martin that I can sail in. Finally I receive the message to come in …

A helicopter hovers over *Guppy* as she heads under full sail to Simpson Bay and there are an increasing number of boats sailing in company. I recognise Dad and Mum, who are on a mega-speedboat. They are amongst a number of people I know, and, after having to look twice, I recognise my little sister, Kim, who now has bright-red hair and is waving like crazy. I wave back and my face breaks into a satisfied grin. I lower all the sails just before I get to the bridge, while the cameras follow me. I slowly steer *Guppy* through the same bridge that I sailed through a year ago with an enormous string of boats trailing behind.

There are a lot of people who are apparently there for me. I'm so overwhelmed that I can't distinguish between dream and reality half the time. The whole afternoon goes by in a haze of activity, embraces and interviews. That evening we enjoy a meal on board the *Sherikan*, a luxury mega-yacht that we've been invited to.

After a good night's rest, I manage to see the world around me with more clarity the next morning. But the feeling — the very normal feeling that I've sailed around the world on my own — still hasn't changed. I take it easy in the days that follow my amazing reception, and spend much time with my family. I swim, run along the beach with Kim, walk through Philipsburg and am not too bothered about the mess I've left *Guppy* in.

My mum and sister go back to the Netherlands after almost a week on the island. Slowly, but surely, I get *Guppy* ready for departure, and once my Gran and Granddad are on their flight back home I sail from Saint Martin for Bonaire together with Dad. There's a strong breeze and we are getting the most out of *Guppy* who has a huge white smile on her bow as she takes off. We cover the 470 miles in two and a half days! We leave *Guppy* in Bonaire while I fly to the HISWA Boat Fair in Amsterdam to give some presentations that will help to fill the boat's kitty.

After this I really want to carry on sailing with *Guppy*; through the Panama Canal for a second time and then across the beautiful Pacific with New Zealand as my destination — the country in which I want to build my life. I may travel through Australia and backpack my way around South America; or go to Iceland or Alaska. I may even sail to Antarctica to see if the infinite white gives me the same sense of peace as the ocean. Plenty of dreams to fulfil, but I know one thing for sure — and that's that I will always continue to sail and enjoy being at one with nature.

Afterword

One of the questions I was asked the most after finishing my trip was: 'What are you going to do now?' I had, of course, thought about this a lot myself during the trip, but never had a very good answer. And when the trip was over, I still didn't have a great answer. I felt like people wanted me to say I was going to sail around the world again, or go to Alaska, or maybe to the moon. They wanted to hear about my next exciting goal, but I wasn't able to give them anything exciting, and I still can't. Well, I guess that depends on what you find exciting, but it surely wouldn't be the equal of sailing around the world at 16. Honestly, what could I possibly do to top that?

It was, and is, of no great importance to me. I didn't set out to break a record, or to seek recognition. I simply wanted to do it; it was a dream, a great adventure through which I wanted to explore my boundaries, and get to know nature and myself. I found all those things and much more I never could have imagined. What came next may not seem as exciting to others, but it is to me. You'd think after sailing around the world, everything else would seem easy by comparison; but actually trying to settle somewhere, to enter the real world, was a lot harder.

After my trip had officially ended in Saint Martin, I gave myself a week off with family and friends. After that week I sailed with my father to the island of Bonaire, where I stayed for a while to clear my head. I had such a jumbled mix of emotions at that time: I was happy that I had achieved my goal of sailing around the world, but was still trying to process it. At the same time I was sad, because the great journey was over. Then there were feelings of liberation: I had proven that I could actually do it, and there was no need to prove anything to anyone any more; no more rules, no more people telling me what to do and what's best for me.

This was true in some sense, but eventually I realised that — having been the centre of attention for so long — people would always have an

315

opinion about me. This was not an easy thing to accept. At first I hated all the attention, as I had very much hoped to live a quiet life after the trip's end. But when that attention just didn't go away, I decided it was better to tell my story myself, rather then try to vanish from the public eye and leave people wondering what had happened to me.

I started giving presentations all over the world for all kinds of audiences. And, to my great surprise, sharing my story has brought me a lot of joy. I've received many positive comments from people who had been inspired by my voyage and now wanted to fulfill their own dreams.

After the break in Bonaire I began to pursue my next dream: sailing to New Zealand. I followed the same route I had taken on my trip, through the Panama Canal towards French Polynesia. From Tahiti I sailed straight to my birth place, Whangarei, New Zealand, where I arrived on 1 September 2012. New Zealand had been a place I had wanted to go to for a very long time, and getting there was very special. It didn't take much time before I'd decided that this was going to be my home base.

But I had never remained in one place for a long time, and wasn't about to start now. I stayed in Whangarei for a while, but my urge to keep moving grew stronger. I worked for a scuba-diving company in the North Island for a time, bought myself a car and road-tripped through the whole of New Zealand with some new-found friends.

After that, many more land-based travels followed: through Southeast Asia, Europe, North America and many more places. I never liked the overland travels more then the ocean, but I found them more interesting in many ways. Land brings man-made things, but also animals, and an amazing amount of nature. At sea, though, I was given the opportunity to learn a lot about myself, and about the beautiful ways of nature. I learnt to accept being a small meaningless dot alone out in the open, with the winds and strong seas ruling over my life. I learnt to find happiness in little things. I learnt to get by on the bare necessities of life.

Between my travels I return to *Guppy*, who is now berthed in the marina of Whangarei. We've done some shorter trips around New Zealand and up to Norfolk Island, but she mainly functions as my home now, waiting faithfully for me while I am gone, and greeting me with many good memories when I come back. I try to travel in the New Zealand winters, when living on board *Guppy* can get a little fresh!

There are many ideas in my head of what to do next, and more come every day as I travel to all corners of the world and come across the different cultures and lifestyles that influence me. After bouncing around for two and a half years, I am starting to realise that it doesn't really matter where I am; being in a certain place doesn't bring me happiness. One place might bring more joy then another, but it certainly doesn't bring happiness. Neither does money, fame or having achieved many goals. I am happy if I am able to appreciate the basic essentials of life, like having a dry, non-salty place to sleep, food and hopefully some good souls around me to share the experience with. I hope to inspire other people to pursue their dreams, and to stand up for what they feel is right.

August 2014

Appendix: *Guppy*

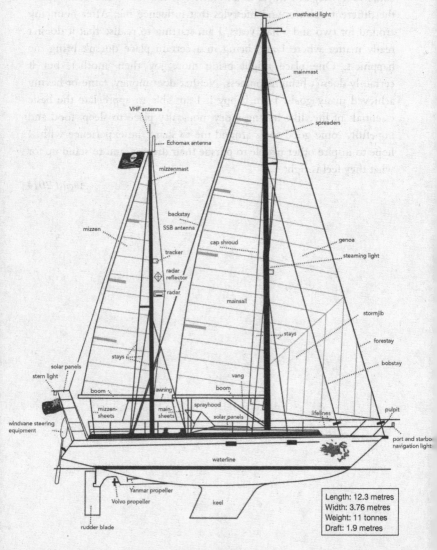

masthead light

mainmast

spreaders

VHF antenna

Echomax antenna

mizzenmast

genoa

backstay
SSB antenna

cap shroud

mizzen

steaming light

tracker

radar
reflector

radar

mainsail

stormjib

forestay

stays

bobstay

stays

solar panels

stern light

vang

boom

boom

awning

mizzen-
sheets

main-
sheets

sprayhood

solar panels

lifelines

pulpit

windvane steering
equipment

port and starbo[...]
navigation light[...]

waterline

Yanmar propeller

Volvo propeller

keel

rudder blade

Length:	12.3 metres
Width:	3.76 metres
Weight:	11 tonnes
Draft:	1.9 metres

Appendix: *Guppy*

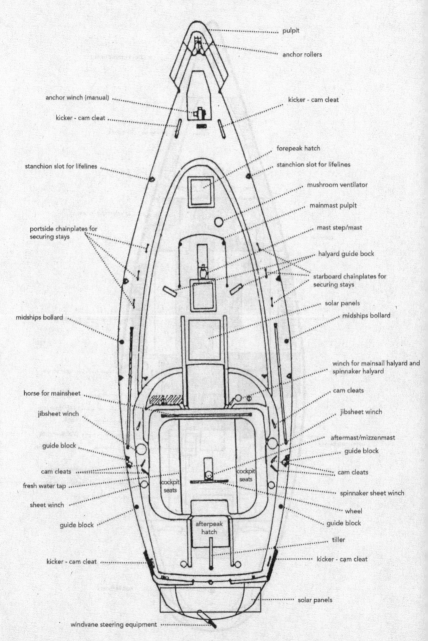

pulpit

anchor rollers

anchor winch (manual)

kicker - cam cleat

kicker - cam cleat

forepeak hatch

stanchion slot for lifelines

stanchion slot for lifelines

mushroom ventilator

mainmast pulpit

portside chainplates for
securing stays

mast step/mast

halyard guide bock

starboard chainplates for
securing stays

solar panels

midships bollard

midships bollard

winch for mainsail halyard and
spinnaker halyard

horse for mainsheet

cam cleats

jibsheet winch

jibsheet winch

guide block

aftermast/mizzenmast

guide block

cam cleats

cam cleats

fresh water tap

cockpit
seats

cockpit
seats

spinnaker sheet winch

sheet winch

wheel

guide block

afterpeak
hatch

guide block

tiller

kicker - cam cleat

kicker - cam cleat

solar panels

windvane steering equipment

one girl, one dream

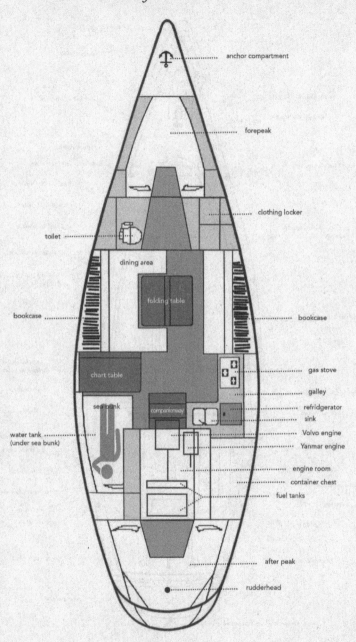

anchor compartment

forepeak

clothing locker

toilet

dining area

folding table

bookcase

bookcase

gas stove

galley

chart table

refridgerator

sea bunk

companionway

sink

Volvo engine

water tank
(under sea bunk)

Yanmar engine

engine room

container chest

fuel tanks

after peak

rudderhead